THE MARKET VALUE PROCESS

Market
Value

Customer Value

Employee Teams
Building
Precision Strategies
with the
Market Value Process

Shareholder
Value

THE MARKET VALUE PROCESS

Bridging Customer and Shareholder Value

Alan S. Cleland and Albert V. Bruno

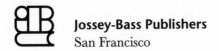

Jossey-Bass Publishers
San Francisco

Substantial discounts on bulk quantities of Jossey-Bass books are available to corporations, professional associations, and other organizations. For details and discount information, contact the
special sales department at Jossey-Bass Inc., Publishers (415) 433–1740; Fax (800) 605–2665.

For sales outside the United States, please contact your local Simon & Schuster International Office.

Manufactured in the United States of America. Printed on acid-free recycled paper that contains at least
50 percent recycled waste, including 10 percent postconsumer waste.

Library of Congress Cataloging-in-Publication Data

Cleland, Alan S., 1939–
    The market value process : bridging customer and shareholder value
/ Alan S. Cleland and Albert V. Bruno. — 1st ed.
      p. cm. — (The Jossey-Bass business & management series)
    Includes bibliographical references and index.
    ISBN 0–7879–0275–6 (alk. paper)
    1. Strategic planning.   2. Marketing.   3. Consumer satisfaction.
  4. Corporations—Valuation.   I. Bruno, Albert V. II. Title.
  III. Series: Jossey-Bass business and management series.
  HD30.28.C578 1996
  658.8—dc20
                                      96–10106

Credits are on page 243.

FIRST EDITION
HB Printing 10 9 8 7 6 5 4 3 2 1

THE JOSSEY-BASS

BUSINESS & MANAGEMENT SERIES

CONTENTS

PREFACE

A̲ll of us are constantly witnessing breathtaking turns in the fortunes of business enterprises both large and small. Virtually every issue of *The Wall Street Journal* overflows with compelling stories of enterprises whose growth suddenly halts or whose stock price abruptly collapses—symptoms of a deeper problem. Readers of these stories usually look for complex reasons to explain the dramatic differences between the victor and the vanquished. But the cause of success or failure is seldom complicated.

When an enterprise hits air pockets in its growth and stock price, the deeper problem is usually the imprecision with which its strategies detect and meet its customers' shifting needs—needs that the customer may be only dimly aware of or not aware of at all. As a consequence of their imprecision, these strategies do not create enough value for either the enterprise's customers or its shareholders, and the strategies do not work. We call this the *combined-value problem*.

Precision does not require complexity. Strategies that meet shifting needs with precision can be summarized on a single page, as we shall see in Chapter Nine. This summary should be so easy to understand that any employee can use it when deciding how to put the enterprise's resources to best use.

How to Solve the Combined-Value Problem

To solve the combined-value problem, an enterprise needs to empower employee teams to build precision strategies that meet its customers' shifting needs with accuracy and profit. The graphic on the title page of this book depicts the explosive power of cross-functional employee teams banding together to build these strategies. The book presents a practical, easy-to-use, twelve-step process that employee teams can follow to build strategies that will win customers and shareholders for their enterprise. We call this the *Market Value Process*[SM1] because it measures and maps the value that an enterprise creates in both the product markets and the securities markets. Through the maps it presents, this book transforms concepts like "customer value" from empty slogans into measurements as precise as profit and cash flow.

What Makes This Book Unique

The Market Value Process offers a uniquely balanced and clear approach to solving the combined-value problem. Its precision strategies balance the importance given to customer and shareholder value, and the process for building these strategies is remarkably clear and straightforward.

Recent books about value creation have tended to fall into one of two categories. The first takes the position that customer value drives shareholder value. The authors of these books assert that if an enterprise has an enthusiastic set of customers, shareholder value will fall into place almost automatically.

The second category of books takes the opposite position: that shareholder value drives customer value. These books hold that focusing on maximizing shareholder wealth almost automatically necessitates pleasing customers.

We believe that neither one automatically leads to the other. An enterprise must work with equal intensity on building value for customers and for shareholders if it hopes to deliver superior results to both constituencies. The building blocks of customer value and shareholder value are different. The building blocks of customer value are the quality the customer receives with a purchase compared to the purchase price. Those of shareholder value are revenue growth and profit margin. While we do believe that customer value needs to be created first, this is because customer value simply opens the possibility for the financial payoff opportunities—revenue growth and profit margin—that build shareholder value. Customer value is a necessary but not sufficient condition for shareholder value. There is nothing automatic about either one leading to the other. Instead, an enterprise must use the careful management provided by the Market Value Process to make sure that its customer value strategies deliver vigorous revenue growth and the profit margins needed to beat its cost of capital and thereby build wealth for shareholders. This idea of neither value discipline leading automatically to the

Exhibit P.1. Two Mental Models That Don't Work and One That Does.

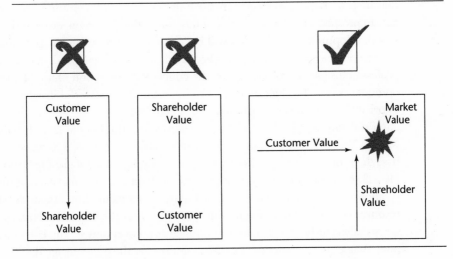

other is so central to the development of this book that we depict it in Exhibit P.1. The figure with the check mark on the right is a simplified version of the graphic on the title page.

The defining characteristic of the Market Value Process is the precision with which it systematizes your problem solving. The book first maps the problem of creating value for customers and shareholders that an enterprise faces in each of its markets. Then it breaks this challenge into pieces, each of which constitutes a step in the Market Value Process. For each step, the book provides you with both a concept and a tool to solve the piece of the problem you are facing. This "just-in-time, problem-to-solution" approach is user friendly and satisfying because it resolves each market-based challenge on the spot before moving on to the next step. The solution of each problem becomes the *carried value* that is input to the next step of the process.

Who Should Read This Book

This book is designed for everyone who wants to learn an approach to strategy building that highlights the contribution each management function needs to make in order to solve the combined-value problem.

Top executives will be able to use the Market Value Process to build global strategies for their enterprises. Business unit managers can use it to build precision strategies for their units. Marketers will be able to use it to map the customer value that their marketing strategies create. Sales professionals can use it to communicate to prospects the value of their enterprise's offering. Engineering and research and development professionals will be able to use it to assess the potential market acceptance of the innovations they are developing. New-product development professionals can adopt it to guide the concept-investigation phase of the development process. Product managers will use it to gain powerful insights into how to price their products to optimize combined value.

Professionals in other business functions will also benefit from learning the Market Value Process. Financial managers will be able to use it to make sure they base their forecasts of shareholder value on a strong market logic. Operations people will see from it how their concern with both quality and internal cost uniquely positions them to create customer and shareholder value simultaneously. Human resources professionals will gain insights into what the content of training programs needs to be in order to give managers an overview of the corporate purpose. Academicians will find it useful in illustrating the tight linkage that must exist between customer and shareholder value.

How Examples Bring the Market Value Process into Focus

Each chapter of the book showcases an example of corporate success or failure in the 1990s that illustrates the chapter's key topic. As we all know, this is the Information Age. In the 1990s, U.S. industry has been spending more on computers and communications equipment than on all other capital equipment combined. The book draws many of its examples from this information economy. Of course, since these are snapshots of a fast-moving situation, specific conditions may well have changed by the time you read the example. But this simply illustrates how the Market Value Process can be used to view a snapshot in time and how important it is to use the Market Value Process to update this view when the snapshot changes in a material way.

Most of our readers will learn the most from case studies. For this reason, we couple our discussion of the Market Value Process with an extended illustration; "Sportmed" is a disguised $100 million sports medicine instruments corporation that faced the combined-value problem. Both its customers and shareholders were unhappy because Sportmed's strategies were not creating enough value to satisfy either group. We describe how Sportmed organized its top thirty people into three cross-functional teams in order to implement the Market Value Process in Sportmed's three markets. The Sportmed story provides an excellent example of how an enterprise can reinvent itself in the marketplace by using the concepts and tools presented in this book.

How Ford Has Grappled with Balancing Customer and Shareholder Value

As you dive into Chapter One, you may object that we are being inconsistent, since we first advocate a balanced focus on customer and shareholder value but then suggest that an enterprise needs to create customer value first. Remember that we start with customer value because it opens the opportunity for shareholder value, although it by no means leads automatically to it.

A compelling illustration of this appeared in a July 18, 1995, article in *The Wall Street Journal* that carried the title "Alex Trotman's Goal: To Make Ford Number 1 in World Auto Sales."[2] Its telling subtitle was "But Some Fear the Chairman May Slight Profitability—The Art of Finding a Balance." The jury is still out as to whether the customer value that generated Ford's recent sales gains will come down to the bottom line for shareholders and thereby solve the combined-value problem; this story elaborates on that point.

The article reported that Alexander Trotman is trying to engineer a new world order in the automobile industry. Simply put, the chairman of Ford Motor Company wants the automaker to be number one worldwide, supplanting General Motors for the first time since 1932.

For more than a decade, Ford has been on a tear, seizing market share from GM, Chrysler, and foreign makers. Ford's U.S. sales of cars and trucks hit 3.9 million in 1994, up 1.7 million vehicles from 1981, and its market share is up a remarkable seven percentage points (with one point now representing $2.5 billion in sales).

The real question is whether Ford is focusing too much on market share and not enough on profitability. Critics note that the costs of Ford's push for market share have hurt its profit margins, while Chrysler, though smaller, has been setting the profitability standard for the industry.

Should management focus on being big or on being profitable? "It's a very complex and fundamental issue in management strategy," says Paul McAvoy, a management professor at Yale University. He observes that Japanese electronics and auto companies have proved that the short-term costs of gaining market share can be offset by fatter long-term profits. But he cautions that management should avoid the trap of pursuing growth for its own sake.

As an example, one of the first things GM's new president, John F. Smith Jr., did to stop his company's profit hemorrhaging was to halve its cut-rate car sales to daily rental fleets. Its U.S. market share has eased to 32.3 percent by mid 1995 from nearly 35 percent in 1991, but profits are healthy again.

Similarly, since taking Ford's top job in January 1994, Mr. Trotman has taken significant steps to raise profitability, cutting three layers of management and combining its North American and European arms in a single $92-billion-a-year business. Importantly, however, in 1992 Ford spent heavily, aggressively combining rebates, special lease deals, and fleet discounts to push its Taurus ahead of the Honda Accord as America's best-selling car. Sales to fleet customers through May 1995 accounted for 59 percent of Taurus sales, compared with just 5 percent for the Honda Accord, according to registration data compiled by R. L. Polk and Company. "There's a great plus in being the leader," Mr. Trotman says. "Our customers and dealers see it as important." Ford still uses that sales crown in its marketing, and it does the same thing with its best-selling F-series trucks and Explorer vehicles. Now it is striving to top Chrysler in minivan sales.

Yet the Ford chairman contends that gaining market share is not his chief goal. "Our objective is to optimize our ongoing profitability," he declares, adding that "we don't have a share number written on the wall."

But keeping the drives for profitability and market share in balance "is an art," Trotman acknowledges. How is it done? "If I could give a precise answer, I would put it on a floppy disk and go home," he says. "The answer changes every day."

The company still has some way to go to become the most profitable automaker. Despite record earnings of $5.31 billion in 1994, a boom year in the U.S. market, its return on sales ran just 4.1 percent, below its goal of averaging 5 percent over the business cycle—and below Chrysler's robust 7.1 percent. At the time of the article, Ford common was trading at just six times annual earnings per share, compared to a ratio of seven for GM. While the jury is still out on the long-term outcome, at the time of the article Ford had not brought its market-share-winning customer value down to the bottom line for shareholders.

We stop well short of promising that you will be able to put the solution to the combined-value problem on a floppy disk and go home. But we also do not believe that the answer changes every day; rather, the answer is embodied in the Market Value Process. We believe that in the realm of business books the Market Value Process is the most comprehensive and practical solution to the combined-value problem. And as the Sportmed example illustrates, the process works.

How This Book Is Organized

The book's organizational structure traces the solution of the combined-value problem through the three phases of the Market Value Process—the Diagnosis, the Bridge, and the Payoff, as depicted in Exhibit P.2. The Diagnosis shows how

Exhibit P.2. Creating Value for Customers and Shareholders.

The Market Value Process solves the combined-value problem.

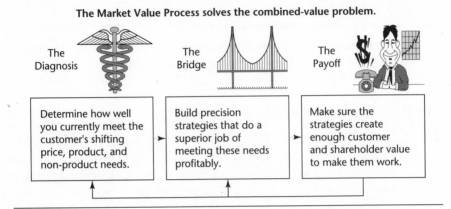

The Diagnosis	The Bridge	The Payoff
Determine how well you currently meet the customer's shifting price, product, and non-product needs.	Build precision strategies that do a superior job of meeting these needs profitably.	Make sure the strategies create enough customer and shareholder value to make them work.

well an enterprise is currently meeting customers' shifting price, product, and non-product needs, which are explained in Chapter One. The Bridge provides the concepts and tools for building precision strategies that do a superior job of meeting these needs profitably. The Payoff shows how to determine whether these strategies create enough combined value for customers and shareholders to make the strategies work. The feedback arrows in the sketch indicate that you must frequently reexamine the underlying needs in order to detect shifts and rebuild strategies that respond to these shifts.

To make the decisions that create combined value and to package these decisions into precision strategies, an enterprise must have both sound concepts and sophisticated tools. Having one without the other is not enough. Concepts without tools give the enterprise a philosophy without a method; tools without concepts give it a method without a philosophy. Each chapter in this book provides both the concepts and the tools an enterprise needs to make decisions that solve value problems.

Part One: Introduction and Principles

Chapter One describes the twelve steps that constitute the Market Value Process. It provides a self-assessment exercise so that you can measure how well your enterprise is currently using these concepts to solve its combined-value problems. Chapter Two discusses the following six principles, which underlie the Market Value Process:

1. Put customer value before shareholder value.
2. Understand price, product, and non-product needs.
3. Measure and map your progress toward meeting these needs.

4. Carry forward the value from one step to the next.
5. Build integrated customer value strategies.
6. Allocate resources to the highest combined value.

Chapter Two also introduces the maps that will allow you to measure and to visualize your enterprise's decisions at each step.

Part Two: The Diagnosis

In Part Two, Chapters Three, Four, and Five cover how to define markets based on differences in price, product, and non-product needs, how to envision market evolution, and how to prioritize these markets for investment attractiveness. Chapters Six, Seven, and Eight help you diagnose how well your enterprise is currently meeting each market's price, product, and non-product needs, as well as how well it is managing its own internal product and non-product costs in each market.

Part Three: The Bridge

Chapter Nine shows how to pull the considerations of product and non-product quality, price, and internal cost together into precision strategies. These strategies bridge the gap between what the seller is currently doing and what the seller must do to offer customers a price, product, and non-product benefit package that customers will perceive as superior to the competition. These strategies are comprehensive but can be summarized on a single page.

Part Four: The Payoff

Chapters Ten through Fourteen show the payoff of these precision strategies. Chapter Ten shows how to measure the relative customer value that a strategy will deliver once the strategy is in place. Chapter Eleven describes the *value-based revenue outlook*, a ground-breaking approach that teaches you how to envision the sales growth that a strategy can deliver. This approach removes the bias that traditionally accompanies envisioning future sales and replaces it with objectivity. Chapters Twelve and Thirteen demonstrate how to select the best among several promising customer value strategies in each market, based on the combined customer value and shareholder value that the strategies create. In Chapter Fourteen we discuss the implementation of the Market Value Process, and the precision strategies that an enterprise builds in using the process.

Appendix: An Overview of a Precision Strategy

To maximize the usefulness of the book, we collect Sportmed's key maps in the Appendix. These maps will serve as a complete blueprint for building your own precision strategies and mapping the customer and shareholder value these strategies create. If you prefer to see detailed conclusions before you begin, then you should probably review the Appendix before starting Chapter One.

Glossary

Throughout the book, we build a body of definitions that form the language of combined value. At the end, we include a glossary of the words that comprise this language. These terms, such as *precision strategies,* appear in italics the first time we use them. The glossary provides a convenient reference for the definition of these frequently used words.

Acknowledgments

Our thanks for valuable suggestions and comments to Karen Cavanaugh, Henry Claycamp, Dev Dion, Jim Kouzes, Ed McQuarrie, Robert Nolte, Barry Posner, Sidney Schoeffler, Charlie Tonkin, Tyzoon Tyebjee, Ted Yasinsky, Dave Zuckerman, and Dirk Zwemer. And special thanks for very close and detailed readings of multiple drafts of the manuscript to Carol Cleland and Ted Frey.

Palo Alto, California   Alan S. Cleland
June 1996   Albert V. Bruno

THE AUTHORS

This book grew out of the authors' work with Cleland Associates, Inc., a consultancy located in Palo Alto, California.

Alan S. Cleland is the president of Cleland Associates. Prior to founding the company, he was vice president and manager of the West Coast office of PIMS (Profit Impact of Market Strategy) Associates, part of the Strategic Planning Institute. Previously he was vice president of corporate planning for the $2 billion Carlson Companies in Minneapolis; director of corporate planning and chief financial officer for Canada for International Harvester during its restructuring; financial vice president for Lehigh Portland Cement; an investment banker at Shearson American Express; and a project engineer for Combustion Engineering Lummus.

Cleland is a graduate of Yale University, holds a master's degree in mechanical engineering from Massachusetts Institute of Technology, and a master's in business administration from Harvard Business School.

Albert V. Bruno is the Glenn Klimek Professor of Marketing at the Leavey School of Business and Administration, Santa Clara University, and vice president of Cleland Associates. Bruno joined Santa Clara University's faculty in 1971. He was chair of the Marketing Department from 1976 to 1983, and acting and associate dean of the business school from 1989 to 1992. In 1989, he received Santa Clara's Dean's Award as the outstanding teacher on the business faculty.

At Santa Clara, Bruno teaches undergraduate, graduate, and executive-level courses in the fields of marketing management, new-product policy, and business policy. He has written more than sixty articles that have been published in a variety of professional business journals and periodicals.

Bruno holds a bachelor's degree from Purdue University, and a master's degree in business administration and a doctoral degree from the Krannert Graduate School, also Purdue University.

The authors would be pleased to hear from anyone with comments or questions about the book. You can contact them at Cleland Associates' offices in Palo Alto, California. Telephone: (415) 323-0953; or fax: (415) 323-6651.

THE MARKET VALUE PROCESS

PART ONE

INTRODUCTION AND PRINCIPLES

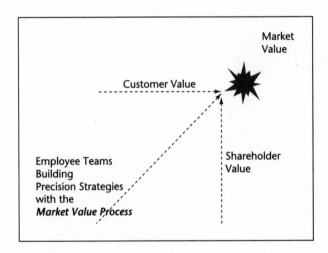

CHAPTER ONE

USING THE MARKET VALUE PROCESS

Customers buy a seller's offering in order to satisfy three kinds of needs, some of which are conscious and some subliminal. The first is the need for the best possible *price;* this is clear-cut. The second set of needs includes such issues as superior performance, solid reliability, broad variety, and ease of use. We call these *product needs.* The third set includes needs that are less tangible, such as up-to-date information provided by consultative selling, ready availability provided by a strong distribution system, top-notch customer service, and reassurance provided by the image and reputation of the seller. We call these *non-product needs.*

Sellers, in turn, offer customers a benefit package to meet these needs. We give the name *product quality* to the precision with which these benefits meet the customer's product needs. We give the name *non-product quality* to the precision with which these benefits meet the customer's non-product needs. Whenever we use the word *quality* in this book, we mean it in this broad sense, including both the product and the non-product aspects. In short, quality encompasses how well a seller meets all of the nonprice needs that affect the buying decision.

Buyers choose the best *customer value*—that is, the best quality for the price—they can find in the marketplace. Successful sellers build precision strategies that bridge the gap between what the seller is currently doing and what the seller must do in order to offer customers a price, product, and non-product benefit package that customers perceive as superior to that offered by the competition. At the same time, these strategies must build wealth for shareholders. By following the Market

Value Process, an enterprise can get a strong handle on whether its strategies are likely to work for both constituencies, customers and shareholders, before it begins to put the strategies in place. Let's look at some examples.

Turning Chips into Crumbs at Borden

Enterprises that fail to build strategies that precisely meet price, product, and non-product needs destroy, rather than create, value for customers and shareholders. On January 25, 1994, *The Wall Street Journal* carried a front-page story entitled "Elsie's Executives: Borden's Bottom Line Has Been Damaged by Conflicting Styles."[1] The article painted a devastating picture. While Elsie the cow was once one of America's respected corporate identities, the company, at the time the article was written, had never been in worse shape. Romeo Ventres, appointed chief executive officer in 1986, dreamed of transforming the company from a sleepy conglomerate into a major food marketer. To do this he embarked on a series of ninety-one acquisitions between 1986 and 1991, buying such brands as Laura Scudder's potato chips, Fisher Cheese, Steero Bouillon, and Krazy Glue; Anthony D'Amato, who became CEO in 1991, was left to sort out these acquired operations.

Borden's strategy was to grow by marketing its own and its recently acquired regional brands beyond their home turf. It did not carefully consider whether the regional brands would appeal to a national audience or whether markets needed to be defined region by region. Borden's pasta business paid the price for this error. The company had assembled a number of strong regional brands, such as Prince and Pennsylvania Dutch brands, becoming the number one marketer of brand-name pasta in the United States. To build on this success, Borden tried to transform its best-selling Creamette pasta into a national brand. By doing so, it undercut its own strong regional brands and also placed Creamette in direct competition with popular local brands. The pasta business, once the gem of its food portfolio, had begun to lose market share by November 1993, and Hershey Foods Corporation was threatening to become the market leader.

The company, in its acquisition spree, ignored some of the well-known brand names it already owned, such as Lady Borden ice cream. Its scenarios for the ice cream market missed the trend toward high-quality, super-premium ice cream, and it failed to extend Lady Borden into this attractive arena.

The company felt it had a core competence in low-cost manufacturing and, through its acquisition strategy, hoped to fill unused manufacturing capacity. As part of its overfocus on cost in a market in which quality was important, it moved the manufacture of Laura Scudder's potato chips out of California into Salt Lake City. At the time, Laura Scudder's was one of the strongest regional potato chip brands in the country, with the number two spot in the huge California market. Delivering the product over the Sierra Nevada, however, created a lot of broken potato chips and inspired *The Wall Street Journal* article's subtitle: "Turning Chips into Crumbs." This was a disaster for product quality.

Borden struggled to consolidate the disparate distribution systems its acquisitions created, but limited availability of its products for purchase hurt the company's non-product quality. In the face of these product and non-product quality problems, the company did not price its product low enough to compete with the mounting competition from private labels.

The imprecision with which Borden's strategy met its customers' price, product, and non-product needs destroyed customer value. In January 1994, sales in every major division were declining. Destruction of shareholder value accompanied the destruction of customer value. Borden's stock, which peaked in 1991 at $38.75 a share, had declined to $15 by January 1994.

Borden's poor strategy design was accompanied by poor implementation. Ventres failed to deal with the operational complexities that his acquisition program created. He rarely got involved in day-to-day operations, spending most of his time in Borden's small Park Avenue offices in New York, far from the hub of the company's operations in Columbus, Ohio.

Let's take a look at how the Borden story relates to the Market Value Process.

Building Strategies That Work with the Market Value Process

Borden's strategy was filled with value mistakes that led to disaster. To avoid these mistakes and to build precision strategies that create rather than destroy value for customers and shareholders, an enterprise needs to follow twelve logical steps. Each step accomplishes a key task in the Market Value Process. For now we simply list the tasks. We consider the twelve steps in more detail as a group in Chapter Two. Then, we examine each step individually in Chapters Three through Fourteen.

 As you review these steps, depicted in Exhibit 1.1, make a mental note each time you see a task that Borden failed to accomplish. We use the steel girder icon on this chart to convey the idea that we are building a framework piece by piece, carrying forward the key result of the prior step as input to a future step. Think about how the steps that Borden took built on themselves to create the final disastrous outcome.

The Diagnosis

1. Define your markets creatively.
2. Envision market evolution with scenarios, not forecasts.

Exhibit 1.1. The Market Value Process: Concepts.

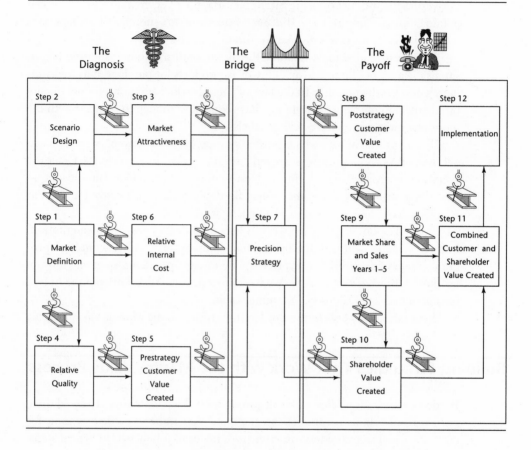

3. Determine whether a market will reward your investment.
4. Deliver quality through product and non-product benefits.
5. Price low enough to please customers and high enough to satisfy stockholders.
6. Manage internal costs to support your quality and price targets.

The Bridge

7. Build precision strategies that do a superior job of meeting needs profitably.

The Payoff

8. Map the customer value your precision strategies create.
9. Map the revenue growth your customer value will deliver.

10. Map the shareholder value your revenue growth and profit margins create.
11. Map the combined value your precision strategies create.
12. Implement your precision strategies quickly and easily.

This twelve-step framework tightly links customer and shareholder value by showing how to seize the financial payoff opportunities—revenue growth and profit margin—that customer value opens.

We saw how Borden's strategy failed to achieve this payoff. Now that we know the steps of the Market Value Process, we are ready to consider a dramatically different example; here is a company that followed these steps. As you read through this example, make a mental note each time you see one of the twelve steps being skillfully executed.

Keeping the Magic Going at Compaq

Around the same time as the Borden story, an article appeared in the February 21, 1994, issue of *Fortune* magazine, entitled "How Compaq Keeps the Magic Going."[2] The article tells a very different tale from the Borden story.

Since Eckhard Pfeiffer became CEO of Compaq in October 1991, he has engineered a stunning and complete turnaround. This turnaround has transformed Compaq from a supplier of PCs to corporations into something much broader: a maker of machines for every market from servers (high-powered PCs that anchor office networks) to consumer products—and all at a blisteringly competitive price.

Prior to the appointment of Pfeiffer as CEO in October 1991, Compaq was a company in trouble. Compaq had built its strategy on the scenario that its markets would continue to be quality sensitive, as they had been in the 1980s, and that customers would pay large price premiums for the features its high-end computers offered. Compaq failed to respond when a shift to a scenario of extreme price sensitivity took place in the microcomputer market. The failure to respond to this shift left Compaq's products overpriced in the marketplace and triggered a major loss in market share. The company reported its first-ever quarterly loss in 1991 and sacked 1,700 people.

The new management immediately identified a market for low-end machines and developed the Pro Linea line of desktop computers to serve this consumer and small business market. In August 1993 Compaq introduced the Presario line of home computers. These machines were designed to attract technophobes, with friendly features like factory-installed software and a built-in telephone answering machine. The Presario quickly became not only Compaq's hottest new

PC ever but also mass merchants' top-selling computer under $1,500. Now Compaq is in the vanguard of a trend toward designing computers for specific market segments and advertising them aggressively. Product quality in all markets is sky-high.

Traditionally, Compaq had focused heavily on selling to corporations through "resellers"—intermediaries dedicated to that purpose. However, when surveys revealed that consumers thought Compaq products hard to find, Pfeiffer added thousands of retailers to the distribution scheme. By early 1994, retailers accounted for 20 percent of Compaq's shipments, versus only 5 percent in 1992. In designing a key marketing display, one Compaq marketer spent $240,000 putting eye-catching cardboard strips around Compaq's monitors. The glossy, multicolored "monitor hood" displays information about the computer's features. With these actions, non-product quality in the form of information and availability for purchase shot through the roof. Sales of models with the hood jumped 11 percent.

Compaq's historic core competence had been to be the high-quality competitor, and Pfeiffer's actions reinforced this. But to operate successfully in a world of price-sensitive markets, Compaq also needed to develop a core competence in low internal cost. Pfeiffer squeezed manufacturing costs and ordered Compaq's factories to operate round the clock. To save money, Compaq began to outsource subassembly work to subcontractors in 1992, abandoning its practice of assembling every nut and bolt itself. In 1993, while volume doubled from 1.5 million to three million computers, total manufacturing costs fell almost $10 million. In a major departure, Compaq changed its entire manufacturing system to a "build-to-order" rather than a build-for-inventory approach. In 1993, fewer than 5 percent of Compaq's PCs were built on order; Pfeiffer wants to hit 100 percent. Compaq's cost strategy is based on the reality that only the most efficient manufacturers will be able to continue to reduce prices while still achieving acceptable profit margins.

As a result of the precision with which it has met its customers' shifting price, product, and non-product needs, Compaq, since it changed course, has more than doubled its share of the $35-billion-a-year PC and workstation market, going from 3.8 percent in 1991 to 10 percent at the time the *Fortune* article was written. Compaq has also created value for its shareholders, making more money in 1993 than IBM and Apple combined. Its stock price quadrupled from $20 a share in mid 1992 to $82 in January 1994, the time of the *Fortune* article. The microcomputer market is a volatile one, and Compaq's future success is by no means assured. Still, its good moves had given it strong momentum when this snapshot was taken.

Taking the Self-Assessment Exercise

Now that you know the steps of the Market Value Process and have seen them in action in the Borden and Compaq stories, we invite you to apply this process to some aspect of your own business. Use Exhibit 1.2 as a guide. Any "no" response flags a need for corrective action.

How the Market Value Process Evolved

An enterprise can keep its magic going, as Compaq did, or create the magic if it is not there, by following the Market Value Process. Cleland first conceived the idea of what became the Market Value Process in 1980, shortly after joining the Profit Impact of Market Strategy (PIMS) Program of the Strategic Planning Institute. He had spent his early career as an investment banker and chief financial officer, immersed in shareholder value. In client meetings, he saw that most participants understood one or another of these value disciplines, but few understood both. The outlines of the Market Value Process began to take shape in his mind. In 1986, Cleland and Bruno met through the Executive Development Center at Santa Clara University, where Cleland was presenting an early version of the Market Value Process. We shared a common interest in the combined value problem. Together, we worked on the continuing evolution of the Market Value Process.

The Market Value Process has been proven in action for more than five years by more than one thousand managers who have attended our worldwide programs in the Americas, Europe, and Asia. After each program, we have further refined the material and then used a new draft of this book with each succeeding group. These managers have come from organizations as diverse as high-technology, banking, retailing, heavy manufacturing, name-brand consumer goods, and health care enterprises. In all of these arenas, the Market Value Process has consistently demonstrated its capacity to solve hundreds of combined-value problems.

The Market Value Process as presented in this book has grown out of our experiences in all of these situations. You will notice that we have broadened the applicability of commonly used terms. Understanding quality as a benefit that addresses the customer's non-product as well as product needs is one example. As a result of this broadening, the concepts of the Market Value Process become universal, and the Market Value Process works in any marketplace.

Exhibit 1.2. Self-Assessment Exercise:
Solving the Combined-Value Problem.

Check the appropriate column: <u>Yes</u>   <u>No</u>

The Diagnosis

Do you define your markets differently than you did five years ago?   ____ ____

Have you envisioned several scenarios for the future evolution of
each market?   ____ ____

Is there a fit between your core competencies and what your
scenarios tell you it takes to succeed in each market?   ____ ____

Do you have a dominant position in your market-perceived product
and non-product quality relative to your competition?   ____ ____

Do you price your quality at a level low enough to please customers
and high enough to please shareholders?   ____ ____

Do you have a product and non-product internal cost structure that
supports your quality and price targets?   ____ ____

The Bridge

Do you have a precision strategy in each market to bridge the gap
between your current and desired performance?   ____ ____

The Payoff

Have you measured the relative value you will offer customers once
your precision strategy is in place?   ____ ____

Have you envisioned the revenue growth that the difference
between your prestrategy and poststrategy customer value will
deliver?   ____ ____

Have you assessed the shareholder value that your revenue growth
and profit margins will create?   ____ ____

Have you determined whether your strategy will deliver enough
combined customer and shareholder value to make it work?   ____ ____

Do you have a structure in place to make sure the people that build
the strategy will be empowered to implement it?   ____ ____

Any "no" response flags a need for corrective action.

CHAPTER TWO

LEARNING THE PRINCIPLES

This chapter describes the six principles of the Market Value Process. For each one, we offer an example that shows the principle in action. This chapter will provide you with a solid understanding of the language of the Market Value Process. And with this understanding, you'll have smooth sailing through the rest of the book.

Principle One: Putting Customer Value Before Shareholder Value

An enterprise gives itself the best chance to achieve its goals of creating value for both customers and shareholders if it focuses on customers first and shareholders second—not the other way around. Customer value opens the opportunity for shareholder value. This is why the customer value steps precede the shareholder value steps in the Market Value Process. It is amazing how many enterprises believe that they can serve shareholders best by putting shareholder value first.

In a financially driven world that pays too much attention to short-term earnings, it is all too easy to lose the crucial focus on customer value. In a successful enterprise, customers come first, employees come second, and shareholders come third. This does not suggest that shareholders are unimportant. Instead, it says that if an enterprise has enthusiastic customers and empowered employees who build strategies to keep customers happy, then it is highly likely that the results will turn out well for shareholders. An enterprise can make certain that this is the case by seizing the opportunities for financial payoff—that is, revenue growth and profit margin—that customer value opens.

We can depict the combination of customer value and shareholder value that a precision strategy creates in the Customer and Shareholder Value Map, Exhibit 2.1. We measure customer value created—the result of the marketing strategy—along the horizontal dimension and shareholder value created—the result of the financial strategy—along the vertical dimension. The reader will immediately recognize that Exhibit 2.1 is the graphic on the title page transformed into an interpretive chart. In both the graphic and this chart, customer and shareholder value grow toward, and converge in, the upper right corner to solve the combined-value problem. We will constantly return to, and build on, this chart throughout the

**Exhibit 2.1. Customer and Shareholder Value Map:
A Vision for Making Strategy Work.**

Create customer value first and shareholder value second.

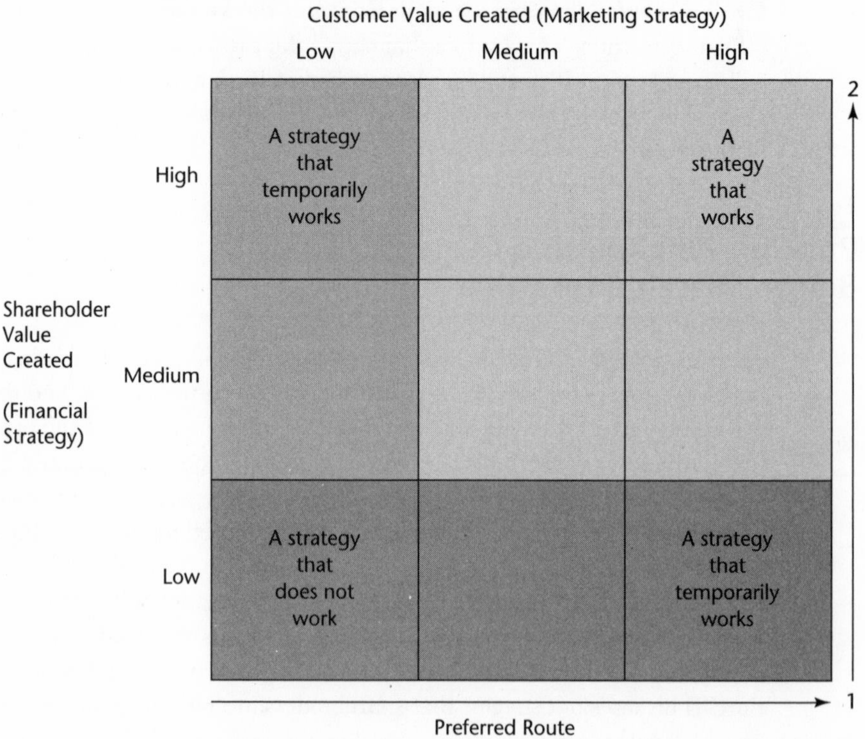

Customer Value Created (Marketing Strategy)

	Low	Medium	High	
High	A strategy that temporarily works		A strategy that works	2
Shareholder Value Created **Medium** (Financial Strategy)				
Low	A strategy that does not work		A strategy that temporarily works	

Preferred Route → 1

book. In this section we discuss the concepts of the chart and the best direction of movement on it. Under Principle Six, we show generally how to use the chart to select strategies, set objectives, and prioritize markets for investment. And in Chapter Thirteen, we will show you how to turn it into a specific tool to select the best among your enterprise's strategies.

An enterprise wants to develop a strategy that will achieve a position in the light-shaded, upper right corner of the chart—in other words, a strategy that creates high value for both customers and shareholders. The biggest failure is a strategy that lands in the bottom left corner—one that creates value for neither customers nor shareholders. An enterprise must not undertake a strategy that leaves it anywhere in the dark-shaded bottom row—a strategy that destroys rather than creates value for shareholders.

Let's take an example where an enterprise has a strategy that is stuck in the "does not work" corner; obviously, it needs to improve the strategy. It would be ideal to go straight from the worst corner to the best corner. Many strategies envision this happening, but it is more easily said than done. In practice, the enterprise often has to work its way along the perimeter. Then the temptation is to move straight up to the neutral-shaded upper left corner where shareholder value is high and customer value is low. After all, this takes the enterprise out of the bottom row where all strategies result in shareholder value destruction. The enterprise can execute this move by cutting costs to improve margins and pruning excess assets to increase turnover. Unless it can then immediately put customer value in place, this strategy will work only temporarily. Soon the enterprise will end up right back in the "does not work" corner because short-term, financially driven fixes that are not coupled with customer value fixes are destined to fail.

A good example of a financially driven fix is the classic Schlitz beer story of the 1970s. Schlitz was the number two beer maker in America, but management was dissatisfied with the company's stock price. Certainly, Schlitz was not in the worst corner of the chart. Perhaps it was in the middle. In any event, Schlitz's management embarked on a purely financially driven strategy to improve the company's situation. Management analyzed the income statement and decided to cut expenses and increase margins by using a less expensive hops in its beer. They analyzed the balance sheet and decided to reduce the assets tied up in the business by cutting the time Schlitz aged the beer. Sure enough, profit margins increased, asset turnover went up, and the stock price jumped. But then something happened in the marketplace. Customers noticed that Schlitz didn't taste as good anymore, and they deserted the brand in droves. The stock price plunged, and Schlitz ended up in the bottom left corner, having destroyed both customer and shareholder value. Schlitz never regained its former position. It serves as a classic example of the danger of focusing on shareholder value before customer value. Having a position in the upper left corner means that you have a strategy that will work only temporarily.

To make the trip from the worst to the best corner of the chart by going along the edges, it is always best to put customer value in place first. Temporarily, this leaves an enterprise in the dark-shaded bottom row, with increasing customer value but continued low shareholder value. The enterprise still must turn on a dime and put in place the profit margins it needs to create shareholder value. But this is easier to do when an enterprise's sales are growing as a result of its high customer value than when sales are tumbling, as they did for Schlitz.

There are, however, many companies who fail to make this turn. One example took place about the same time as the Schlitz story. Bowmar Instruments was the early leader in the handheld calculator market. In the late 1960s, these calculators sold for around $200. Prices tumbled, however, as they commonly do in high-technology markets. A year later the price was $100. Eventually, it dropped below $20. In the face of this, Bowmar was never able to turn its market leadership into acceptable margins and move out of the bottom right corner. Market leadership passed to Texas Instruments, a low-cost producer of the semiconductors that powered the calculators.

The message of these examples is that an enterprise's strategies must create value for both customers and shareholders. Neither one automatically leads to the other. It is highly desirable for an enterprise to create value for both constituencies at the same time, rather than one after the other. But if an enterprise can't, it is better to create customer value first. It is easier to move to a position of high combined value from the lower right corner than from the upper left corner. In our two examples, it would have been far easier for Bowmar to enter into a strategic alliance with a semiconductor manufacturer in order to get low-cost componentry for their market-leading calculator than for Schlitz to find an alliance that would save a brand that had been fatally wounded in the customers' eyes.

The most successful enterprises begin their thought process by determining how they can meet customer needs with more precision than their competition, not how they can create wealth or how they can use a new technology. Once they have done this, they check to see whether they are creating shareholder value and whether their technology is sound—but that's not where they begin. The most successful enterprises begin by seeing existing needs or imagining potential needs. *National Geographic* made this point in a story about Alexander Graham Bell:

> Impressed by Thomas Edison's "invention factory," Bell tried to replicate it on a small scale. But his approach to invention was different. Edison tried to identify a commercial need and then look for a way to meet it. Bell was more likely to be struck by a physical phenomenon and then look for a way to use it.[1]

This piece of wisdom is timeless. The idea of putting customer value first applied in the era of Edison and Bell; it still applies in the information economy of the 1990s.

Principle Two: Understanding Price, Product, and Non-product Needs

Precision strategies take their name from the precision with which they meet customers' price, product, and non-product needs. It is important to nail down an understanding of these needs as you begin because they underlie each of the twelve steps in the Market Value Process.

We established in Chapter One that customers buy to satisfy three needs: price, product quality, and non-product quality. Customers buy the best value, the most quality for the price, they can find in the marketplace. Sellers, in turn, offer customers a price, product, and non-product benefit package to meet these needs. Exhibit 2.2 illustrates this.

To create customer value, an enterprise must be driven by benefits, not finances. A benefits-driven enterprise directs all its activity toward meeting the needs that customers currently want to satisfy, or may in the future want to satisfy, when they buy the enterprise's offering. Before we look at an example, let's consider why we choose the words *product* and *non-product* to describe the nonprice needs.

Other writers have used different pairs of words to distinguish between these two sets of needs. One alternative, for example, would be "tangible" and "intangible." But in some purely service businesses, such as investment banking or consulting, all needs are intangible. Another alternative would be "product" and "service." This pair also creates problems since it seems to refer only to

Exhibit 2.2. Understanding the Needs-Benefits Link.

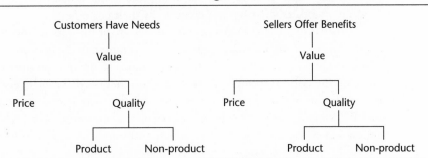

manufacturing businesses that offer a tangible product, such as a computer, surrounded by intangible services. We use the terms *product* and *non-product,* as we have defined them, to describe the nonprice needs because these terms apply equally well to both manufacturing and service enterprises. Customers of both manufacturing and service enterprises have needs at the core of their buying decision, and they also have needs that surround those at the core. The words *product* and *non-product* will help you use the Market Value Process in both manufacturing and service markets. To drive this point home, we'll look at an example that illustrates the use of the word *product* in a pure service business.

One important financial decision that an enterprise must make is the choice of an investment banker. Let's think about how an enterprise makes this choice. We remember that product needs are the tangible or intangible needs that are at the core of the customer's buying decision. In choosing an investment banker, an enterprise considers, at the core of its buying decision, how well each Wall Street firm executes certain key transactions. These key transactions, which are the product needs, include public offerings, private placements, acquisitions, and major corporate restructurings. The use of the word *product* to describe these needs is by no means artificial. Investment bankers regularly refer to these transactions, in conversations among themselves, as their "products."

We also remember that non-product needs are those that surround the product needs. We can depict this "surrounding" concept for our investment banking example with the two concentric circles in Exhibit 2.3.[2] The non-product needs are the ongoing activities listed in the outer circle, which surround the key transactions in the inner circle. These non-product needs include research analyst support for a stock following a public offering, market-making activities if the stock trades over the counter, ongoing financial advice, and the reassurance provided by the image and reputation of the investment banking firm.

An enterprise makes a choice among investment banking firms that meet these needs with at least threshold levels of competence. Meeting these threshold levels qualifies these firms to compete for the enterprise's investment banking business. Together, these four product and four non-product needs constitute the *quality* of investment bankers' offerings as perceived by their customers.

Just because the customer's product needs are at the core of the buying decision doesn't necessarily make them more important than the non-product needs. In any specific situation, the collective importance of the non-product needs can outweigh the collective importance of the product needs in the overall quality picture. To the customer of an investment banker, research analyst support of its stock following a public offering can be enormously important. Having a research analyst widely regarded as the best in that customer's industry can be the decisive factor in being chosen as that customer's investment banker. Returning to

Exhibit 2.3. Customers' Product and Non-product Needs: Investment Banking.

**Customers have both product needs and non-product needs.
Non-product needs may be more important than product needs.**

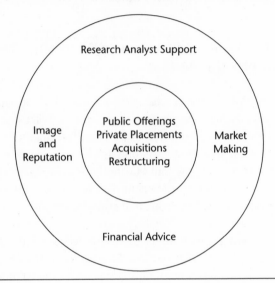

Exhibit 2.3, the larger area of the surrounding circle dramatizes the greater importance of these non-product needs. In fact, one important reason to separate product from non-product needs is that we have a natural tendency to overfocus on core needs and to underestimate the importance of the surrounding needs in the customer's buying decision. In situations like investment banking, the surrounding non-product needs can dominate the outcome of the buying decision.

Occasionally, it may not be obvious whether a given need belongs in the product or non-product category. In these instances, an enterprise should not agonize over the distinction but should simply make a judgment that seems reasonable. The Market Value Process automatically adjusts for this judgment, as we will see in Chapter Three.

Finally, after considering quality, the enterprise finishes making its choice among investment bankers by looking at price. To a customer seeking a public offering, price is the fee that competing investment bankers charge for the transaction. The customer considers the relative value—the quality for the price—offered by competing investment bankers and chooses the banker who offers the best relative value.

In response to customer needs, Wall Street firms develop competing *offerings*—price, product, and non-product benefit packages—that meet these needs. The winning player will be the one who offers the best value in the marketplace.

Next, we will see how to measure and map the relative value that a benefits-driven competitor offers its customers.

Principle Three: Measuring and Mapping Your Progress Toward Meeting Needs

The concept of *customer value* as the measurement of what quality for the price an enterprise is offering is a powerful one, and we will use it throughout the book. We saw in the Preface, however, that to build strategies that meet needs with precision, an enterprise must have tools as well as concepts. In this section we will show you how to use a highly sophisticated but easy-to-use tool to measure and map the value that an enterprise's benefit package offers its customers. This will give you an introduction to the maps that you will encounter at each step of the Market Value Process.

Measuring something is important because without measurement, concepts such as customer value become fuzzy at best. At worst they become empty slogans. In contrast, the visual impact of mapping what an enterprise measures is profound. Mapping provides a visual record of the enterprise's rate of progress toward meeting needs, and this record provides the insight that can lead to action. At each step of the Market Value Process, this book will show you how to use maps, such as the one we are about to see, as powerful tools to measure and depict the result of your enterprise's value-creating decisions. Let's look at an example.

We can see how to measure and map customer value by examining the Customer Value Map in Exhibit 2.4.[3] This map shows relative product and non-product quality along the horizontal dimension and relative price along the vertical dimension. Remember, we are measuring both quality and price relative to the competition. The zero point on the relative quality axis does not mean rock-bottom quality. It means quality that is the average of the quality offered by the key competitors in the market, including the enterprise itself. The zero point on the relative price axis doesn't mean that an offering is given away for free. It means a price that is the average of the price offered by the key competitors.

To continue the investment banking example, let's say the customers in the investment banking market are equally sensitive to quality and price. This means that if an investment banker is offering a package of product and non-product quality that is 10 percent above average, customers will accept a price that is 10

Exhibit 2.4. Customer Value Map.

We must be able to measure and map customer value created
(quality-for-the-price) in order to give it meaning.

percent above market average. We show this equal tradeoff customers make between quality and price by the forty-five-degree line that we call the *"market wants"*
line. This line depicts the tradeoff between quality and price that customers are
prepared to accept. Now suppose that competitors A, B, C, and D are, respectively, 30 percent above, 15 percent above, 15 percent below, and 30 percent below
average on both quality and price. In this case, they will all fall on the "market
wants" line and their market shares will be stable, because each competitor's benefit package offers a relative customer value—quality for the price—that customers
are willing to accept.

Now let's change the example in Exhibit 2.5. Suppose the government puts
a regulatory process in place requiring the four competitors to sell at a single
price—one lower than D is currently charging. Suddenly, then, all competitors
have a zero relative price because all are charging the same low, mandated price.
Relative quality positions, however, remain unchanged. We call this new competitive lineup the *"market gets"* line. The market, however, remains willing to view
quality and price as a fifty-fifty tradeoff, so the "market wants" line remains unchanged. Then competitors A and B will gain market share at the expense of C
and D because A and B offer the customer a superior relative value.

The power of the Customer Value Map is that it provides insights that are
both static and dynamic: it shows the position of each competitor at an instant
in time, and it also indicates the changes in market share that will take place as a

Exhibit 2.5. Customer Value Map Where Price Is Constant.

**A competitor creates a superior customer value by offering a
better quality-for-the-price tradeoff than the customer requires.**

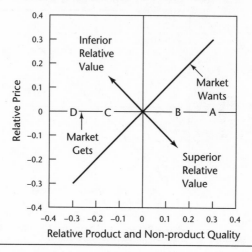

result of that position. Any competitor positioned below the "market wants" line is offering a superior relative value—a better quality-for-the-price tradeoff than the market requires—and will gain market share. Any competitor positioned above the "market wants" line is offering an inferior relative value—a worse quality-for-the-price tradeoff than the market requires—and will lose share. Let's suppose that Competitor C is our Wall Street firm. In order to avoid losing market share, it must immediately begin to develop a precision strategy to improve its product and non-product quality.

In the next section, we will see the entire collection of maps that the Market Value Process uses as tools to solve the combined-value problem.

Principle Four: Carrying Forward the Value from One Step to the Next

This section is a road map for the Market Value Process. In Chapter One we listed the twelve steps that comprise the three parts of the Market Value Process—the diagnosis, the bridge, and the payoff. We showed how enterprises use the steps with varying degrees of skill in the Borden and Compaq examples. Now we build on this introductory material to accomplish four key tasks. First, we go beyond simply listing the steps and enlarge on the concept that each step embodies. Next, we see in greater detail how the strategies of Borden and Compaq illustrate the concept in action. Then, we introduce the map that is the tool for measuring and depicting the decisions an enterprise makes at each step. Finally, as the title of this section suggests, we pinpoint the step's key result that becomes the carried value for a future step. These carried values create a framework that tightly links customer value and shareholder value. This link between the two consists of the financial payoff opportunities—revenue growth and profit margin—that superior customer value opens.

　　　The road map we will use to do these four things is shown in Exhibit 2.6. This is similar to Exhibit 1.1, but inside each box we have replaced the name of the step with the name of the map that depicts the result of that step.

　　　Above each step in Exhibit 2.6, we have placed a globe icon. This icon flags the map as one of the important tools of the Market Value Process. Whenever

Exhibit 2.6. The Market Value Process: Tools.

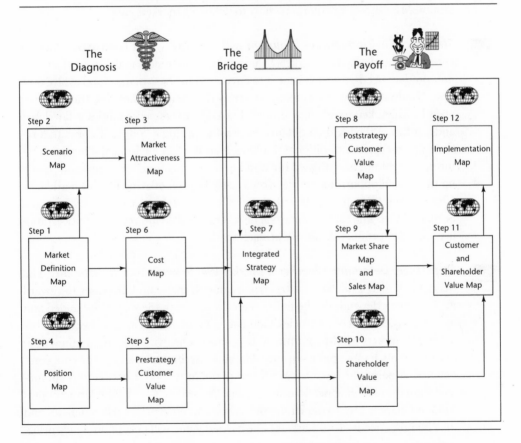

this globe icon appears on a map in later chapters, it reminds you that we are looking at one of the key maps from among our larger group of exhibits in this book.
We collect these key maps in the Appendix. Now let's take a closer look at this road
map, starting with Step One at the far left of the chart.

The Diagnosis

 Step One: Define Your Markets Creatively. An enterprise wins customers by creatively identifying differences in their price, product, and non-product needs. The
"power users" in Compaq's high-end markets needed powerful features and were
willing to pay for them. The technophobes in Compaq's low-end markets wanted
ease of use at a low price. Recognizing these differences was key to Compaq's
resurgence. The company carried forward this market definition into every subsequent step in building its strategies. In Chapter Three we see how to map these
differences in customers' price, product, and non-product needs. The Market Definition Map shows an enterprise how to define its markets creatively.

 Step Two: Envision Market Evolution with Scenarios, Not Forecasts. Once an
enterprise has defined its markets by uncovering differences in price, product, and
non-product needs, the next issue is to envision how these markets will evolve over
time. To do this, you must create scenarios that help you imagine the different
ways in which key trends may unfold. Looking at these possibilities is far richer
and safer than relying on a detailed forecast for a single "official future" that reflects an enterprise's traditional thinking. Had Borden envisioned alternative futures, it might not have missed the trend to super-premium ice cream and passed
up the golden opportunity to develop a Lady Borden offering for this market. In
Chapter Four we will show how to develop several alternative futures by using the
Scenario Map. The carried value will be several possible futures for the price, product, and non-product sensitivity of each market.

 Step Three: Determine Whether a Market Will Reward Your Investment. The
degree to which a market is attractive to an enterprise and promises to reward
its investment depends on the fit between the direction the market is headed and
an enterprise's core competencies. Compaq got into trouble in 1991 because it believed its markets would continue to be quality sensitive when in fact they were
becoming much more price sensitive. Compaq, at that time, lacked the core competence of being the low-cost producer, so the fit was poor between its competence and the emerging needs of its markets. We will use the Market Attractiveness
Map in Chapter Five to depict the fit between an enterprise's competencies and
the emerging needs of its markets. The carried value will be a preliminary prior-
itizing of markets for investment.

Step Four: Deliver Quality Through Product and Non-product Benefits. In Step Four we measure and map how an enterprise's customers perceive its quality relative to the competition's quality. We consider both the product and non-product dimensions of quality in detail. The sales of Compaq's Presario line of machines to its low-end market were enhanced by the product quality provided by its user-friendly, factory-installed software. Sales also benefited greatly from the non-product quality of the information that the glossy, multicolored "monitor hood" provided. Chapter Six shows how to measure and map the relative quality an enterprise offers in each market by using the Position Map. We carry this relative quality forward as a key input to the customer value an enterprise offers.

 Step Five: Price Low Enough to Please Customers and High Enough to Satisfy Shareholders. Once an enterprise knows its relative quality, it turns to price. The enterprise must price its quality at a level that creates a superior value. Borden failed to do this and lost ground to mounting competition from private-label products as customers focused increasingly on price.

While pricing must be low enough to create value for customers, it must also be high enough to create value for shareholders. In Chapter Seven we use the Customer Value Map to show how to strike this crucial balance. We call the result the enterprise's *prestrategy customer value*. We carry forward the prestrategy customer value as a key input to building precision strategies to enhance it.

 Step Six: Manage Internal Costs to Support Your Quality and Price Targets. Now that an enterprise knows the quality and price it needs to offer the marketplace in order to provide a superior customer value, it must ensure that its cost structure is low enough to provide profit margins that create value for shareholders. To do this, it needs to evaluate its internal cost structure along both the product and non-product dimensions. Compaq took strong steps to cut *product costs* by moving to round-the-clock manufacturing and to a "build on order" model. Borden struggled to reduce its *non-product costs* by rationalizing the multiple distribution systems it inherited from its many acquisitions. Chapter Eight shows how to use the Cost Map to depict an enterprise's performance along each of these critical cost dimensions. We then carry forward the enterprise's relative cost position as another key input to building strategies.

The Bridge

 Step Seven: Build Precision Strategies That Do a Superior Job of Meeting Needs Profitably. An enterprise's prestrategy customer value created plus its relative internal cost and its market attractiveness are the carried values that serve as input to building integrated customer value strategies in Step Seven. In Exhibit 2.6, we can see how Steps Three, Five, and Six feed into Step Seven at the center of the chart. *Integrated customer value strategies* integrate quality, price, and cost. All integrated customer value strategies are precision strategies. Despite their broad scope, they should not exceed a single page in length. We use the Integrated Strategy Map in Chapter Nine to show how to build these precision strategies. We carry forward the quality, price, and cost actions that comprise the strategies as an input to the poststrategy customer value the enterprise offers and the shareholder value it creates.

The Payoff

 Step Eight: Map the Customer Value Your Precision Strategies Create. By Step Eight we are ready to measure and map the customer value an enterprise offers once its strategy is in place. We call this the *poststrategy customer value.* Compaq's strategy dramatically enhanced customer value. Borden's strategy just as dramatically destroyed it. In this step we return to the Customer Value Map to depict these different degrees of success. We carry forward the enterprise's poststrategy customer value as a key input to its revenue growth.

 Step Nine: Map the Revenue Growth Your Customer Value Will Deliver. This is one of the most cutting-edge steps in the Market Value Process. We use the *value-based revenue outlook* to compare the enterprise's prestrategy and poststrategy Customer Value Maps and measure the financial payoff of customer value—that is, the revenue its strategies are likely to deliver in each market. We use the Market Share Map and Sales Map to do this and carry the enterprise's future revenue growth forward to the next step as a key driver of shareholder value. Depending on the precision with which the enterprise's strategy meets price, product, and non-product needs, its market share will respond accordingly. Compaq's market share increased from 3.8 percent to 10 percent of the PC and workstation market. Borden's sales were declining in every major division.

 Step Ten: Map the Shareholder Value Your Revenue Growth and Profit Margins Create. An enterprise must always create value for both customers and shareholders. *Shareholder value* has two parts: the cash flow that a strategy generates and the increase in value in the business that the strategy causes. We use the Shareholder Value Map in Chapter Twelve to show the amount of shareholder value each strategy creates and to show how it is built up from these two parts. Customer value creates the sales growth and profit margins that drive shareholder value. Compaq's stock price quadrupled from $20 a share in mid 1992 to $82 in January 1994. Borden's stock, which peaked in 1991 at $38.75, declined to $15 by January 1994.

Step Eleven: Map the Combined Value Your Precision Strategies Create. We measure the total impact of a precision strategy by using the Customer and Shareholder Value Map to depict the combined value it creates. In Chapter Thirteen we show how to measure combined value and use the result to select the best among several strategies in each market. We also show how to use the result to allocate resources among markets.

 Step Twelve: Implement Your Precision Strategies Quickly and Easily. The last step, discussed in Chapter Fourteen, is to implement the Market Value Process and the strategies an enterprise builds with it. We use the Implementation Map to make certain the enterprise delivers the price, product, and non-product benefits that its precision strategies have created.

 The mapping tools and carried-value concepts we have introduced in this section are powerful integrating techniques. They give an enterprise the means to build precision strategies that create enough combined customer and shareholder value to make sure the strategies work. Together, they are the vital keys to solving the combined-value problem. Each time a world globe icon or steel girder icon appears in this book, it is a reminder that the reader is seeing an application of these mapping or carried-value techniques.

Next we will see in broad outline how to build a precision strategy.

Principle Five: Building Integrated Customer Value Strategies

In this section we preview the principles for building strategies—Step Seven in the Market Value Process. Then we apply these principles to outline a precision strategy for our investment banking example from Principles Two and Three.

First, in developing a strategy for a particular market, an enterprise identifies several possible *objectives* for its position in that market. Examples of these objectives are to gain, hold, or lose market share. Each objective is usually associated with a particular level of investment in human and capital resources relative to the competition. For example, if an enterprise is equally productive in using its resources as the competition, then investing on a par with the competition would be consistent with a hold share objective. Investing more or less aggressively would be consistent with a gain or lose share objective. The question is which objective and its associated level of investment are the "right" ones for that particular market.

To answer this question, the enterprise builds a precision strategy for deploying the resources needed to attain each objective. In building strategies, the correct sequence of attack is quality, price, and cost. For example, to support a gain share objective, an enterprise designs an aggressive set of actions to improve its product and non-product quality. Next it sets a price that together with its quality, offers customers a superior value. Then, an enterprise sets its internal costs at a level that provides the profit margins necessary to create shareholder value. Low internal cost is part of a customer value strategy because it signals to the market, through business press articles like the Compaq story, that an enterprise can sustain low pricing and still reward its shareholders.

Finally, the enterprise measures how well the strategy supporting each objective meets the enterprise's ultimate goal—creating a high combination of customer value and shareholder value. The "right" objective and supporting strategy are the ones that create the highest combined value.

In summary, the sequence of thought is objectives, strategies, and goals. This mirrors the classic "design, build, and test" cycle that enterprises use in developing new products.[4] Here, the "design" is the choice of objectives, the "build" is the strategy supporting that objective, and the "test" is the combined value the strategy creates. The enterprise will select the objective and supporting strategy that pass the test by the widest margin and thereby do the best job of solving the combined-value problem.

You may object that this thought process seems too open ended and that an enterprise could end up building candidate strategies forever. The answer lies in never losing sight of the ultimate goal: creating combined value. With this goal in mind, you have a standard for discarding obviously weak strategies early in the process. This discarding leads quickly to a focus on a few strong strategies that will contend for the winning position.

We are now ready to apply the principles and build a strategy. For our example we return to the investment banking business. We can see a visualization of the sequence of objectives, strategies, and goals for our investment banker in Exhibit 2.7, which we will now explore in some detail.

We begin by carrying forward the product and non-product needs from Principle Two. We display them in the far left column as the major building blocks of strategies. Then, in the other three columns we consider different objectives our Wall Street firm might set for the market—gain, hold, or lose share. These objectives form the "design" backdrop for the investment banker's strategies. Often an initial reaction is to reject the idea of losing share in a market, because this seems an unworthy objective. Several markets often compete for an enterprise's limited resources, however, and opportunities may be better in some markets than in others. In this case, the lose share objective might be appropriate for some markets. Many Wall Street firms engage in both the investment banking and the retail brokerage markets, for example. Both require a major investment of resources. It may not be possible to expand both simultaneously. This is why it is important to consider multiple market share objectives in each market.

Exhibit 2.7. The Sequence of Objectives, Strategies, and Goals.

1. We identify alternative objectives we might set in each market.
2. Then we build an integrated customer value strategy to attain each objective.
3. Finally, we measure combined customer and shareholder value created by each strategy.

Market: Investment Banking

1. Alternative Objectives	Gain Share	Hold Share	Lose Share
2. Strategies			
Quality			
Product	Aggressive	Moderate	Mild
Public Offerings			
Private Placements			
Acquisitions			
Restructuring			
Non-product	Aggressive	Moderate	Mild
Research Support			
Marketing Making			
Financial Advice			
Image and Reputation			
Price	Low	Moderate	High
Cost			
Product	Support quality	Support quality	Support quality
Non-product	and price	and price	and price
3. Goals			
Customer Value Created	?	?	?
Shareholder Value Created	?	?	?

Next, continuing in each of these three columns, the investment banking firm develops integrated customer value strategies to support each of the three objectives—the "build" step. Here we simply use single-word strategy descriptions like "aggressive," "moderate," and "mild" to characterize the level of resource investment, but we will greatly enlarge on these strategies in Chapter Nine.

The strategy to support the gain share objective involves an aggressive program to meet each product and non-product need. The investment banking business requires both human and capital resources for growth. Consequently, the firm will need to develop or acquire top-notch skills in the core product needs of public offerings, private placements, acquisitions, and restructurings. It will also need an abundance of skills in the surrounding non-product needs of research support, market making, financial advice, and image. Pricing should be on the low side to create the superior customer value necessary to gain share.

In contrast, the strategy supporting the lose share objective might require only mild moves to meet product and non-product needs. Coupled with pricing on the high side, this strategy would provide attractive margins but offer an inferior customer value that is consistent with a lose share objective.

The strategy supporting the hold share objective would be somewhere between these two.

Each of the three strategies should include putting in place the internal cost structure—product and non-product—that is required to support the strategy's quality and price actions.

In the next principle, we turn to the question marks at the bottom of Exhibit 2.7, which ask how much customer value and shareholder value each of these strategies creates—the "test" step. This combined-value creation is the enterprise's ultimate goal.

Principle Six: Allocating Resources to the Highest Combined Value

Now that the enterprise has built strategies to support each of its objectives, it needs to measure the combined customer and shareholder value that each of these strategies creates. These are the question marks at the bottom of Exhibit 2.7, and Principle Six gives a preview of how the Market Value Process resolves them. Once an enterprise makes this measurement, it can identify the winning strategy—the one that creates the highest combined value. We will see how to make this measurement later. The enterprise then sets the objective that the winning strategy was built to support. This is the "right" objective for the enterprise in this particular market.

It is important to realize that setting objectives at the end of the thought process, as we have just done, runs counter to conventional wisdom. Conventional wisdom holds that an enterprise should set objectives on some intuitive basis at the beginning of the process and that everything else will flow from these objectives. But an enterprise should not set objectives on an intuitive basis. The enterprise cannot know the right objective for each market until it works through the Market Value Process and knows the combined value created by the strategies supporting the objectives. Only then can the enterprise be sure that it has identified the winning strategy and accompanying objective. Only then can the enterprise be confident that it has set the objective that provides the best solution to the combined-value problem.

Finally, the enterprise extends the combined-value test beyond looking at a single market to identifying the best among several markets in which it competes. To do this, it simply compares the combined value created by the winning objective and supporting strategy in the different markets. The market in which the winning objective delivers the highest combined value gets first priority for resources. Consequently, by measuring and mapping combined value, an enterprise can both select the best objective in each market and set priorities for resource allocation among multiple markets. By following the Market Value Process, an enterprise touches all the bases needed to propel itself to leadership in the markets where it can deliver the most value to both its customers and its shareholders.

For an example of how an enterprise uses the combined-value test, we turn once again to our Wall Street firm. We worked through the "design" and "build" part of its strategy in Principle Five; now we complete the "test" part. We saw in Principle Five how this firm built three integrated customer value strategies for its investment banking business, one to support each of the gain, hold, and lose market share objectives. The firm then prepared strategies to support these same three objectives in its retail brokerage business. Next, the firm measured and mapped the customer and shareholder value created by these six strategies. We will show how to do this in Chapter Thirteen. For now, however, let's focus on the end result.

To do this we look at Exhibit 2.8, another version of the Customer and Shareholder Value Map. We used this chart to depict the Schlitz and Bowmar examples in Principle One, but we use it here in quite a different way. In Principle One we used it to show that the best way to move from unfavorable to favorable terrain was to create customer value first and shareholder value second. Here, instead of using the Customer and Shareholder Value Map to assess direction of movement, we will use it to make judgments about the merit of strategies based on the combined value they deliver once they are in place. Exhibit 2.8 shows the information that our Wall Street firm needs in order to make the following two key decisions.

The first decision is to decide which of the integrated customer value strategies and accompanying objectives to choose in the investment banking and the retail brokerage markets. The correct choice is the strategy and accompanying objective that promise the highest combination of customer and shareholder value. This is the strategy located closest to the upper right corner of the chart. In the investment banking (IB) market, this is the gain share (G) objective and its supporting strategy. In the retail brokerage (RB) market, this is the hold share (H) objective and its supporting strategy.

The second decision is to decide what priority to give these two markets for the investment of human and capital resources. The correct choice is to give top priority to the market whose best strategy promises to deliver the highest combined

Exhibit 2.8.

**By measuring and mapping combined value, we can set
priorities within markets and priorities among markets.**

Customer Value Created (Marketing Strategy)

		Low	Medium	High
	High	Invest —Selectively	Invest IB(H)	Invest —Priority IB(G)
Shareholder Value Created (Financial Strategy)	Medium	Invest —Selectively RB(G) RB(L)	Invest RB(H) IB(L)	Invest
	Low	Withdraw	Improve Financial Performance or Withdraw	Improve Financial Performance or Withdraw

IB, RB = Investment Banking, Retail Brokerage
G, H, L = Objective to Gain, Hold, or Lose Share

value. To do this, we inspect the chart again. We see that the strategy supporting the gain share objective in the investment banking market, IB(G), is closer to the upper right corner and therefore delivers greater combined value than the strategy supporting the hold share objective in the retail brokerage market RB(H). Consequently, our Wall Street firm gives priority for allocation of human and capital resources to the investment banking market rather than the retail brokerage market.

Summary

To sum up, we have introduced in this chapter the six principles of the Market Value Process:

1. Put customer value before shareholder value.
2. Understand price, product, and non-product needs.
3. Measure and map your progress toward meeting these needs.
4. Carry forward the value from one step to the next.
5. Build integrated customer value strategies.
6. Allocate resources to the highest combined value.

We used an example from the service industry—investment banking—to illustrate these ideas. Now we are ready to move to Part Two, "The Diagnosis." We will use an example from high technology—sports medicine instruments—to illustrate the twelve logical steps of the Market Value Process and to measure and map the price, product, and non-product result of each step.

PART TWO

THE DIAGNOSIS

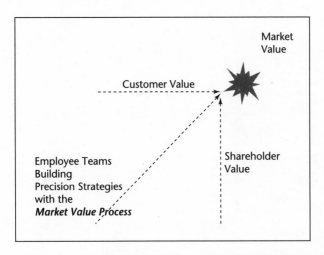

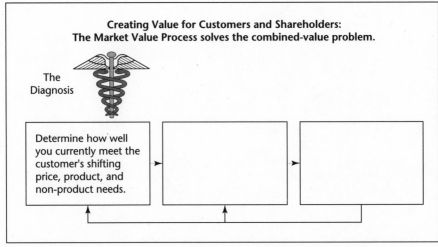

CHAPTER THREE

WINNING CUSTOMERS WITH CREATIVE MARKET DEFINITION

A s a first step in the diagnostic process, an enterprise assesses whether it is doing a good job of defining its markets. Let's begin to make this assessment by looking at markets, market definition, and creative market definition.

A *market* is a group of customers whose price, product, and non-product needs are similar to one another's and different from those of other customer groups. For example, Compaq's power users and technophobes had dramatically different needs. Power users want the latest features and are willing to pay for them, but they don't need a lot of support. Technophobes want ease of use above all, are more price sensitive, and need support from the seller.

Market definition is a two-step process, a creative act followed by an analytic act, and it precedes the development of strategy. The creative act is to develop a variety of alternative approaches to definition, such as geography—United States versus the rest of the world—or upper versus lower income; these represent different ways to divide the enterprise's business area into markets. The analytic act is to determine which of several promising approaches is the best.

Market definition is, of necessity, the first step in the Market Value Process because we build precision strategies for specific markets. In quality-sensitive markets, these strategies emphasize product and non-product quality. In price-sensitive markets, the strategies emphasize price, product cost, and non-product cost.

An enterprise can achieve dramatic success in the marketplace by finding a new way to divide customers into groups whose needs differ distinctly. Creative market definition gives an enterprise a huge leg up on competitors who have not yet identified these new distinctions or have not yet perceived their full importance.

It follows immediately from this line of reasoning that we use the word *creative* in a special sense when we talk about market definition. Creativity, in the context of market definition, is the idea that new is not necessarily beautiful, although it may be, but big is most certainly beautiful. *Creative market definition* is figuring out the way to divide customers into groups having bigger differences in needs among them than any other way of defining can produce. Then the enterprise offers each market a benefit package that is unmistakably tailored to meet that market's uniquely different needs. Customers are easily able to distinguish among, and buy, the distinctly different offerings of enterprises that define creatively. Compaq's power users and technophobes are an excellent example. It was very apparent to the power users and the technophobes which offerings were intended uniquely for them. Customers are less able to distinguish among, and buy, less distinct offerings that arise from less creative definition.

An enterprise should not shortchange the amount of time it spends on creative market definition. All too often this effort is brief and perfunctory. We suspect that this is because the imaginative process of defining markets can be frustrating. There is often a feeling that you are thrashing around and getting nowhere. This feeling is perfectly normal. But the reality is that this is some of the most important thrashing around an enterprise can do if the result is creative market definition. And while the reward for success is high, the penalty for failure is great. Because strategies belong uniquely to specific markets, getting market definition wrong automatically means getting everything else in the process wrong.

With these thoughts about the importance of market definition in mind, let's examine the scope of the business area that an enterprise will divide into markets.

Choosing the Scope of the Business Area

The scope that an enterprise uses to bound its business area has profound consequences for everything that follows in the Market Value Process. Taking an example from the pharmaceutical industry, let's consider anti-inflammatories, the pain-easing drugs. One way to define the business area would be "branded prescription anti-inflammatories." This would narrow the scope of the competitive arena to large drug companies. Enlarging the scope to "prescription anti-inflammatories" would bring generic prescription drugs into the picture. Enlarging the scope still further to "physician-influenced anti-inflammatories" would bring "high-end" over-the-counter (OTC) drugs into the picture. A good example of this is Naprosyn, a branded prescription anti-inflammatory from Syntex

Corporation. In early 1994, Naprosyn was approved by the Food and Drug Administration for OTC marketing by Syntex and Procter and Gamble under the brand name of Aleve. Aleve now competes with prescription drugs. Physicians often recommend to their patients these OTC products that have recently been approved for nonprescription sale. It is important to set the scope of the business area broadly enough to bring all serious competitive threats into the picture.

It is, however, important to define the business area tightly enough to exclude unqualified competitors. If the customer needs an intercontinental missile, a business area entitled "airborne missiles" would include sellers of short-range missiles whose offering fails to meet the threshold distance qualification. On the other hand, an enterprise should not make the mistake of thinking that customers have set threshold qualifications when in fact they have not. For example, if customers do not require branded prescription products, it is important to include generic prescription drugs and high-end OTC products in the competitive arena.

Introducing the Sportmed Example

To illustrate creative market definition in some depth, let's consider an enterprise that sells medical instruments and supplies to physicians who practice sports medicine—the treatment of sports-related injuries. We will call this real but disguised $100 million company "Sportmed" and use it as a continuing example throughout the rest of the book. We briefly mentioned Sportmed in the Preface as an excellent example of an enterprise that solved the combined-value problem and reinvented itself in the marketplace by using the concepts and tools described in this book. Sportmed's work with creative market definition, which we will describe here, formed the foundation for this reinvention.

Determining Customers' Price, Product, and Non-product Needs

Sportmed set the boundaries of its sports medicine instruments business area to be global in scope in order to encompass the full range of both its customer base and its competitive threats.

An enterprise must constantly monitor the ever-shifting needs of customers in its business area—both those needs of which customers are well aware and those of which they may be only dimly aware but which may foreshadow important shifts in their needs. Monitoring begins with informal everyday contact with these customers, and it continues more formally with the study of industry publications and reports. Monitoring often culminates with scientifically designed, third-party market research studies. The important thing is not to rely on any single one of these sources but to use them all.

Exhibit 3.1 shows the product and non-product needs of sports medicine instrument customers. The customers for these instruments seek to satisfy product needs of advanced features, multiple functions (the instruments can test for several injury or disease conditions), accuracy, and ease of use. Customers seek to satisfy non-product needs of ongoing education, service, reassurance through the company's image and reputation, and information provided through consultative selling. These needs become the elements of product and non-product quality and also product and non-product cost.

Sportmed wanted to divide this business area of global sports medicine instrument customers into markets based on differences in their price, product, and non-product needs. In this business area, Sportmed felt that all customers in the sports medicine instruments business area have the same broad set of four product needs and four non-product needs. This means that customers differ only in the importance they attach to each of the needs. A common set of needs is frequently a competitive reality in global markets. Importantly, however, the assumption of a common set of needs is not required to make the Market Value Process work. The task an enterprise faces is to look for differences. Differences

Exhibit 3.1. Customers' Product and Non-product Needs: Sports Medicine Instruments Business Area.

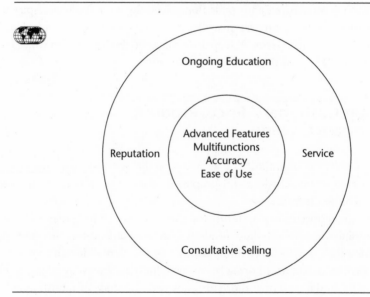

would be much easier to detect if they were differences in kind rather than differences only in importance, as we are assuming here.

We will identify each key Sportmed map from among our larger group of exhibits with the globe icon in the upper left corner. This indicates that it is one of the important tools to map our path through the concepts of the Market Value Process. Exhibit 3.1 is the first of these key maps.

To maximize the usefulness of this book, we collect these key maps in the Appendix. This accomplishes two things. First, you will be able to see, in a streamlined way, the flow of the Sportmed example. Second, you will be able to use this collection of maps as the step-by-step master road map for building your own strategy and for mapping the customer and shareholder value this strategy creates. Following this master road map will ensure that the strategy an enterprise creates delivers the highest possible combined value for its customers and shareholders.

Now we will look at the creative and analytic acts necessary to divide customers in the global sports medicine instruments business area into different markets based on the differing importance they attach to the needs in Exhibit 3.1.

Taking on the Creative Act

The creative act is to develop approaches to definition that disclose major differences in the underlying markets. Creativity lies in conceiving approaches to definition, such as age, that divide customers into markets, such as old and young, that attach different importance to price, product, and non-product needs. For example, a young sports medicine physician practitioner may be just out of medical school and setting up her practice. She may be price sensitive because she is just getting started and doesn't have a lot of money to spend. She may attach high importance to product needs such as advanced features because she has been instructed very recently in medical school regarding their value. She may attach low importance to non-product needs such as information provided by consultative selling because the information she learned in medical school is fresh in her mind. An older sports medicine practitioner may be less price sensitive because he has a greater financial cushion after years of successful practice. He may be less product sensitive because he has seen that he can get along nicely using the current technology. He may be quite non-product sensitive, however, since his medical school education is no longer as current as his young colleague's, and he knows he needs the information provided by consultative selling to update his knowledge. If these premises stand up, the age approach to market definition is a promising one. The age approach uncovers clear differences in the weight of importance the customers in its markets, young practitioners and older practitioners, attach to their common set of price, product, and non-product needs.

The enterprise must not stop, however, after identifying a single approach to establishing the different markets; otherwise, it may miss a more important one. It must consider multiple approaches, and we will now introduce an aid to doing this.

Using an Aid to the Creative Act

As an aid to the creative act, it helps to think of approaches to market definition in three categories. We depict these categories in the three columns in Exhibit 3.2.

The first category, described in the left column, examines *whose* price, product, and non-product needs are being met. Approaches in this category include age and medical specialty. The markets in the age approach are young practitioners and older practitioners. The markets in the medical specialty approach are sports medicine specialists (SMs) and general practitioners or generalists (GPs) with less extensive medical education.

The second category, described in the center column, examines *what* price, product, and non-product needs are being met. Approaches in this category include practitioner psychographics and patient diagnosis. *Psychographics* relates to "what" mind-set the customer has. The markets in the practitioner psychographics approach are *Progressive* practitioners (the need to be an early adopter of new tech-

Exhibit 3.2. Alternative Approaches to Market Definition.

Business Area: Sports Medicine Instruments

"Whose price, product, and non-product needs are being met"	"What price, product, and non-product needs are being met"	"How price, product, and non-product needs are being met"
Approach: Age Market: Young Practitioners Market: Older Practitioners	Psychographics Progressive Traditional	Technology for Delivering Results Computer Display Printout
Approach: Specialty Market: Specialist—SM Market: Generalist—GP	Patient Diagnosis Muscle and Tendon Other	Testing Technology Nonmicroprocessor Based Microprocessor Based

nology) and *Traditional* practitioners (the need to be a late adopter). An organization's sales force typically has little difficulty in classifying customers in the marketplace into the Progressive and Traditional categories—both the organization's own customers and those of competitors. The markets in the patient diagnosis approach are practitioners making muscle and tendon diagnoses and practitioners making other diagnoses such as fractures.

The third category, described in the right column, examines *how* price, product, and non-product needs are being met. The "how" often takes the form of alternative technologies. Approaches in this category may include the technology for delivering results and the testing technology. The markets in the approach that looks at the technology for delivering results are practitioners who prefer computer display and practitioners who prefer printout of results. The markets in the testing-technology approach are practitioners buying microprocessor-based technology and practitioners buying nonmicroprocessor-based technology.

While we have limited our discussion to two approaches in each category, there is no limit to the number of approaches an enterprise should consider in each. The more approaches considered, the better the chance of finding a more creative one.

Remember, the same set of four product and four non-product needs from Exhibit 3.1 underlies the buying decision in each market under each of the "who," "what," and "how" categories in Exhibit 3.2.

The enterprise needs to make a judgment regarding which approach in each category discloses the greatest differences in importance that customers in its markets attach to these common needs. Sportmed highlighted in Exhibit 3.2 the approach it felt to be the most promising one in each category. It chose the medical-specialty approach over the age approach, the psychographics approach over the patient-diagnosis approach, and the testing-technology approach over the technology-for-delivering-results approach.

Visualizing the Creative Act

In Exhibit 3.3 we see how Sportmed visualized its choice of the approaches that reveal the greatest price, product, and non-product differences along each of three dimensions. Sportmed depicted its most promising choice in the "who" category, medical specialty, along the vertical dimension, its most promising choice in the "what" category, psychographics, along the horizontal dimension, and its most promising choice in the "how" category, testing technology, along the diagonal (front-to-back) dimension.[1] This presentation allows us to visualize the intersections among markets. Inside this cube are all the practitioner customers in the global sports medicine instrument business area—including both Sportmed's

Exhibit 3.3. Approaches That Reveal the Greatest Differences Along Each Dimension: Sportmed.

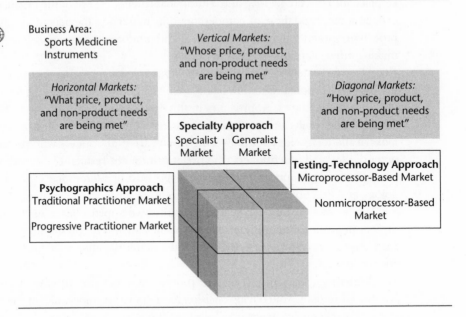

Business Area:
Sports Medicine
Instruments

Vertical Markets:
"Whose price, product,
and non-product needs
are being met"

Horizontal Markets:
"What price, product,
and non-product needs
are being met"

Diagonal Markets:
"How price, product,
and non-product needs
are being met"

Specialty Approach
Specialist | Generalist
Market | Market

Testing-Technology Approach
Microprocessor-Based Market

Nonmicroprocessor-Based
Market

Psychographics Approach
Traditional Practitioner Market

Progressive Practitioner Market

customers and its competitors' customers. Each customer can be assigned simultaneously to one of the two markets in each approach along each dimension. That is, everyone is simultaneously an SM or GP, Progressive or Traditional, and a buyer of microprocessor-based or nonmicroprocessor-based instruments.

Now that we see how to set up the cube, we can use it to define markets in any business area, as the following example from the Information Age shows.

Hitting a Snag from New Technology: The Dialog Story

A small article buried deep inside *The Wall Street Journal* on May 6, 1988, carried the title "Lockheed's Efforts to Sell Dialog Unit May Hit Snag from New Technology."[2] The article went on to report that Dialog Information Services, widely described as the world's largest on-line information service, faced a challenge from a (then) relatively new disk technology, CD-ROM.

Dialog doesn't own the hundreds of databases its customers— librarians or researchers in manufacturing companies and service businesses—dial up on the company's mainframe computers. These databases range from Toxline, which lists the adverse effects of chemicals, to the full text of the *Financial Times,* to a compendium on coffee production. Dialog licenses the databases and pays royalties to the database suppliers. In doing this, the company functions as a "value-added re-seller" with the value added being the breadth of selection among several hundred databases through a single distribution system. In 1988, however, analysts began to predict that some suppliers would record their databases onto CD-ROM disks and sell them directly to customers who would use them on personal computers.

Roger K. Summit, then Dialog's president, said he believed that it would be less lucrative for most database suppliers to switch to the CD-ROM disks from on-line. But he added that the CD-ROM disk was "an interesting technology" and that Dialog was developing an offering of several databases that used the new technology. The reader of this *Wall Street Journal* article was left with the impression that Dialog did not perceive CD-ROM to be a major threat and did not consider CD-ROM to be central to its business area.

The article went on to say, somewhat ominously, that CD-ROM makes sense for information that doesn't have to be updated more frequently than monthly, while on-line access is virtually the only way to retrieve up-to-the-minute information such as stock quotes and other financial data. The article concluded that as many as half of Dialog's databases could be more efficiently distributed on disks.

With this background, let's consider the implications of changing the boundaries of Dialog's business area from the "on-line information industry" to the "electronic information industry," which would bring CD-ROM into the picture.

The cube in Exhibit 3.4 depicts the company's base of existing and potential customers. Along the "who" dimension, the industry approach divides the electronic information business area into customers competing in manufacturing industries such as Sportmed and customers competing in service industries such as law firms. Along the "what" dimension, the updating-frequency approach divides the business area into customers with needs for frequent information updating and those with infrequent updating needs. Along the "how" dimension, the distribution-technology approach divides the business area into customers receiving the information on-line through a modem connected to the selling company's mainframe computer and customers receiving information on CD-ROM disks. Had Dialog viewed its business area this way, it might have felt a greater sense of urgency in developing CD-ROM offerings.

Lockheed subsequently sold Dialog to Knight-Ridder, Inc., of Miami, which owns a large number of newspapers including the *San Jose Mercury News*. On August 16, 1993, the *Mercury News* carried an article headlined "The Cost of Success."[3] The article described how Dialog's sales growth had slowed dramatically and profits had plunged. The reason was that Dialog had run out of room for easy growth in its established on-line market. During the past decade, Dialog had

Exhibit 3.4. Approaches That Reveal the Greatest Differences Along Each Dimension: Dialog.

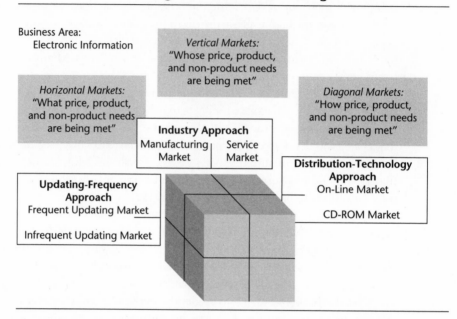

successfully signed up most of the large corporations whose professional librarians and researchers could afford Dialog's premium-price on-line service. The article reported that the average cost to access Dialog is $90 an hour, with some databases costing as much as $300 an hour. These high rates limit the appeal of Dialog to big companies that need the information right away and are willing to pay for the privilege.

To get back on the track of double-digit increases, Dialog would need to make risky innovations, such as pushing through the wall of the company library to reach the desks of workers who want direct access to Dialog's storehouse of information. These knowledge workers typically have PCs sitting on their desks equipped with CD-ROM drives, and Dialog needs a strong CD-ROM offering to serve them fully. The single picture in the article showed the new CEO, Patrick J. Tierny, holding up a CD-ROM platter bearing the title "Dialog OnDisc." The company's full-page magazine ads for Dialog OnDisc stress its benefits in offering all the power and flexibility that Dialog delivers on-line with the convenience of CD-ROM. They also stress the cost effectiveness of unlimited searching at a fixed cost that CD-ROM provides. Dialog was responding forcefully to its new challenge, but it had missed the opportunity to be a pioneer—and therefore a leader—in CD-ROM technology.

Taking on the Analytic Act

Once an enterprise like Sportmed or Dialog has subjectively selected the most promising approach along each dimension of the cube, the analytic act is to determine which of these several promising approaches is the best.

The Dangers of Defining by Technology

A first step in the analytic act is to realize that it can be dangerous to define markets using approaches along the diagonal dimension, alternative technology. This is true because the next step, after selecting the technology approach, is often to overfocus on only one of the technology markets—your own—and to overlook others. This is the mistake Dialog made when it believed that the on-line solution was the only solution its customers needed. It is risky to define markets in a way that encourages an enterprise to exclude competing technologies from its thought process.

An excellent historical example of this is ocean transportation at the time when steam power came into existence. Makers of sail-powered ships responded not by converting to steam but by making more elaborate sail-powered ships. This was natural because sail power was their technology. These ships were vessels of remarkable beauty with sails positioned to catch every breath of wind. The problem was that the fastest of these sailing ships was slower than the slowest steamship. To be committed to sail-powered technology was to be doomed to extinction in the commercial ocean transportation market where speed was critically important. If we define markets using a technology approach and then a better technology comes along, we risk ignoring the new technology and becoming a "sailing ship" enterprise—one that defines its markets in a way that excludes, rather than includes, competing technologies.

Now, let's consider how the danger of defining by technology relates to the Sportmed example. It may be superficially comforting for one of Sportmed's competitors to say that it is the market leader in the market for nonmicroprocessor-based instruments. This is small comfort, however, if the market for nonmicroprocessor-based technology is disappearing. All too often, the leader in one generation of technology fails to translate that achievement into leadership in the next generation. An enterprise must not let this happen to it by defining its business area with a diagonal market, alternative-technology approach to definition and then overlooking the market that is buying a competitor's technology. Following this line of reasoning, Sportmed decided not to use the testing-technology approach to define its markets.

The Usefulness of Management's Informed Intuition

The second step in the analytic act is to score the total differences in price, product, and non-product needs among the markets in each of the two remaining approaches; in the Sportmed example, these are the psychographics and medical-specialty approaches. Then we will compare these two total difference scores. The approach with the higher total difference score is the approach to use for creative definition.

Since we will be using assessments based on management's informed intuition to measure difference scores, we need to ask ourselves in advance how accurate this informed intuition is likely to be. Two factors are key to the answer. First, all Sportmed managers participating in the assessment process were people whose jobs entailed contact with customers. Second, these managers were making an intellectually honest effort to make these assessments from the standpoint of the customer. We have had substantial experience in testing these management assessments against subsequent third-party customer interviews we have conducted for clients. Our experience strongly suggests that management assessments of this kind are sufficiently accurate to allow the enterprise to draw realistic conclusions on which to build strategies. The informed intuition of knowledgeable managers with regular customer contact is rarely far wide of the mark.

This is not to say that an enterprise should not conduct in-depth market research. An enterprise should, whenever time and budget permit, confirm its assessments with information provided directly by customers, particularly when a high-stakes decision turns on the assessments. But an enterprise should not feel that it is unable to proceed with the Market Value Process if it does not have reams of large-scale market research. Traditional market research has both strengths and limitations. Its strengths are its scientific methods. Its limitations include its very limited ability to assess customer response to "frame-breaking" innovation with which customers are unfamiliar. Management must see or sense this response in firsthand contact with its early adopter customers. Some advocates of informed intuition take the position that it is more important to lead the customers where they want to go but don't know it yet, rather than study in depth the needs they express today.[4] We like this idea, since this pushes the concept of meeting shifting needs to its outer limit.

Measurement of Total Difference Scores

Sportmed assessed the importance that customers in each market attached to the customers' common set of price, product, and non-product needs in making the buying decision. These assessments appear in the top half of Exhibit 3.5, and we will examine each of them in turn.

Exhibit 3.5. Difference Scores of Alternative Approaches to Market Definition.

	Assessments Specialty Approach			Assessments Psychographics Approach	
	SM		**GP**	**Progressive**	**Traditional**
Price	40		60	35	65
Quality	60		40	65	35
Product	50		65	50	60
Non-product	50		35	50	40

	Measurements Specialty Differences			Measurements Psychographics Differences		
Price	40	20	60	35	30	65
Product	30	4	26	32.5	11.5	21
Non-product	30	16	14	32.5	18.5	14
Total Difference Score		40			60	

To measure the total difference score for the psychographics approach, simply bring down to the bottom half of Exhibit 3.5 the 35 price assessment for the Progressives. Then divide the 65 quality assessment for the Progressives, giving 50 percent of it, or 32.5 points, to product and the other 50 percent, or 32.5 points, to non-product. Similarly, for the Traditionals, bring down the 65 price assessment. Then divide the 35 quality assessment for the Traditionals, giving 60 percent of it, or 21 points, to product and the other 40 percent, or 14 points, to non-product.

Comparing the scores for the Progressives and the Traditionals in the "Differences" column inside the box, we see a 30 percent difference in price (65 percent minus 35 percent), an 11.5 percent difference in product, and an 18.5 percent difference in non-product. Adding these three, we arrived at a total difference score of 60 for the psychographics approach.

Following a similar thought process for the specialty approach on the left side of Exhibit 3.5, Sportmed arrived at a total difference score of 40.

Let's begin with the assessments for the psychographics approach in the upper right corner. With input from its sales force, Sportmed assigned all customers, those of its competitors as well as its own, into either the Progressive or Traditional Market. The Progressives were the customers who wanted to be the early adopters of new technology in the market and were willing to "pay up" for the competitive edge that this technology gave them in their medical practice. Sportmed felt that Progressive practitioners, when allocating 100 percent of their *total buying decision,* attached an importance of 35 percent to price and 65 percent to quality (the eight nonprice needs shown in Exhibit 3.1). Sportmed felt that the Progressives, in making their *quality buying decision* attached an importance of 50 percent, collectively, to the four product needs in Exhibit 3.1 and 50 percent to the four non-product needs. We can see these assessments in the "Progressive" column.

The Traditionals were the more cautious customers who wanted to wait to adopt new technology until it had been broadly accepted in the market. They were willing to forego competitive advantage in their medical practice in order to "play it safe." When they finally purchased the technology, it was no longer new. Sportmed felt that Traditional practitioners, when allocating 100 percent of their buying decision, attached an importance of 65 percent to price and 35 percent to quality. Sportmed also felt that the Traditionals attached an importance of 60 percent to the four product needs and 40 percent to the four non-product needs. These assessments appear in the "Traditional" column on the far right. These assessments result in a total difference score of sixty points in the way Progressives and Traditionals make their buying decision, as described at the bottom of Exhibit 3.5.[5]

Next, attention turned to the medical-specialty approach. Management's customer contact indicated that the sports medicine specialists, the SMs, with their more extensive medical education, attached more importance to quality than to price. Sportmed felt that a 40–60 split between price and quality and a 50–50 split between product and non-product needs best characterized this buying decision. These assessments appear in the upper left corner of Exhibit 3.5.

On the other hand, customer contact with generalists, the GPs, suggested a different picture. GPs, with their less extensive medical education, were less quality sensitive and more price sensitive than the SMs. The management team felt that a 60–40 split between price and quality and a 65–35 split between product and non-product needs best characterized this buying decision. These assessments produced a total difference score of 40 points, as described at the bottom of Exhibit 3.5, in the ways that SMs and GPs made their buying decisions.

We said in Chapter Two that when it is not obvious whether a given need, such as ease of use, is product or non-product, an enterprise should make its best judgment and the Market Value Process would adjust for that judgment. This example depicts the adjustment. If ease of use is important, one simply notes the category that it is part of and assesses the product/non-product category importance split with that in mind. Some of you may object that occasionally making an arbitrary assignment renders the category assignment unimportant and not worth doing. The reason for doing it, however, is that enterprises typically underestimate the overall importance of non-product needs in the customer's buying decision. Making no attempt to distinguish them would reinforce this tendency. It would result in building strategies that are dangerously deficient in meeting non-product needs, even though these needs can sometimes collectively outweigh product needs in importance.

Mapping Market Definition

We can depict these difference measurements in the Market Definition Map, shown in Exhibit 3.6. This chart maps the scores inside the shaded boxes in Exhibit 3.5. We can see on the right the psychographics total difference score of 60 and the medical specialty total difference score of 40; a distance of 20 points separates them. The chart allows us to compare, side by side and graphically, the price, product, and non-product buildup of the 60 and 40 scores. Of the 60 total difference score for the psychographics approach, 30 comes from the differences in importance Progressives and Traditionals attach to price, 11.5 from differences in product, and 18.5 from differences in non-product. Exhibits 3.5 and 3.6 are the first example of Sportmed's measuring and mapping results that the concepts and tools of the Market Value Process make possible. We will use this measuring and mapping sequence again and again in each chapter as the means of building precision strategies.

Exhibit 3.6. Market Definition Map:
Sports Medicine Instruments Business Area.

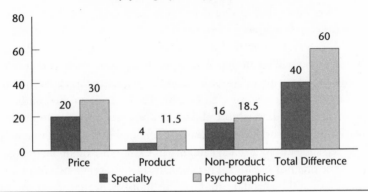

The Market Definition Map helps us visually to make two decisions. The first decision is whether the specialty and psychographics approaches individually are good approaches. In reaching this decision, we will use a rule of thumb based on experience. As described in Exhibit 3.7, our experience suggests that total difference scores of 30 to 40 points or more indicate that an approach is a good one. Since the total difference score for the medical-specialty approach is 40 and the total difference score for the psychographics approach is 60, both approaches pass this test. The 40 score tells us that important differences in price, product, and non-product needs exist between SMs and GPs. The 60 score tells us that important differences exist between Progressive and Traditional practitioners.

The second decision, now that we know both approaches are good, is to determine which is better. This is an issue of the distance between the total difference scores of the competing approaches. Our experience, again described in Exhibit 3.7, suggests that a distance of 20 to 30 points or more between the total difference scores of competing approaches suggests that one approach is clearly better than the other. We can see the distance of 20 (60 minus 40) between the psychographics and the medical-specialty approaches in the disparity between the height of the two "Total Difference" bars on the far right of Exhibit 3.6. Of this 20 distance, 10 comes from price, 7.5 from product, and 2.5 from non-product, as we can see from the difference in height from these three side-by-side pairs of bars. The score of 20 means that the psychographic approach is the better one, since the distance between the two falls into the 20-to-30 comfort zone. This means that the difference in the way Progressive and Traditional practitioners make buying decisions is greater than the difference in the way SMs and GPs make buying decisions by an important margin. For this reason, Sportmed chose psychographics as the approach it would use for creative market definition.

There are two final aspects of the scoring process to consider. First, you will notice that each of the approaches we have scored consists of only two markets. We have found that this suffices for a great many business areas. The scoring process can, however, be extended to approaches having more than two markets. For those interested, this extended scoring process is described in Exhibit 3.8. Second, you will recall that Sportmed previously made several subjective assessments among approaches in Exhibit 3.2, which determined the final candidates for selection that we scored in Exhibit 3.5. Once Sportmed understood the scoring process, it returned to Exhibit 3.2 and scored each candidate it had considered there. The additional scoring confirmed that the approach Sportmed had selected subjectively in each category in Exhibit 3.2 did in fact have a higher score than the one not selected. This confirmed these previous assessments.

Sportmed realized it could use this simple scoring process to test any new approach that might come to mind in the future against the winning psychographics

Exhibit 3.7. Rules of Thumb.

Total Difference Scores

During the public and private programs we have conducted, thirty-six management teams made scoring assessments for their own most promising vertical and horizontal approaches, similar to Sportmed's scoring assessments in Exhibit 3.5. It is important to remember that all the approaches being scored had passed an earlier screen for promising candidates, illustrated in Exhibit 3.2, where the best approach along each dimension was selected judgmentally. We divided the winning approaches from a scoring contest similar to Exhibit 3.5 into high, middle, and low thirds of twelve each based on the winning approach's score, the counterpart for the 60 score for the psychographics approach. The middle third showed a score ranging from 30 to 40 difference points. While not rigorously scientific, this mid-tier range of difference scores between the markets of approaches, prescreened for their promise, provides a useful guideline because it represents the middle third of the prescreened best. Based on this experience we believe that as a useful rule of thumb, total diference scores of 30 to 40 points or more are high. Scores like this indicate that there are clear differences between markets within an approach. Since the total difference score for the medical specialty approach is 40 and the total difference score for the psychographics approach is 60, both approaches pass this test. The 40 score tells us that important differences in price, product, and non-product needs exist between SMs and GPs. The 60 score tells us that important differences exist between Progressive and Traditional practitioners.

The Distance Separating the Two Total Difference Scores

Next, let's consider the distance separating the two total difference scores. The question is how great the distance of separation needs to be before we feel comfortable saying one approach is better than the other. While again not rigorously scientific, the assessments of the thirty-six management teams sample can provide a clue. We can divide these thirty-six into thirds again, this time based on the distance between the total difference scores. The distances of the middle twelve companies range from 20 to 30 points. Based on this experience we believe that as a useful rule of thumb, if the total difference scores are more than 20 to 30 points apart, the distance between them is high. A distance of this magnitude or higher gives us some level of comfort in characterizing one approach as better than the other. We can see the distance of 20 (60 minus 40) between the psychographics and the medical specialty approaches in the disparity between the height of the two "Total Difference" bars on the far right of Exhibit 3.6. The score of 20 means that the psychographic approach is the better one, since the distance between the two falls into the 20-to-30 comfort zone. This means that the difference in the way Progressive and Traditional practitioners make buying decisions is greater than the difference in the way SMs and GPs make buying decisions by an important margin. For this reason, Sportmed chose psychographics as the approach it would use for creative market definition.

Exhibit 3.8. An Alternative Way to See That Both the Specialty and Psychographics Approaches Are Good, but the Psychographics Approach Is Better.

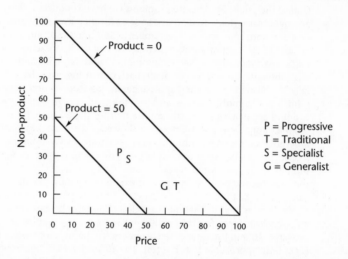

We see here an alternate way of visualizing the two conclusions that both approaches are good but psychographics is better. Since price, product, and non-product scores add up to 100, any time we know the importance of two, we know the third. If price and non-product are each 25, product must be 50. If price is zero and non-product is 50, product must be 50. This kind of reasoning defines the diagonal lines of product = 50 and product = 0. The distance between two points on the chart gives a quick visualization of the magnitude of the price, product, and nonproduct differences between them. We located points P, T, S, and G using the price and non-product assessments in Exhibit 3.5. The fact that S and G are far apart shows that the specialty approach is good. The fact that P and T are far apart shows that the psychographics approach is good. The fact that P and T are farther apart than S and G shows that the psychographics approach is better. The advantage of the bar chart visualization in Exhibit 3.6 is that it allows us to measure the 40 and 60 total difference scores mathematically. When there are three or more markets in an approach, however, the mathematics of scoring becomes more complex. The advantage of the visualization in Exhibit 3.8 is that it allows us to get around mathematics and to visualize how good an approach is with three or more markets by observing the distances among its markets. The greater the distances, the better the approach, because great distances reflect great differences in needs.

approach to see if the new approach was better. Sportmed planned to repeat the scoring process annually to make sure the winning psychographics approach continued to hold its lead against other candidates as needs shifted over time.

Now it is time to put this scoring to work to outline precision strategies for each market in the winning approach.

Outlining Precision Strategies in Each Market

Sportmed now knew that if it tailored offerings to the Progressives and the Traditionals, these offerings would be more distinctly different from each other than offerings tailored to SMs and GPs. Progressives and Traditionals would easily recognize which offering's benefit profile matched their need profile, and they would move quickly to buy that offering. Offerings tailored for SMs and GPs, on the other hand, presented a higher risk of being indistinct from each other; this could more easily create confusion between SMs and GPs regarding which offering had been tailored for which group, and such confusion would result in lost sales. The net result is that Sportmed would get higher sales from the global sports medicine instrument business area by defining markets with the psychographics approach than it would with the specialty approach. Sportmed, therefore, began to build precision strategies to serve the Progressive and the Traditional Markets.

Sportmed knew that the buying decision in the Progressive Market was 35 percent price and 65 percent quality. Its strategy in this market would be to offer a line of high-end instruments reflecting the reality that price was only one-third of the buying decision while quality was two-thirds of the buying decision. The 65 percent for quality was evenly divided between the product needs and non-product needs, so Sportmed knew its high-end offering would have to do an equally good job of meeting both these need sets.

Sportmed knew that the buying decision in the Traditional Market was 65 percent price and 35 percent quality. Its strategy in this market would be to offer a line of low-end instruments reflecting the reality that price was fully two-thirds of the buying decision and quality was only one-third of the buying decision. The 35 percent for quality was divided 21 percent for product needs and 14 percent for non-product needs. Sportmed realized that whatever modest attention it gave to quality in this low-end market would emphasize product needs rather than non-product needs.

This simple but powerful first cut at a precision strategy for each market amply rewarded the effort Sportmed had invested in creative market definition by winning customers.

Underscoring the Importance of Market Definition

It is crucial to spend a generous amount of time with this first step of the Market Value Process. To do this, an enterprise needs to develop a tolerance for ambiguity. Such tolerance gives the enterprise the room it needs to cast about for new and sometimes unconventional approaches to definition without rushing to a premature conclusion. By taking the time to think "outside the box,"[6] the enterprise may come up with a more creative approach to definition, just as Sportmed did with psychographics. If it does, the enterprise will stand the market on its head, and customers will flock to buy its more distinctly different offerings. This step of the Market Value Process gives us the concept (measuring differences in price, product, and non-product needs) as well as the tool (the Market Definition Map) that we need to visualize these differences and to make a first cut at building precision strategies that win customers and shareholders.

Making Market Definition a Key Ingredient in Mission Statements

Two of the key ingredients in a mission statement are an enterprise's goal and its market definition. We have already seen that an enterprise's goal is to create value for its customers and shareholders. Market definition provides the market context in which the enterprise builds precision strategies to solve the combined-value problem. Sportmed's mission statement incorporated the insight that its mission was to create value for customers and shareholders in the Progressive and Traditional Markets and summarized the price, product, and non-product value proposition that it would offer to customers in each market.

Organizing Planning Teams

Sportmed's thirty-person top management group, including the president, divided itself into planning teams to build integrated customer value strategies in each of the markets it had defined. Since the top management group itself had reached the definition decision after considerable discussion, there was naturally a high level of commitment to this definition. There was also a high level of commitment to fleshing out these first-cut strategies that would give Sportmed its best chance for success in each market. Importantly, since the strategies were being built by the top group of operating managers, the same group that built the strategies would have responsibility for implementing them successfully. All of these elements became keys to Sportmed's success, as we shall see.

Now let's look at the key results of our work with market definition that become carried value to future steps of the process.

Carried Value

Each of the twelve steps of the Market Value Process ends with a key set of results that becomes a carried value to future steps. This carried value creates a framework that tightly links customer and shareholder value by showing the financial payoff of customer value.

Sportmed summarized the key results of its market definition step in Exhibit 3.9. The top line comes from Exhibit 3.1, where Sportmed identified the product and non-product needs that become the elements of quality and cost. Sportmed had previously assessed the next two lines, "Quality/Price" and "Product/Non-product," in Exhibit 3.5. Sportmed was able to make the remaining assessments quickly since it had earlier identified, with input from its sales force, the market—Progressive or Traditional—into which each of its own customers and competitors' customers fell. These assessments reflected the instruments that Sportmed had sold to customers in each market during the current year and the prior year.

As a road map for our journey through the Market Value Process, we will use a carried value chart. We can see the first of these in Exhibit 3.10. At each step of the process we will replace the girder image with the identity, shown in the shaded blocks, of the value item we are carrying forward as we build the entire framework. We will also show the number of the step into which we are moving each item of carried value. The reader will be able to trace each item of carried value from Exhibit 3.9 to the steel girder carried-value chart. We will see again each item of carried value when we come to the step of the Market Value Process that uses it. The rhythm of measure, map, and carry will become increasingly apparent to you with each succeeding chapter.

Exhibit 3.9. Items of Carried Value from the Market Definition Step.

	Progressive Market	Traditional Market	Carried Value to Step Number
Elements of Quality and Cost	Exhibit 3.1	Exhibit 3.1	2, 6
Quality/Price	65/35	35/65	2, 5
Product/Non-product	50/50	60/40	2, 4
Last Year Size in Units (Instruments)	6,500	625	9
Last Year Market Share in Units	32%	10%	9
Last Year Unit Price	$10,000	$8,000	9
This Year Unit Price	$10,500	$8,040	9
Last Year Operating Profit Margin*	7%	6%	10

*Earnings before interest and taxes as a percent of sales

Exhibit 3.10. Carried Value: Creative Market Definition.

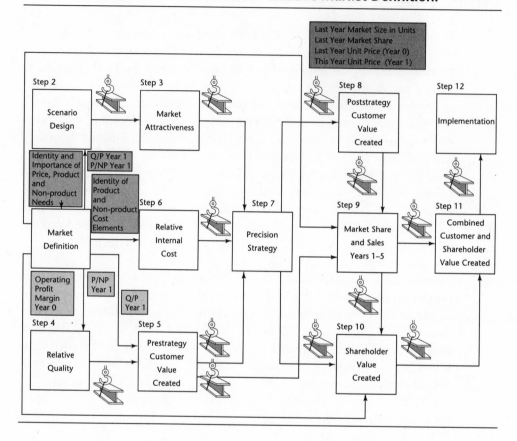

CHAPTER FOUR

USING SCENARIOS TO ENVISION MARKET EVOLUTION

Once an enterprise has defined its markets by uncovering differences in customer needs, the next issue is how best to envision the way in which these needs will evolve over time. To do this, we first consider why extrapolations and forecasts have fallen into disuse. Then, we introduce *scenarios*, the powerful tool that has replaced them. Next, we examine why scenarios are the most dependable way to envision an undependable future. Finally, we consider why scenarios encourage an enterprise to be proactive about shaping its own future.

Since the 1980s, scenarios have replaced extrapolations and forecasts as management's preferred tool for dealing with an uncertain future.[1] The reason for this is that even the most sophisticated forecasting techniques are built on the dangerous premise that an enterprise can use the past to predict the future. This is particularly dangerous if the enterprise's markets are impacted by changes in technology. Technological change is much more likely to be discontinuous from the past than demographic change. Consequently, extrapolations and forecasts are particularly weak tools for envisioning a future impacted by technology.

A scenario is a play, written to portray evolution in the marketplace, whose acts and events lead to an ending that is often surprising. To use scenarios, an enterprise first writes several plays with dramatically different endings for each market. These different endings represent a range of futures for the market. Then, the enterprise prepares a strategy that is appropriate for each play's ending and keeps the strategy ready in the event the scenario materializes. Scenario writers and Shakespeare have a lot in common.

By envisioning a range of futures, the enterprise increases its chances of capturing the one that will ultimately materialize. For this reason, scenarios are a more dependable way of envisioning the future than extrapolations or forecasts. Successful enterprises envision dramatically different futures and have appropriate strategies ready in case an unlikely future—but one they have rehearsed by writing the play—actually materializes.

Successful enterprises also realize that since they are writing the play, they can write themselves into it. By taking actions to influence the future shape of the marketplace rather than simply waiting for this shape to unfold, they become proactive, not reactive, participants. One of the major benefits of scenario writing is that it encourages this proactive state of mind.

Now, for a specific example, let's see how the quality-versus-price sensitivity of a market evolves over time and how an enterprise can impact the outcome.

How Market Needs Evolve over Time

To begin thinking about the way market needs evolve over time, we need to return to the Customer Value Map we examined briefly in Exhibit 2.4. We used an example in which customers were equally sensitive to quality and price. This means that if a competitor is offering a package of product and non-product quality that is 10 percent above average, the market will accept a price that is 10 percent above market average. We showed this equal tradeoff that customers make by a forty-five-degree line that we called the "market wants" line.

Now let's move to the example on the left side of Exhibit 4.1. This shows a quality-sensitive market where customers attach twice as much importance to quality as they do to price. What happens to the slope of the "market wants" line? The slope becomes steeper than forty-five degrees. In quality-sensitive markets, customers are prepared to "pay up" for quality. The high slope of the "market wants" line reflects the pleasant reality that customers are prepared to reward every unit in quality increase with a price increase of two units. In this case, the market is prepared to reward a quality package that is 10 percent above average with a price that is 20 percent above average.

Let's change the example once more; look this time at the right side of Exhibit 4.1. Assume that we are in a price-sensitive market in which customers attach twice as much importance to price as they do to quality. The low slope of the "market wants" line reflects the unpleasant reality that customers are prepared to accord every unit in quality increase with only a half unit in price increase. The

Exhibit 4.1. Depicting Differing Quality-Versus-Price Sensitivities.

**The slope of the "market wants" line reflects
the quality-versus-price sensitivity of the market.**

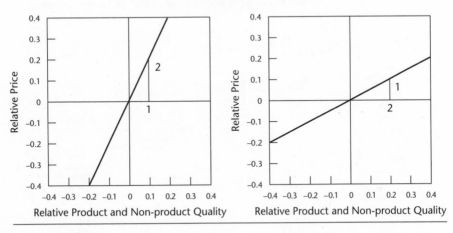

Relative Product and Non-product Quality   Relative Product and Non-product Quality

market is now prepared to accord only a 5 percent price premium to a quality package that is 10 percent above average. In summary, high-slope markets are quality-sensitive markets, and low-slope markets are price-sensitive markets.

The slope of the "market wants" line is not static. It changes over time, often in a discontinuous way. Usually what changes the market slope is innovation in product and non-product quality. A major technology innovation in product and non-product quality can create a very high-slope market because customers are often willing to "pay up" for what they perceive to be major breakthroughs in innovation. On the other hand, if the pace of innovation slows appreciably, the market will become increasingly price-sensitive, since customers are usually unwilling to "pay up" for stale technology.

Examining the Difference Between Price Sensitivity and Price Decrease

It is important to distinguish clearly between the price sensitivity of a market and its unit price decrease over time. Markets can be quality sensitive even when unit prices are declining. We can see this happening with microprocessors in Exhibit 4.2. It shows how high product and non-product innovation can simultaneously cause the market average unit price to decline and the slope of the "market wants" line to remain steep. The chart reflects the evolution of the microprocessor

Exhibit 4.2.

**High product and non-product innovation can simultaneously
cause the market average unit price to decline
and the slope of the "market wants" line to remain steep.**

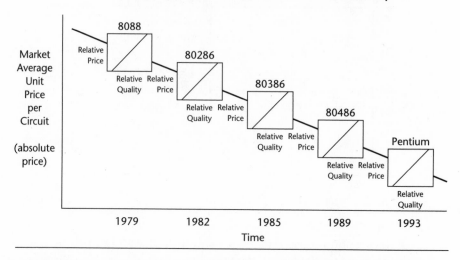

market, dominated by Intel Corporation, over the past decade. The unit of measurement in this market is the individual electric circuit. Because of submicron technology, the number of circuits per microprocessor has been increasing dramatically over time, and the price per circuit has declined dramatically. Yet the market has perceived each new Intel microprocessor to be a major innovation. This sense of innovation has kept the market quality sensitive even while prices have fallen. But this quality sensitivity exists within the new standard of lower price and higher quality that has been set by each new Intel offering. We call this *double-win one* in the Market Value Process. The innovator scores a double win by simultaneously creating a high-slope, quality-sensitive market and becoming the quality leader in that market. We will see examples of different kinds of double wins later.

Describing Both Market Structure and Competitive Position with Comprehensive Scenarios

The concept of a double win leads us to an important point about scenario writing. Some strategy books distinguish between environmental scenarios and competitive scenarios. Environmental scenarios describe events that impact market structure in such ways as government regulation impacting price levels. Competitive scenarios describe events that affect competitive position in such ways as innovation impacting competitors' market shares.

We make no such distinction between these types of scenarios. Instead of writing separate environmental and competitive scenarios, an enterprise should combine them through a three-step thought process. First, the enterprise determines the greatest uncertainty that the market faces, regardless of whether this threat is environmental or competitive. Often the greatest uncertainty is the future quality sensitivity of the market, which translates to the future slope of the "market wants" line. Next, the enterprise identifies the driver of this uncertainty. In the case of quality sensitivity, the driver is the timing, source, and magnitude of the next major breakthrough in product and non-product technology. Finally, the enterprise writes several plays whose events depict different degrees of innovation by competitors. The magnitude of the innovation determines the magnitude of the future slope of the "market wants" line.

When the innovation is large enough to break everyone's frame of reference, it affects both market structure and competitive position. This frame-breaking innovation increases future market slope, a key measure of market structure. Simultaneously, the breakthrough improves the innovating competitor's market share, a key measure of competitive position. Intel is a prime example of an innovating enterprise simultaneously building a winning market structure and a winning competitive position. It is much more natural to think of these simultaneous impacts of innovation in a single, comprehensive scenario than to use separate environmental and competitive scenarios.

Examining Historic Scenarios

Exhibit 4.3 examines historic scenarios in the microcomputer market for three different five-year periods; this shows us how innovation can impact quality sensitivity. These scenarios reveal how the level of product and non-product innovation in one time period creates the slope of the "market wants" line in the following time period. In the early 1980s, the historic scenario was one of rapid product and non-product innovation, shown in the upper right corner. During this time, Apple Computer brought two major innovations to the microcomputer market. It brought product innovation in the form of a graphical interface that made computers easier to use. It brought non-product innovation in the form of a highly trained dealer organization to provide major after-sale support to customers. Customers perceived these to be major innovations and were willing to "pay up" for them. This is another excellent example of how the competitive strategy of a key player shapes the structure of the entire marketplace—the double win we just discussed.

Exhibit 4.3. Historical Scenarios.

**The level of innovation in the microcomputer market
has historically determined the slope of the "market wants" line.**

Innovation by Apple Macintosh
Driver 1: Non-product Innovation

Driver 2: Product Innovation		Low	Medium	High
	High			Early 1980s: Graphical Interface Dealer Support 1985 Slope: High Slope
	Medium		1990s: Voice Recognition? Dealer Support? 2000 Slope: Moderate Slope?	
	Low	Late 1980s: Low Innovation 1990 Slope: Low Slope		

By 1985 the market was very high slope, and Apple was enjoying high revenue growth and profit margins as result of its superior quality. But during the last half of the 1980s, the scenario was different. It changed to the one shown in the bottom left corner of the chart. During this time period, customers perceived that the microcomputer market was experiencing low levels of product and non-product innovation. They became less willing to pay up for these less rapid increases in quality. By the end of the 1980s, the profit margins of all competitors, including Apple, were experiencing downward pressure.

What scenario will unfold in the 1990s? Perhaps voice recognition and the need for dealer support of this development will be perceived as medium innovation, and the market will regain a moderate slope. Perhaps some other future will unfold.

How can you best prepare for an uncertain future? The answer is to use a scenario design process that defines and develops several alternative scenarios, a topic we are about to explore in some depth. This process leaves an enterprise ready to shift strategy more rapidly than its competitors can, should a future materialize that is different from the past; it also allows an enterprise to shape that future. In early 1994, Apple introduced the Power MacIntosh, a powerful line of computers that would run programs written for the Windows operating system as well as allow voice recognition. This was Apple's response when it realized that its earlier scenario, which called for proprietary operating systems, was not going to materialize. It was also an attempt to shape the future into one that called for microcomputers that can run both MacIntosh and Windows application programs equally well, rather than one or the other exclusively.

Defining Scenarios at Sportmed

To illustrate scenario definition, we return to our sports medicine instrument company, Sportmed. In Chapter Three, we saw that Sportmed defined two markets, the Progressive and the Traditional Markets, and assigned planning teams to each market. The next issue each planning team faced was to envision how these two markets would evolve over time. To envision evolution in the Progressive Market, Sportmed used a Scenario Space Map, shown in Exhibit 4.4, that was similar to the one we just saw for Apple. We call this chart the Scenario Space Map because it defines scenarios in the space created by differing degrees of innovation along the product and non-product dimensions.

The sides of the chart show varying degrees of innovation in the four product needs and the four non-product needs listed in Exhibit 3.1. Inside the chart, we need to assess how differing degrees of innovation will drive the importance that customers in year five would attach to quality needs relative to price needs (Q/P) and attach to product needs relative to non-product needs (P/NP). We have continually stressed that an enterprise must keep on top of shifting needs. Changes in Q/P and P/NP are two of the most important shifts to envision. Scenarios are the tool we use to accomplish this.

The time frame for an enterprise's scenarios usually coincides with its strategy period. The *strategy period* is the time period over which an enterprise attempts to envision the value it can create for customers and shareholders. Many enterprises use a strategy period of five years. Companies whose offerings have short life cycles often plan for several generations of products at the same time—the successor to the current offering, as well as the successor's successor. Consequently,

Exhibit 4.4. Scenario Space Map: Progressive Market.

Driver 1: Non-product Innovation
Education
Service
Reputation
Consultative Selling

Driver 2: **Product Innovation**		Medium	High	Very High
Advanced Features Multifunctions Accuracy Ease of Use	Very High	"Engineering Innovation" Scenario Q/P = 65/35 P/NP = 60/40		"Creative Destruction" Scenario Q/P = 80/20 P/NP = 50/50
	High		Conventional Wisdom "Business as Usual" Scenario Q/P = 65/35 P/NP = 50/50	
	Medium	"Falling Asleep" Scenario Q/P = 50/50 P/NP = 50/50		"Marketing Innovation" Scenario Q/P = 65/35 P/NP = 40/60

their strategy period may still be five years, even if their product life cycle is considerably shorter.

The scenario definition process begins by identifying what levels of product and non-product innovation the Progressive Market experienced over the past five years. The level was high for both. Next, envision a future end state, named "Business as Usual," that reflects a continuation of past levels of product and non-product innovation. Then place the "Business as Usual Scenario" at the center of the Scenario Space Map by labeling the midpoint of each dimension as "High." This leads to a labeling of Medium, High, and Very High along each side of the Scenario Space Map. Locating "Business as Usual" in the center is important because it frees you to envision how the future might be different from the past in all directions on the map.

Next Sportmed asked itself what combination of future product and non-product innovation reflected the "Conventional Wisdom Scenario," the belief held by most customers and competitors in the market. Sportmed felt that conventional wisdom predicted that "business as usual" would continue to prevail. Consequently, Sportmed placed this in the same position on the Scenario Space Map. It's important to note that these two futures may not always coincide as they did for Sportmed. Sometimes, the conventional wisdom says that the future will be very different from the past. For example, the advent of powerful managed health care customers will almost certainly cause the future for pharmaceutical manufacturers to be different from recent history.

Sportmed then imagined four additional end states that could materialize by the end of its five-year time frame. We can depict the additional end states it envisioned for the Progressive Market in the corners of Exhibit 4.4. Notice that in completing the Scenario Space Map, Sportmed was quite specific about the importance that customers in year five would attach to Q/P and P/NP under each scenario.

Sportmed decided to develop in detail the scenarios it had named "Business as Usual," "Falling Asleep," and "Creative Destruction." It is important to give your enterprise's scenarios names that convey with some emotional impact the future that each scenario envisions. "Creative Destruction," for example, envisions competitors deliberately destroying their own old offerings by introducing new offerings well before the old ones reach the end of their normal life cycle. "Falling Asleep" means a slowing of innovation, such as the one we just described in the microcomputer market in the latter half of the 1980s. As we have said, "Business as Usual" reflects the conventional wisdom that future innovation in sports medicine instruments would continue at the same high level of the past five years.

Notice that in the conventional wisdom "Business as Usual" scenario, the customer's quality-versus-price sensitivity remained at the historic and current ratio of 65 to 35—the ratio that Sportmed had used to define its markets in Chapter Three. In fact, this ratio is carried value from our work with market definition in Chapter Three. It seemed logical to Sportmed that a continuation of the historic level of innovation would result in a continuation of the historic Q/P. The very high level of innovation envisioned in the "Creative Destruction" scenario drove Q/P in year five up from 65/35 to 80/20. The medium level of innovation in the "Falling Asleep" scenario dropped Q/P from 65/35 to 50/50. Under all three scenarios, Sportmed envisioned an equal balance between product and non-product innovation, and consequently, the market continued to attach the same 50/50 importance in year five to product and non-product needs in all scenarios as it did today.

Developing and Mapping Sportmed's Scenarios

Next, each Sportmed team needed to be as precise as it could about the specific events in the key drivers—product and non-product innovation—that would lead to each end state. At this point we can begin to see how writing a scenario is very similar to writing a play.[2] A playwright envisions an ending that is a dramatic outcome of the play's dominant theme. Then the playwright creates the detailed acts that lead to this ending in a sequence of cause and effect. In the case of our scenarios, the dramatic end state is the quality-versus-price and product-versus-non-product sensitivity that results from the innovation. Once these are determined, the scenario writer details the innovation theme in events that lead to each end state.

An enterprise should not hesitate to write extreme scenarios. This "outside the box" thinking can be very valuable in envisioning major discontinuities in market evolution. Shakespeare anthologies often divide his plays into histories, romances, tragedies, and comedies. This is probably not a bad way to think about scenarios. Histories would represent the "Business as Usual" scenario, the continuation of the past into the future. The romance might be the future that an enterprise shapes to its greatest advantage. The tragedy might be the scenario an enterprise fears the most. The comedy might be the scenario where absolutely nothing goes as planned. Romances, tragedies, and comedies represent the extreme futures that have a way of materializing in an enterprise's markets more often than you might think.

We can see the scenario development process in the Scenario Map shown in Exhibit 4.5. We show the theater masks to remind us that each of the three columns of boxes constitutes a play Sportmed wrote to depict three different futures, each with a different strategy implication for the Progressive Market. The middle column is a history. The right column is a romance because it leads to a very high-slope, quality-sensitive market where customers are very willing to "pay up" for quality. The left column is a tragedy because it leads to a moderate-slope, balanced market where customers are as sensitive to price as they are to quality.

Today's slope, a Q/P of 65 to 35, is carried value from our work with market definition in Chapter Three. The scenario identity, trends in drivers, and end states in year five are from the work with scenario definition on the Scenario Space Map, Exhibit 4.4, that we just finished.

The events that lead us from today to year five are the acts of our plays, which we will now write. We will write very simple plays to illustrate the principle, but in practice the plays in most markets will be more complex. We saw earlier that the key driver in the market is often the timing, source, and magnitude of the next

Exhibit 4.5. Scenario Map: Progressive Market.

Sportmed wrote three plays with three different end states and strategy implications.

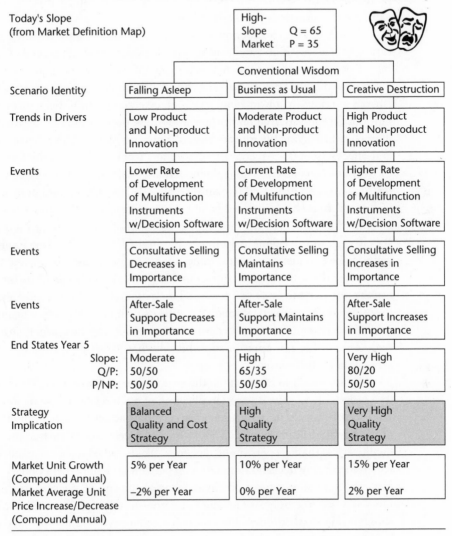

	Today's Slope (from Market Definition Map)		High-Slope Market Q = 65 P = 35	
		Conventional Wisdom		
Scenario Identity	Falling Asleep	Business as Usual	Creative Destruction
Trends in Drivers	Low Product and Non-product Innovation	Moderate Product and Non-product Innovation	High Product and Non-product Innovation
Events	Lower Rate of Development of Multifunction Instruments w/Decision Software	Current Rate of Development of Multifunction Instruments w/Decision Software	Higher Rate of Development of Multifunction Instruments w/Decision Software
Events	Consultative Selling Decreases in Importance	Consultative Selling Maintains Importance	Consultative Selling Increases in Importance
Events	After-Sale Support Decreases in Importance	After-Sale Support Maintains Importance	After-Sale Support Increases in Importance
End States Year 5 Slope: Q/P: P/NP:	Moderate 50/50 50/50	High 65/35 50/50	Very High 80/20 50/50
Strategy Implication	Balanced Quality and Cost Strategy	High Quality Strategy	Very High Quality Strategy
Market Unit Growth (Compound Annual) Market Average Unit Price Increase/Decrease (Compound Annual)	5% per Year –2% per Year	10% per Year 0% per Year	15% per Year 2% per Year

major breakthrough in product and non-product innovation. Here, everyone knows that Competitor B is about to introduce a new multifunction instrument with decision software, but no one knows how major an innovation the Progressive Market will perceive B's offering to be.

Each scenario should be quite specific in the third row of boxes from the bottom about the degree of innovation initiated by the enterprise and by key competitors. Scenarios are the source of information about competitor future performance ratings that will come into play in Step Eight, poststrategy customer value created, discussed in Chapter Ten.

In the Creative Destruction scenario in the right column, B's offering is perceived to be a very highly innovative, frame-breaking event. It represents a higher rate of development in multifunction instruments driven by decision software than has occurred in the past. Because of this, all competitors scramble to destroy their current offerings by introducing new ones to keep up with B. Because everyone is introducing sophisticated new product offerings, non-product needs also increase in importance. (Note the repeated use of the word *because*. This reflects the cause-and-effect sequence of scenarios.) Customers will need increased information in the form of consultative selling, increased after-sale support to service their new instruments, and increased reassurance provided by the reputation of the seller.

The Business as Usual and Falling Asleep scenarios reflect the flow of events resulting from a decreasing customer perception of the degree of innovation in B's offering. In the Falling Asleep scenario in the left column, B's offering is perceived to be a moderate advance rather than a major breakthrough, and Q/P declines over the scenario horizon from 65/35 to 50/50 because customers are usually unwilling to "pay up" for small incremental gains in technology. This is the "tragedy" of markets experiencing little or no innovation. Once again, P/NP is 50/50 across all scenarios because the level of innovation, whether medium, high, or very high, is envisioned to be split 50/50 between product and non-product in each scenario.

It is important to highlight, in the shaded row of boxes second from the bottom in Exhibit 4.5, the strategy implication of each scenario. We define quality-sensitive markets as those in which the customer attaches more than 60 percent of the buying decision to quality. We define price-sensitive markets as those where quality is less than 40 percent of the story. We define balanced markets as those where the buying decision is between 60 percent and 40 percent quality. Clearly, in markets envisioned to be quality sensitive at the end of the scenario, competitors will want to emphasize product and non-product quality in their precision strategies. In markets envisioned to be price sensitive, strategies will emphasize being price competitive while decreasing product and non-product cost. In balanced markets, a balanced quality and cost strategy is appropriate. The message of the third row of boxes from the bottom of Exhibit 4.5 is that quality is half or more of the buying decision in all scenarios, since Q/P is always 50/50 or higher. Importantly, however, the top figure in the ratio varies greatly. In the Creative Destruction scenario with Q/P of 80/20, a very high quality strategy is imperative. In the Business as Usual scenario with Q/P continuing to hold at 65/35, a continuation of the high quality strategy of the past is appropriate. In the Falling Asleep scenario with Q/P of 50/50, low internal cost assumes equal importance with quality in the strategy picture, and a balanced strategy is appropriate.

The final piece of work that the Sportmed teams did appears in the bottom row of boxes. Sportmed was specific about the outcomes they envisioned in the market's compound unit growth and the market average unit price increase or decrease over the scenario time frame. Frequently, an increase in innovation triggers an increase in the market unit growth rate. Sometimes innovation also causes unit prices to decrease, as we saw in Exhibit 4.2.

How Market Value Process Scenarios Differ
from Conventional Scenarios

Scenarios in the Market Value Process differ importantly from scenarios that you will encounter elsewhere. They are more tightly focused. They point toward the bottom three rows of boxes in Exhibit 4.5 as their final outcomes. These rows show the Q/P and P/NP at the end of the strategy period, the strategy implication, and the market growth and unit price change over the strategy period. This information provides the carried value necessary to build the enterprise's post-strategy Customer Value Map and to measure the revenue growth a precision strategy can deliver. We will look more closely at these areas in Chapters Ten and Eleven.

Battling to Retain Microprocessor Supremacy at Intel

It's worth continuing the Intel story we looked at in Exhibit 4.2 to understand the importance of scenarios. Intel's workhorse technology is CISC (complex instruction set computing). The fly in the ointment for Intel's domination of the microprocessor market is that it is not the pioneer in RISC technology, which could become the wave of the future in this high-slope market. In a May 8, 1994, article entitled "Congratulations, Apple, for Making a Mac That's Much More Than a Mac," the *San Jose Mercury News* suggested that it helps to think of traditional CISC chips as trucks that try to carry every tool that any job might ask for.[3] RISC chips are motorcycles that can carry only one tool at a time. But these bikes are tuned for speed. They're such hot rods that they can run back and forth many times for the tools they need in the time it takes the truck to get there in the first place. A CISC chip might perform some complex division operation with a single instruction that needs fifty ticks of the microprocessor's clock. A RISC chip might need to break that operation down into five simpler tasks, but if those tasks take only five ticks each, the total is still only half the time taken by the CISC chip.

When the IBM/Motorola PowerPC chip was introduced in the spring of 1994 in Apple's Power MacIntosh, it represented a major product innovation that posed a significant threat to Intel. The catch for the PowerPC, however, is that a new chip has to be surrounded by non-product innovation in the form of application software (spreadsheets and word processors); this software is not created by chip makers. Most of the application software on the market in 1994 had been written to use the full capability of Intel's CISC chip, not the new RISC chip. Until more software appears that uses the full capability of this new motorcycle, its potential can't be realized. Consequently, the magnitude of the risk to Intel is the speed with which this non-product innovation in support of RISC will take place. Unless Intel developed state-of-the-art RISC technology, a scenario of high non-product innovation would threaten its historic dominance of the microprocessor market. Intel had to build a strategy to respond in the event this scenario materialized.

On June 9, 1994, *The Wall Street Journal* revealed Intel's strategy for this scenario in an article headlined "H-P, Intel Form Broad Alliance on Computers."[4] The article reported that this alliance would develop a new chip that will run both the software written for Intel's line of chips and the more elaborate software for Hewlett-Packard workstations and larger computers that can run entire companies. H-P, while a leader in RISC, was making limited headway in getting other companies to build computers around its version of the technology. The new design will represent a new degree of product innovation by using RISC and also several technologies that are newer still. The end result will be an entirely new RISC chip that runs at blazing speed while maintaining complete compatibility with two prior generations of software—HP's and Intel's.

The message of this story is simple and powerful. Successful enterprises envision alternative futures and have a strategic response ready to meet whatever future actually materializes.

Avoiding Assigning Probabilities to Scenarios

Many enterprises want to work with a single set of market growth and market unit price assumptions rather than with the three sets that emerge from the bottom row of Exhibit 4.5. Often, they accomplish this by assigning probabilities to the scenarios they write. Then, they blend all the scenarios into a single "expected" scenario by weighting each of the original scenarios with their assigned probability and combining them into one. The result is an "expected" scenario with numbers, but with no event stream that has meaning. Moreover, in this process the "low-probability" scenarios lose their identity.

Extreme scenarios with "low probability" of materializing have enormous value in helping an enterprise avoid surprises. They provide the means for rehearsing the romance or tragedy of a discontinuous future that may be created by an enterprise itself or by the competition. In fact, "low-probability" scenarios have a way of materializing with astonishing regularity, because an enterprise frequently underestimates the probability of their occurrence. An enterprise is so often blinded by the conventional wisdom of the customers and competitors in its marketplace that it underestimates the probability for discontinuous change. Extreme scenarios need to be held up to the light and examined constantly to determine whether they are indeed in the process of materializing. When an enterprise blends extreme scenarios into a single "expected" scenario, the extreme scenarios vanish. It is self-defeating to do the work of writing these creative plays only to merge them into a single "expected" play. That makes as little sense as writing a play that combines *King Lear; Henry IV, Part One;* and *A Midsummer Night's Dream.* Yet enterprises often do just that.

A far better way to work with a single set of market growth and market unit price assumptions is for an enterprise to choose one of the three scenarios, perhaps the conventional wisdom scenario, as the one for which it will build an in-depth strategy. Then it builds summary strategies for the remaining two. Successful enterprises envision dramatically different futures and prepare thoroughly for the future predicted by conventional wisdom. They do, however, have appropriate strategies ready in case an unlikely future—but one they have rehearsed by writing the play—actually materializes. Beyond this, successful enterprises work to make the scenarios that are highly favorable to them a reality through their own actions in the marketplace.

Responding Early, Not Just Quickly

You may object that it is not worth the effort to write several scenarios that envision different event streams. It seems much simpler to wait to see which events actually materialize and build quick response systems to deal with them.

It is important to distinguish here between an early response and a quick response. This is like the difference between moving early in response to clouds on the horizon and waiting until they become a thunderstorm overhead, then moving quickly to shelter. We believe the mind-set of watching the horizon, seeing storm clouds, and responding to the clouds earlier than competitors do is essential to an enterprise's success in dealing with an uncertain future. Writing several scenarios is a powerful tool in developing this early-response mind-set.

One writer recently asserted that the key to managing discontinuities may not necessarily be to see them immediately, or even first, but to see them soon enough to act and to do so earlier or at least better than anyone else.[5] There is wisdom in this. An enterprise doesn't have to be first to see a discontinuity, but it's not a good idea to be last when the storm is breaking overhead.

Carried Value

Let's return to Sportmed's scenario work. Sportmed carried forward to the remaining steps of the Market Value Process the information it had developed in the Scenario Map, Exhibit 4.5. We summarize this information in Exhibit 4.6 and depict it in the steel girder chart shown in Exhibit 4.7. You can trace the items of carried value in Exhibit 4.6 to the shaded boxes in the carried-value chart.

Exhibit 4.7 highlights the items of carried value from the scenario step while retaining the carried value from the market definition step. We will follow this pattern of building carried value, step by step, throughout the book.

Exhibit 4.6. Items of Carried Value from the Scenario Design Step.

	Progressive Market	Traditional Market	Carried Value to Step Number
Scenario Chosen	Business as Usual	Business as Usual	3
Quality/Price, Year 5	65/35	35/65	3, 8
Product/Non-product, Year 5	50/50	60/40	3, 8
Events from the Chosen Scenario	Key Events	Key Events	8
Market Unit Growth	10% per Year	5% per Year	9
Market Unit Price Change	0% per Year	−2% per Year	9

Exhibit 4.7. Carried Value: Scenario Design.

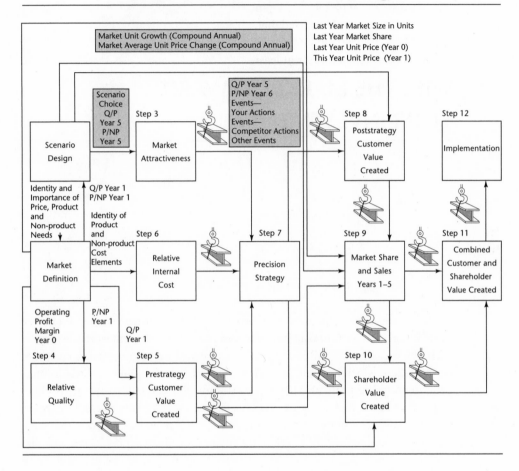

CHAPTER FIVE

WILL THE MARKET REWARD YOUR INVESTMENT?

O nce you have defined your enterprise's markets and envisioned their evolution, you need to consider how well positioned your enterprise is to meet each market's present and future needs. Successful enterprises have at least one *core competence*, which is a bundle of skills and technologies that enables the enterprise to provide a particular benefit to customers.[1] Each enterprise needs to determine whether there is a good fit between its core competencies and the price, product, and non-product benefits the enterprise's scenarios envision that each market will seek in the future. When the fit between an enterprise's competencies and the benefits the market is likely to want is good, then entering and remaining in the market will reward the enterprise's investment. When the fit is poor, the enterprise needs to determine how to stretch to create a fit. It may stretch for a fit through a strategic alliance with an outside partner who has the competence it lacks. It may stretch through a major research and development program or through other means.

To focus still more tightly on fit, we will look at a related concept we call the *value leverage factor* in a market. The value leverage factor is the customer need—quality or price—in which a given move in one direction delivers more value for customers than an equivalent move in the other. For example, in a quality-sensitive market, quality is the value leverage factor. A 10 percent increase in the relative product and non-product quality that an enterprise offers creates greater customer value than a 10 percent decrease in its relative price. In price-sensitive markets, price is the value leverage factor. A 10 percent decrease in relative price creates greater customer value than a 10 percent increase in relative product and non-product quality.

There is a direct relationship between value leverage and core competence. An enterprise's scenarios tell it whether quality or price will be the value leverage factor at the end of the scenario period. It stands to reason that an enterprise should build a core competence that coincides with this envisioned value leverage factor. Quite simply, competence building reflects the desire for global leadership through offering the benefit that customers will come to value most highly. If the scenarios envision that quality will be the value leverage factor, the enterprise will want to build competencies in some or all of the four product needs and four non-product needs that constitute quality. If price will be the value leverage factor, the enterprise should build competencies that allow it to be the low-cost operator in the four elements of product cost and the four elements of non-product cost; this will allow it to be aggressive about lowering prices.

Determining the Market's Value Leverage Factor

With this in mind, let's return to the example presented in Chapter Three where Sportmed defined its markets. We recall that Sportmed felt that the Progressive Market attached a relative importance of 65/35 to quality/price and the Traditional Market attached just the reverse—a relative importance of 35/65 to quality/price (see Exhibit 5.1). We saw in Chapter Two that competitive offerings located on the "market wants" line would hold market share because they were offering the relative value—quality for the price—that the market was willing to accept. A competitor who moves below the "market wants" line is offering a superior relative value—a better quality for the price—than the market is willing to accept. For the moment, assume that competitors are limited to a choice between moving in a purely horizontal or a purely vertical direction in their attempts to get below the line. The Progressive Market is a high-slope, quality-sensitive market. In this market, a competitor can get below the line more quickly by moving horizontally to the right—that is, building a strategy to increase relative quality—than by moving down—that is, decreasing relative price. Quality is the value leverage factor in this market. The Traditional Market is a low-slope, price-sensitive market. In this market, a competitor can get below the line more quickly by moving down, building a strategy to decrease relative internal cost and relative price, than by moving right, increasing relative quality. Price is the value leverage factor in this market.[2]

Exhibit 5.1. Value Leverage Factors.

Quality and price are the value leverage factors, respectively, in the Progressive and Traditional markets.

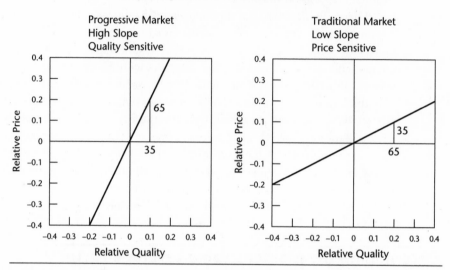

An enterprise needs to understand the importance that customers attach to their quality needs relative to their price needs in each of its markets today. This, together with the importance customers attach to their product needs relative to their non-product needs, is the basis for the market definition work we did in Chapter Three. Our work with market definition tells us the value leverage factor in each market today.

An enterprise also needs to understand the relative importance that it believes customers will attach to these needs at the end of the scenario time frame. This was a key item of carried value from our work in the scenario design step of the Market Value Process in Chapter Four. Our work with scenarios tells us the value leverage factor in each market in the future.

Mapping the Fit Between Value Leverage and Core Competence

The key issue an enterprise faces in considering market attractiveness is the fit between the value leverage factor it envisions in each market at the end of the scenario time frame and its core competence. In assessing this fit, we will focus on the scenario that reflects the "Business as Usual" conventional wisdom of customers and competitors about the direction in which the market will evolve. An enterprise needs to keep an eye on its scenario choice, however, to see whether one of its other scenarios is actually materializing. If so, it may need to develop a different core competence than the one called for by conventional wisdom.

Sportmed made the fit assessment shown in the Market Attractiveness Map (Exhibit 5.2). According to the "Business as Usual" scenario in each market, the importance that customers attach to quality relative to price does not change over the scenario period. The core competence required in the Progressive Market is quality. In our market definition work, we saw that Progressive practitioners were the early adopters who wanted the latest innovation in technology and were willing to "pay up" to get it. The core competence required in the Traditional Market is cost. In our market definition we saw that Traditional practitioners were the late adopters who preferred the older, lower-priced technology. Sportmed has a core competence in quality but not cost. It was unclear to the Sportmed cross-functional teams considering the issue whether Sportmed could gain competence in cost. Consequently, in the Progressive Market, the fit seemed good between the future value leverage factor—quality—and Sportmed's core competence. Sportmed felt it should attach a high priority to this market since the good fit made it attractive. In the Traditional Market, the fit was poor between the future value leverage factor—cost—and Sportmed's core competence of quality. Consequently, Sportmed felt it should attach a low priority to this market.

Exhibit 5.2. Market Attractiveness Map: Sports Medicine Instruments Business Area.

The Progressive market is more attractive than the Traditional market.

Market/ Scenario	Q/P Year 5	Core Competence Required	Have It or Can Gain It	Attractiveness/ Priority
Progressive Practitioner/ "Business as Usual" Scenario	65/35	Quality	Have it	High Good fit between value leverage factor and core competence
Traditional Practitioner/ "Business as Usual" Scenario	35/65	Cost	Don't have it; unclear whether we can gain it	Low Poor fit between value leverage factor and core competence

Now, let's look at an example of the fit between core competence and value leverage in an altogether different business area.

Entering the Digital Era at Kodak

In a June 9, 1995, article entitled "George Fisher Pushes Kodak into Digital Era," *The Wall Street Journal* described how Kodak's new CEO is guiding one of America's most famous brand names to a renewed focus on its core competencies.[3]

The article paints Fisher as a hands-on, high-profile leader who is not afraid of stepping on people's toes. Largely ignoring Wall Street pleas to cut costs, he has charted a risky course of growth, investing heavily in high-tech digital products.

Mr. Fisher's focus on digital technology is causing great tumult at Kodak. He's charging ahead, redirecting dollars and manpower to focus on products that will enable computer users to incorporate high-quality pictures into documents. Among them are cameras that can download images onto a computer and image banks accessible by modem. The key phrase here is high quality. Kodak's core competence is quality, not cost, and Fisher is determined to lead Kodak into areas such as digital imaging where the value leverage factor offers a good fit with this core competence.

Kodak dabbled with this technology for years, aware that it was the future but fearful that it would make the company's traditional film products obsolete. Mr. Fisher has uncovered memos from past executives censuring Kodak's investment in digital businesses. No more. In some areas, digital will replace traditional photography, he notes, while new products like Kodak's CopyPrint stations, which let customers copy and alter photos instantly, should increase film sales.

In March 1995, Kodak announced a series of product and service alliances with companies like International Business Machines, Microsoft, and Sprint. He plans to overhaul Kodak's corporate image with advertising that includes digital products and uses the slogan, "The Picture Is Changing."

"In the past Kodak would have 1,000 people in the room and couldn't make a decision," says Paul Orfalea, chief executive of Kinko's Service Corporation. Now, Kodak plans to offer parts of its Photo CD technology through Kinko's, which will let customers create documents with pictures and store them on compact disks.

But among Kodak's bread-and-butter customers, there are fears of being left behind. Professional portrait photographers threatened to boycott Kodak film after Kodak demonstrated products that make instant digital copies of photographs but make no mention of copyright laws. Kodak has since admitted it was "very, very,

very naive and very stupid" and has promised, among other things, to include copyright warnings with its equipment.

Inside the company, film and paper employees have been equally distressed, feeling they aren't getting the credit they deserve. They note that Kodak's photographic business still pays the bills, accounting for about 90 percent of Kodak's $13.56 billion in revenue in 1994. Moreover, while digital imaging has yet to make a profit, enormous growth is expected in emerging photographic markets such as China and India.

"There used to be a lot of socializing between groups at Kodak. Now there's just this tension," says a digital manager. Adds a former employee, "You've got guys manufacturing film in buildings 29 and 30, and they have terrible office facilities and old desks and furniture because Kodak doesn't want to hurt margins there." To counter the resentment, Mr. Fisher has tried to spotlight photography recently, calling it Kodak's "crown jewel" at the May 1995 annual meeting.

Still, it's clear that Mr. Fisher intends to lead Kodak in the direction where he perceives the greatest fit exists between value leverage and core competence—the quality-sensitive, digital-imaging market.

This strategic direction is creating value for shareholders. The stock price of Kodak climbed by 32 percent to a level of $65 a share in the year prior to the June 9, 1995, article. The stock has continued to climb since then and closed at $72.50 on February 6, 1996.

Carried Value

Sportmed carried forward to the strategy-building step of the Market Value Process the preliminary priorities it assigned to each of its markets in Exhibit 5.2. We depict this in Exhibit 5.3.

Note that this chart accumulates our work from all the steps we have discussed to this point: market definition, scenario design, and market attractiveness. We will use a chart like this at the end of each chapter to show how the concepts of the Market Value Process continue to build, step by step.

Exhibit 5.3. Carried Value: Market Attractiveness.

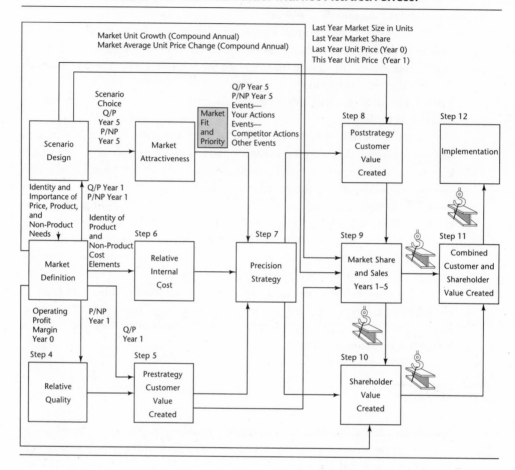

CHAPTER SIX

DELIVERING QUALITY THROUGH PRODUCT AND NON-PRODUCT BENEFITS

The first three steps of the Market Value Process, discussed in Chapters Three through Five, focused on the diagnosis of Sportmed's markets. The diagnostic process now shifts from markets to market share.

In Step Four, an enterprise measures and maps how customers perceive the quality it offers relative to the competition in each of its markets. In doing this, the enterprise assesses the relative benefits its offering provides. It makes this assessment for each of the product and non-product needs that a customer seeks to satisfy in making the buying decision. The assessment begins by weighing each product and non-product need for importance. Then the assessment extends to competitors, rating them for performance on the benefits they deliver to meet each need. Competitors who seek success at the high end of the market may offer customers a 20 percent or greater quality edge over the competition. In our experience, this 20 percent quality edge is the foundation on which high-end competitors build their value proposition.

Defining Relative Perceived Quality

We define relative perceived quality very broadly using three aspects, which we will discuss in a moment. This definition mirrors an approach originally developed by General Electric several decades ago. It was subsequently adopted and refined by the Profit Impact of Market Strategy (PIMS) Program, which does research on a large, diverse, business-unit database.

The first aspect of quality is that it includes all of the nonprice needs, both product and non-product, that customers seek to satisfy. All too often, an enterprise overfocuses on its product quality. This is dangerous because of the large role that non-product quality can play in the buying decision. It's also important to note that we use the term *customer* here to mean all customers in the market—the competitors' customers as well as an enterprise's own customers.

The second aspect of quality is that quality exists only as it is perceived by customers. If customers don't perceive an enterprise's quality, then the enterprise doesn't have quality, whatever the underlying "reality." Perception is reality. Fixing a "quality problem" may entail a profound review of an enterprise's investment in marketing if the enterprise is convinced that the underlying "reality" of the quality it offers is higher than the market perceives that quality to be. Perception in the marketplace is so crucial that an enterprise must treat marketing as an investment that is just as important as capital investment is in a factory. Frequently, an enterprise views marketing as an expense to be cut at the first sign of an economic downturn.[1] This has a devastating effect on relative perceived quality.

The ultimate example of perception as reality is the true story of a small consumer products company that commissioned a market research study of its popcorn-popper market. The result of the study was that the best popcorn popper in the market was identified as one provided by a gigantic competitor. This was astonishing to the small company because the giant didn't make a popcorn popper. The halo effect from the giant's other products, however, was so great that the market perceived not only that the popcorn popper existed but that it was also the best. The small competitor had quite a marketing education program to undertake.

On the other hand, the fix may entail a fundamental overhaul of the product and non-product benefits that an enterprise offers if the negative perception of its quality does reflect the underlying "reality."

The third aspect of quality is that it is measured relative to the competition. If an enterprise offers a miserable package of product and non-product need satisfaction but its competitors' offerings are perceived to be worse, then the enterprise has quality. If an enterprise offers an outstanding package of product and non-product need satisfaction but its competitors' offerings are perceived to be better, then it doesn't have quality. It's as simple as that.

Measuring Relative Perceived Quality

To measure relative perceived quality, we need to examine the customer's buying decision in more detail than we have until now. To do this, we will use Exhibit

6.1. From our work with market definition, we recall that Sportmed felt that Progressive-practitioner customers attached a relative importance of 65/35 to quality/price and 50/50 importance to product/non-product. We see this in the upper left corner of Exhibit 6.1.

Sportmed next assessed the importance weight that customers attached to each of the four product needs relative to each other and to each of the four non-product needs relative to each other. Sportmed allocated the fifty points it had given to the product group to the individual needs comprising that group. For example, Sportmed felt that advanced features, multifunctions, accuracy, and ease of use had a customer perceived importance, in relation to each other, of fourteen, twelve, fourteen, and ten, respectively. It followed a similar process for the non-product needs. Then Sportmed, calling itself Competitor A, identified its three key competitors. These were Competitors B, C, and D. Taking its own price per unit as 100, Sportmed assessed each competitor's unit price as a percent of its own. These were not list prices but prices actually realized after all discounts had been negotiated. B's price, for example was 85 percent of Sportmed's. Finally, in the columns labeled "Competitive Performance Ratings," Sportmed assessed, on a scale of zero to ten,

Exhibit 6.1. Buying Decision: Progressive Market.

Customers make the buying decision by attaching an importance weight and a performance rating to each price, product, and non-product need.

Quality	65	A = Sportmed
Price	35	B = Competitor B
		C = Competitor C
Product	50	D = Competitor D
Non-product	50	

		Competitive Price per Unit (A = 100)			
		A	B	C	D
Price		100	85	95	100

Product Needs	Importance Weight	Competitive Performance Ratings			
		A	B	C	D
Advanced Features	14	8	6	7	8
Multifunctions	12	5	7	7	7
Accuracy	14	10	6	7	8
Ease of Use	10	6	7	7	6
Non-product Needs					
Ongoing Education	13	8	5	5	7
Service	10	9	5	5	3
Reputation	12	9	5	6	7
Consultative Selling	15	8	6	5	3

the relative performance ratings that customers would assign to the benefits that competitors offered for each product and non-product need. In the advanced features row, for example, Sportmed felt that customers would give Competitors A (Sportmed), B, C, and D an eight, six, seven, and eight, respectively.

Let's return to the issue of how an enterprise arrives at these assessments. We saw in Chapter Three that it is always a good idea to confirm management's informed intuition with information that is provided by the customers. The best way to get this information is to ask customers directly during visits to customers. The enterprise should do this both directly, through its own employees, and indirectly, through market research firms. We have conducted many customer interviews to measure customer perceptions. Our experience is that each interview takes about thirty minutes. We spend five minutes explaining the product and non-product needs, which are often developed from information gleaned from customer focus groups. Once we have explained the needs, the customer is almost always able to provide importance weights and performance ratings in fifteen minutes. Customers typically have little difficulty making these assessments. This leaves ten minutes at the end to ask follow-up questions regarding the assessments the customer has just made.

Exhibit 6.2. Relative Total Quality: Progressive Market.

Relative total quality is the perceived performance on each product and non-product need, weighted by its importance to customers.

		Price as a Percent of Average				
		A	B	C	D	Avg.
Relative Price		1.05	0.89	1.00	1.05	95

Product Needs	Importance Weight	Performance as a Percent of Average				
		A	B	C	D	Avg.
Advanced Features	14	1.10	0.83	0.97	1.10	7.25
Multifunctions	12	0.77	1.08	1.08	1.08	6.50
Accuracy	14	1.29	0.77	0.90	1.03	7.75
Ease of Use	10	0.92	1.08	1.08	0.92	6.50
Non-product Needs						
Ongoing Education	13	1.28	0.80	0.80	1.12	6.25
Service	10	1.64	0.91	0.91	0.55	5.50
Reputation	12	1.33	0.74	0.89	1.04	6.75
Consultative Selling	15	1.45	1.09	0.91	0.55	5.50
Relative Total Quality		1.23	0.91	0.94	0.93	

Once we have this model of the customer's buying decision, we can measure Sportmed's relative perceived quality. We show the result of this measurement in Exhibit 6.2. The steps for making the measurement are summarized in Exhibit 6.3. The 1.23 score that we see for Competitor A in the highlighted bottom row of Exhibit 6.2 means that Sportmed's relative quality is 23 percent above the average for the four competitors. The 0.91 score for Competitor B means that B is 9 percent below the average. Whenever this score is above market average quality, we say that a competitor has attained a "high-end" position. Whenever the score is below market average quality, we define this to be a "low-end" position.

The measurement we have just made is a powerful one. It combines all three aspects of the definition of quality—that quality includes both the product and non-product benefits, that quality is perceived by customers, and that quality is not absolute but is measured relative to the competition. We now know Sportmed's overall performance is 23 percent above average, weighted across all of the non-price factors that enter into the Progressive practitioner's buying decision. In our experience, an enterprise that wants to compete successfully at the high end of the market should set a goal of achieving a 20 percent edge in this measure. We define a 20 percent or better quality edge to be a "very high-end" position. Sportmed has exceeded this goal by three percentage points in the Progressive Market.

Exhibit 6.3. Calculating Relative Total Quality.

The first step in calculating relative total quality is to express competitive measures as a percent of average. To do this, we calculate the average of the four prices and the average of the four competitive performance ratings for each product and non-product need. We see the result in the far right-hand column of Exhibit 6.2. For price, 95 is the average of 100, 85, 95, and 100—the prices shown in Exhibit 6.1. For advanced features, 7.25 is the average of 8, 6, 7, 8, in the advanced features row of Exhibit 6.1. Then, we express all competitive performance-rating raw scores as a percent of the market average. For example, the 1.05 score for Competitor A in relative price is simply the 100 raw score from Exhibit 6.1 divided by the average performance rating of 95 found in the right-hand column of Exhibit 6.2. The 1.05 means that A's price is 5 percent above the market average. Similarly, the 1.10 score for competitor A in advanced features is the 8 raw score from Exhibit 6.1 divided by the average performance rating of 7.25 found in the right-hand column of Exhibit 6.2. The 1.10 means that A is performing 10 percent above average in advanced features.

Next, in step two, we calculate for each competitor an overall quality score, which is the weighted average of the eight performance ratings on each product and non-product need. These performance ratings are weighted by the importance weights in the left column. Competitor A's score is $(1.10 \times 14 + 0.77 \times 12 + \ldots)/100$.

The 1.23 score that we see for Competitor A in the highlighted bottom row of Exhibit 6.2 means that Sportmed's relative quality is 23 percent above the four-competitor average. The 0.91 score for Competitor B means that B is 9 percent below the market average.

Mapping Relative Perceived Quality

Exhibit 6.4 helps us visualize the components of Sportmed's overall performance. We will set market average at zero rather than one so that an above-average score will be a positive number and a below-average score will be a negative number. Competitor A, Sportmed, is performing above average in all but two of the eight product and non-product needs. The horizontal bar at the bottom of the chart

Exhibit 6.4. Position Map: Progressive Market—Competitor A.

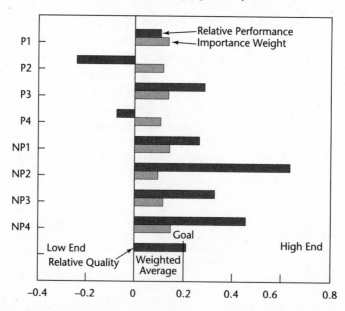

Of the eight pairs of bars in this exhibit, the top bar of each pair measures Sportmed's relative performance in each of the eight needs—the second column from the left in Exhibit 6.2. The bottom bar measures the importance weight customers attach to that need—the far left column of Exhibit 6.2. For advanced features, P1 (the top pair of bars), the upper bar maps Sportmed's score of 1.10, a 10 percent advantage. The bottom bar maps the 14 percent importance weight of advanced features. The upper bar of each pair will be positive or negative, depending on whether Sportmed has a performance advantage or disadvantage in this customer need. The bottom bar of each pair will always be positive because the importance of each need is always greater than zero. We see by looking at the only two black bars to the left that in this market, Sportmed is offering a product and non-product benefit package that is above average in each need except P2, multifunctions, and P4, ease of use.

shows Sportmed's overall score of 23 percent above average. We depict this bar in the horizontal position because relative quality is the horizontal dimension of the Customer Value Map that we saw in Chapter Two and that we are about to discuss in much more detail in Chapter Seven.

This relative quality of 23 percent above average is an excellent score in this performance measurement. We can see that it exceeds the 20 percent goal marked at the bottom of Exhibit 6.4. In our experience, few competitors are able to gain such a clear overall edge in the package of product and non-product benefits they offer to a market. A 20 percent relative quality edge and the very high-end position this represents are challenging goals that an enterprise should set for itself in markets where it is seeking success at the high end.

The Position Map for Competitor B, shown in Exhibit 6.5, presents an altogether different situation. Competitor B has below-average relative performance on two of the four product needs and on three of the four non-product needs. We can see this from the top five black bars to the left in this chart. This results in the relative quality score of minus 9 percent depicted by the bottom bar. Competitors with a low-end position like this must compete on price rather than quality.

Exhibit 6.5. Position Map: Progressive Market—Competitor B.

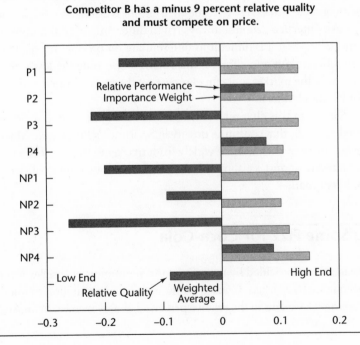

This is not necessarily bad if Competitor B's core competence is low internal cost, which could enable B to be the low-cost competitor in the market. If it is the low-cost competitor, B may be able to price low enough to create both customer value and shareholder value at the same time. The point is that this represents a dramatically different position than the one Competitor A occupies, requiring Competitor B to have a very different strategy for success. Clearly, A competes on quality and B competes on price.

It frequently can be very difficult to differentiate an offering based on product needs, but it is almost always possible to differentiate based on non-product needs. The cement industry is an excellent example. There has been little innovation in this market, so the importance of quality is low. Product innovation is especially low. This means that within quality, product needs are less important than non-product needs. Cement is manufactured to American Society of Testing Materials specifications. Meeting these specifications is the threshold for competition on the product needs, and few competitors attempt to differentiate on product needs once they cross this threshold. Cement can, however, be differentiated based on non-product needs. The customers of cement companies—ready-mix concrete suppliers—often need help with the financial aspects of their business. We knew a vice president of marketing of one cement company who was financially astute. He gained a significant competitive edge by helping his customers solve financial problems, such as whether to lease or purchase their ready-mix concrete trucks. He became their business adviser as well as their supplier.

An enterprise should always try to differentiate on the non-product needs, especially when it is difficult to differentiate on product needs. If the enterprise can differentiate on neither, it must strive to become the low internal cost competitor in the market so it can compete on the basis of price and still create value for its shareholders.

So far in this chapter, we have considered only the four product and non-product needs that constitute quality in Sportmed's Progressive Market. The identity of these needs can vary widely from market to market. Let's widen our focus for a moment and see some of the needs that constitute quality in a completely different market.

Adding Some Fizz for Coca-Cola

Reassurance provided by the image and reputation of a seller is a key customer need in many markets. Consequently, image and reputation frequently have high importance weights in the relative perceived quality picture. In an August 22, 1995, article entitled "Adding Some Fizz: Coca-Cola Is Shedding Its Once-Stodgy Image with Swift Expansion," *The Wall Street Journal* described how Coke is reassuring its customers that the company understands evolving consumer tastes.[2]

The article asserted that in the race to quench the world's thirst, Coca-Cola has always had a reputation as the soft-drink industry's plodding old giant. Though a successful marketer, when it came to speed or innovation, the company faltered. It was swamped by the wave of teas, juices, and flavored waters entering the U.S. market in the early 1990s.

But lately, Coca-Cola is charging around faster than a ten-year-old on a soda buzz—and with equal daring.

In the United States, after nearly a decade without a new product, the company is pushing new drinks out the door at a record pace; these new drinks include everything from Mountain Blast Powerade sports drink to Strawberry Passion Awareness Fruitopia fruit drink. Its new marketing force has unleashed a flood of new packaging and promotions, including its signature curvy bottle, lucratively reborn in plastic. This combines the strength of the old image with the innovativeness of the new. Coca-Cola says the efforts have helped it capture more than 80 percent of the growth in the U.S. soft-drink market in 1995—nearly twice the 1994 rate.

"Nothing energizes an organization like speed," says Roberto Goizeta, the company's chairman and chief executive.

In part, Coca-Cola is adapting to a changing industry, where teas, juices, sports drinks, bottled waters, and other elixirs have transformed a two-cola world. Having recovered from the failure of New Coke, Coca-Cola is more willing to enter the fray and risk its name.

For the most part, though, the changes are an extension of Mr. Goizeta's own careerlong campaign to break institutional habits. During his fourteen-year tenure, he has overhauled the company's financial operations, trimmed the corporate structure, redefined its relationship with bottlers and reined in overseas operations that used to be run as distant fiefs. What is different about the latest moves, he says, is that many of them relate to marketing "and that's what people see."

Clearly, Coca-Cola is still a far cry from becoming the industry's wild child. The company continues to roll over competitors with its heaps of capital and tight control over bottlers, and it remains conservative among scrappier rivals.

What's more, continuing to engineer a faster, more daring Coca-Cola may be a tough task. Obsessed with shareholder value and steady growth, Coca-Cola has gained a reputation as a reliable earnings wonder. Largely on the strength of its international performance, the company's stock was up more than 50 percent in the year preceding *The Wall Street Journal* article. On the date prior to the article, it closed at $63.125, boosting its market value by about $28 billion during that time. The stock continued to climb subsequent to the date of the article and closed at $80.25 on February 8, 1996. A more adventurous company, some say, might become a riskier investment.

"That's the hard balance," says John Kao, a Harvard management professor who recently studied the rise in creativity at Coca-Cola. "They have to simultaneously feed the machine that thrives on efficiency format and market share and at the same time try to be a lab for risk taking and invention." Put another way, Coke must create value for both customers and shareholders.

Today, Coca-Cola seems more willing than ever to swallow its failures such as New Coke in the name of risk and speed.

"You can't stumble if you're not moving," Mr. Goizeta says. "And if you stumble and make a decision that doesn't pan out, then you move quickly to change it. But it's better than standing still."

The Coca-Cola story demonstrates how successful American icons will change their image and reputation in order to meet customers' shifting needs. Now let's return to Sportmed to see what value we carry forward from this chapter.

Carried Value

We carry the measurement of relative perceived quality, together with relative price, forward to Step Five of the Market Value Process, measuring and mapping our prestrategy customer value created. We depict this in the bottom left corner of Exhibit 6.6. Note that many of the girder icons are beginning to disappear as they are replaced by the items of carried value from the steps we have completed.

Exhibit 6.6. Carried Value: Relative Quality and Price.

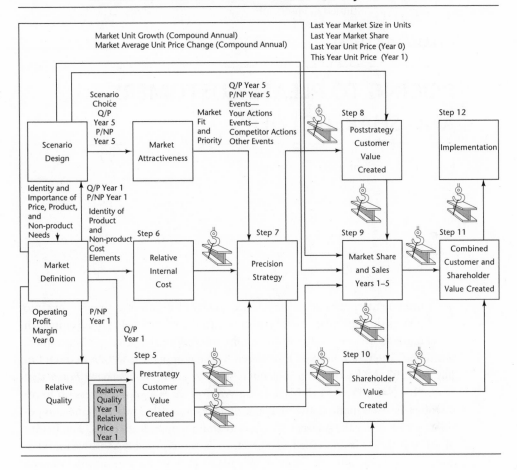

CHAPTER SEVEN

PRICING TO PLEASE CUSTOMERS AND SHAREHOLDERS

O nce an enterprise knows the relative quality of its offering, price comes into play as the enterprise measures and maps the relative value it offers in each of its markets. Relative value is the quality offered for the price, and customers always buy the best relative value offered by the competitors in that market. On July 28, 1992, AST Computer took out a full-page ad in *The Wall Street Journal* that read, "It's Not a Price War, It's a Value War."[1] This is a good expression to remember. In each market, an enterprise engages in a value war with the competition, which it must regularly win if it is to attain market leadership. The nature of this war differs from market to market. In extremely quality-sensitive markets, a value war is a quality war. In extremely price-sensitive markets, a value war is a price war. In most markets, however, it is a combination of both. Achieving a superior quality position opens the possibility for an enterprise to price its offering at a premium. An enterprise must calculate this premium carefully, however, to make sure that together with its quality, the combination offers customers a superior value. We use the Customer Value Map, a powerful tool that we examined briefly in Chapter Two, to accomplish this.

Measuring and Mapping Relative Price

Measuring relative price is simpler than measuring relative quality because it does not require a weighted average process. We can see the measurement process

Exhibit 7.1. Relative Price: Progressive Market.

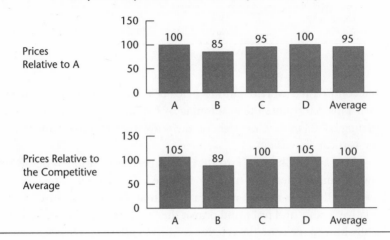

A's price is 5 percent above the competitive average.

Prices Relative to A

	A	B	C	D	Average
	100	85	95	100	95

Prices Relative to the Competitive Average

	A	B	C	D	Average
	105	89	100	105	100

for relative price in Exhibit 7.1. The top row, which shows prices relative to the price of Competitor A, is a graphical representation of the same prices relative to A that we saw in Exhibit 6.1. We calculate prices relative to the competitive average in the bottom row by dividing each price in the top row by 95, the market average. Now, our reference point has changed from Competitor A, Sportmed, to the market average. The 105 measurement for A indicates that A's price is 5 percent above market average. The 89 measurement for Competitor B means that B's price is 11 percent below market average.

Remembering that we have brought each competitor's relative quality forward as carried value from Chapter Six, we can now summarize everyone's relative quality and relative price in Exhibit 7.2.

Now we will see how relative quality and relative price combine to create relative customer value.

Measuring and Mapping Relative Customer Value

We are ready to take the powerful step of measuring and mapping relative customer value. We depict this in the Customer Value Map shown in Exhibit 7.3. The steep slope of the "market wants" line is determined by the quality sensitivity of Progressive practitioners who attach a 65 percent importance to quality and only 35 percent to price. We saw in Exhibit 7.2 that A's quality is 23 percent above

Exhibit 7.2. Relative Quality and Relative Price: Progressive Market.

	Competitor A	Competitor B	Competitor C	Competitor D
Relative Quality	+23%	–9%	–6%	–7%
Relative Price	+5%	–11%	0%	+5%

the competitive average, and its price is 5 percent above the competitive average. This determines the positioning of Competitor A in Exhibit 7.3. The positioning is 0.23 units to the right on the horizontal dimension and 0.05 units up on
the vertical dimension.

We saw in Chapter Two that a competitor positioned below the "market
wants" line is offering a superior relative value—a better quality-for-the-price
tradeoff than the market requires. Now that we have measured Competitor A's
relative quality and price and drawn the "market wants" line, we can see graphically how to measure the relative value A is offering. This measurement simply
reflects the geometric principle that the distance between a point and a line is the
line that passes through the point and that is perpendicular to the line. The length

Exhibit 7.3. Customer Value Map: Relative Customer Value.

**The measure of your relative customer value is the perpendicular
distance between your positioning and the "market wants" line.**

A's position, from Exhibit 7.2, is 0.23 units to the right and 0.05 units up.

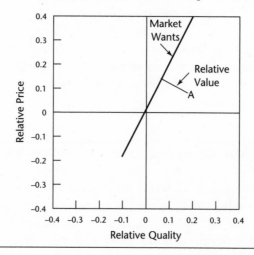

of this perpendicular line from A to the "market wants" line is the measure of the superior customer value A is offering. The length of a comparable line for a competitor positioned above the "market wants" line is the measure of the inferior customer value this competitor is offering.

Fighting Three Value Wars at Sportmed

Now that we understand how to measure and map customer value, we will look at three very different value wars in the Progressive, Traditional, and Commercial Markets.

The Value War in the Progressive Market

Exhibit 7.4 shows the value war in the Progressive Market, the early adopters of technology. We add Competitors B, C, and D to the picture because we know their relative quality and relative price from Exhibit 7.2. Again, the high slope of the "market wants" line is determined by the quality sensitivity of this market. Progressive practitioners attach a 65 percent importance to quality and only 35 percent

Exhibit 7.4. Customer Value Map: Progressive Market.

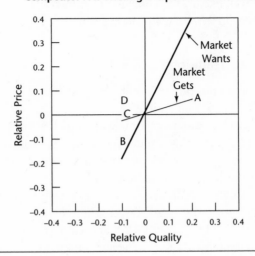

Competitor A is offering a superior relative value.

to price. In our scenario work, we defined quality-sensitive markets as those in which the customer attaches more than 60 percent of the buying decision to quality. Importantly, in quality-sensitive markets, quality is the value leverage factor, and a value war is a quality war. That is the case here.

The "market gets" line is the best straight-line fit for points A, B, C, and D, the points that show the quality for the price that each of the four competitors is offering in this market. In this sense, it depicts what the market is "getting" from competitors. We will focus on its importance shortly.

We saw in Chapter Two that competitors located on the "market wants" line are offering exactly the relative value that the market is willing to accept. For this reason, their market share is not changing. Here Sportmed, Competitor A, is positioned well below the "market wants" line. This means that Sportmed is offering a superior relative value to customers in this market—a better quality for the price than the market is willing to accept. This, in turn, means that Sportmed should be gaining market share. Crucially, the Sportmed planning team for the Progressive Market realized that this was exactly what was happening in this marketplace. This immediately told the Sportmed team that the relative quality and relative price assessments it made in Exhibit 6.1 were consistent with the reality of the marketplace. It confirmed the assessment made in Chapter Five that a good fit existed between the value leverage factor in the market—quality—and Sportmed's core competence.

Competitors B, C, and D are positioned above the "market wants" line. This means they are offering an inferior relative value in this market and would be expected to lose market share. Again, the Sportmed team recognized that this was in fact what was actually happening in the market. This gave Sportmed still further confidence in the validity of its assessments.

The Value War in the Traditional Market

Sportmed's positioning in the Traditional-practitioner market—the late adopters of technology—paints an entirely different picture. Traditional practitioners attach a 35 percent importance to quality and 65 percent to price. In our scenario work we defined price-sensitive markets as those in which the customer attaches less than 40 percent of the buying decision to quality. In price-sensitive markets, price is the value leverage factor, and a value war is a price war. That is the case here, as we can see in Exhibit 7.5. This shows that Competitor A, Sportmed, is positioned well above the "market wants" line. The positioning comes from charts comparable to Exhibits 6.2 and 7.2 that are not included here. This positioning represents an inferior customer value and reflects a share-losing proposition. This is exactly what was happening in this market. Notice that A is actually positioned in the upper left-hand quadrant of the Customer Value Map. Any competitor positioned in this quadrant is offering below-average quality for above-average price. It is asking the customer to pay more for less. We call this quadrant the "Bermuda Triangle" and depict it with the triangle inset in the upper left corner of Exhibit 7.5. Competitors who are positioned in this quadrant will lose market share until they ultimately disappear.

Through contrasting its dramatically different positioning on these two Value Maps, Sportmed had a profound insight. It was offering the identical line of instruments in each of the two markets. This represented a "one size fits all" approach. It was taking the line of instruments tailored for the Progressive practitioner and offering this same line to the Traditional practitioner, a customer who is price sensitive rather than quality sensitive. This was at once a strategy for winning the value war for the Progressives and a formula for losing the value war for the Traditionals. Sportmed realized that it had in fact ignored the purpose of market definition. That purpose is to define markets to uncover differences and then build precision strategies to tailor separate offerings to meet the market's different needs. Instead, Sportmed had used a single strategy that well exceeded what the Progressives were willing to accept and fell far short of meeting what the Traditionals were willing to accept.

Exhibit 7.5. Customer Value Map: Traditional Market.

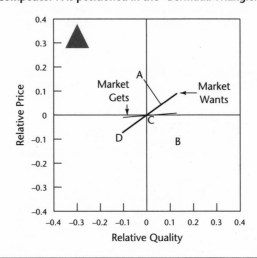

Competitor A is positioned in the "Bermuda Triangle."

The Value War in the Commercial Market

Customers in the Commercial Market consist of practitioners working in public settings, such as university sports facilities, and frequently operating under tight budgets. Commercial customers attach only a 30 percent importance to quality and a large 70 percent of importance to price. In the Commercial Market, a value war is an even stronger price war than it is in the Traditional Market. We can see Sportmed's positioning in this market in Exhibit 7.6. Here A's position is even worse than it was with the Traditionals. Of particular interest, however, is the positioning of Competitor B. Competitor B is positioned deep in the bottom right quadrant. Competitors positioned in this quadrant are offering above-average quality for below-average price. Consequently, they are both the quality leaders *and* the price leaders in the market. We call this a "Take No Prisoners" positioning and depict it with a shell burst in the bottom right corner of Exhibit 7.6. A competitor offering a value as superior as this will gain share so rapidly that it will drive everyone else out of business unless the other competitors dramatically reposition themselves.

Notice that the "market gets" line is tipping down and to the right. This means that customers in this market can get more by paying less, an overwhelming value proposition. This value proposition is created by B's "Take No Prisoners" strategy. Interestingly, it is not uncommon to see a situation like this in high-technology markets. A major technological innovation often creates a breakthrough in which

Exhibit 7.6. Customer Value Map: Commercial Market.

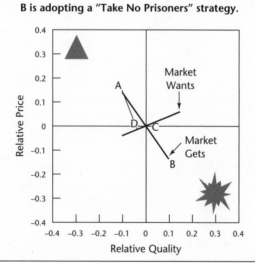

B is adopting a "Take No Prisoners" strategy.

its owner is able to offer more for less. This is why it is so important to write scenarios that include frame-breaking innovation. Such scenarios help an enterprise prepare for these competitive realities.

Repositioning at Procter & Gamble

If an enterprise's markets are decreasing in slope and thereby increasing in price sensitivity, the enterprise must reposition itself. An article in the March 7, 1994, issue of *Fortune,* entitled "Behind the Tumult at P&G," described how Procter & Gamble was doing just that.[2]

Fortune called it the $725 restructuring. Not particularly pricey for a $30-billion-a-year packaged-goods gargantua like P&G. Why $725? That's the premium that a brand-loyal family had to pay in 1993 for a year's worth of P&G products versus private-label or low-priced brands. In the value decade of the 1990s, a premium like that spells trouble. What P&G had was a few hundred bucks of evidence that high prices were slowly transforming the company from mass marketer to mastodon.

The company's new strategy is anchored in value. It recognizes the obvious: P&G had been overcharging for detergents (Tide), toothpaste (Crest), cough syrup (Vicks), and diapers (Pampers). Consumers then began underconsuming. The result is the company's dramatic conversion to everyday low pricing (EDLP) on many of its products—which P&G calls value pricing—as opposed to maintaining high list prices punctured by frequent and irregular discounts. As for P&G's vaunted brands, these once-regal equities will bend to the wishes of consumers everywhere—South America, China, and the United States—and take whatever forms and prices the far-flung customers can afford. Value has made P&G a hunter of revenues rather than a gatherer.

It's axiomatic that P&G could not deliver everyday low prices without incurring everyday low costs. Redefining consumer value means being careful not to charge for costs that do not contribute directly to product and non-product quality. Consequently, P&G is tearing down and rebuilding nearly every activity that contributes to high costs.

Since P&G's CEO Ed Artzt announced in late 1991 that it would convert to EDLP, evidence is mounting that it's working. The company says that in twenty-two of thirty-two categories, domestic market share and revenues are rising. Perhaps "recovering" is a better word, but P&G looks like a big winner.

P&G made the EDLP decision as a result of its experiences of struggling in the churning retail channel. The growth of membership warehouse clubs such as

Costco and Pace and of discount stores like Wal-Mart pulled P&G in a different direction from the one that had worked with supermarkets and drugstores. The new-style retailers weren't interested in yo-yo prices. They wanted goods at the best price day in, day out, in truckload quantities and, in the case of price clubs, delivered directly from the factory, not via a warehouse. As P&G discovered with Wal-Mart, this is an efficient way to do business. Among the consequences, P&G has reduced the number of price changes from fifty-five a day to one and the number of pricing brackets from seventeen to three.

Paradoxically, EDLP has been accompanied by non-product innovation that strengthens, rather than diminishes, P&G's vaunted brands. Once, the company created a new brand image each time it came up with a product innovation. A new formulation like "Tide with Bleach" would have been given a new name. But that strategy left the old brands open to attack. Says Artzt, "We trapped ourselves, at times, into thinking that the best way to bring new technology to the market was to bring it out as a second brand. But you don't deny the new technology to your market leader, or you are going to lose market leadership."

The company learned this lesson the hard way in the diaper business when it developed a new shaped-diaper technology and created a new brand for it, Luvs, instead of extending its main brand, Pampers. Kimberly-Clark immediately incorporated a shaped design into its main brand, Huggies, and gave P&G a thumping.

A similar goof hurt Ivory soap. "My greatest disappointment has been the long-term decline of Ivory, which I have been convinced was due to the fact that we didn't properly understand the Ivory concept," says Artzt. Proctor believed Ivory was soap and soap was Ivory, instead of defining the business area as a pure cleaning product that could retain that identity while taking on new features. Improvements such as soap with cold cream were marketed as new, unrelated brands, to Ivory's detriment.

Similarly, Spic and Span has survived forty-five years of share decline, a statistic that says as much about the lasting value of brand equity as about P&G's ineptitude. In 1993, the company finally imbued it with modern qualities and new formulas—a Spic and Span bathroom spray cleaner, for example—and a turnaround is possible. This is why you're seeing Tartar-Control Crest and Crest With Baking Soda rather than new brands of toothpaste.

The message is clear. A high-end, brand-famous company can be price competitive with store brands without destroying brand equity. At comparable prices, consumers perceive the branded offering to be a better value. Since making the change in 1991, P&G's stock increased from under forty dollars a share to fifty-eight dollars a share at the time of the article.

Learning the Rule of Twenty and Two-Thirds

It is important to price low enough to please customers and high enough to satisfy shareholders. Exhibit 7.7 shows how to achieve this. We stated in Chapter Six
that an enterprise seeking success at the high end of the market should try to
achieve a relative quality edge of plus 20 percent in the package of product and
non-product benefits it offers. If the enterprise achieves this and maintains a competitive internal cost structure, it is in a dominant position to win the value war in
the marketplace. The enterprise can either price up to realize high profit margins
or price down into "Take No Prisoners" territory to gain share rapidly. A useful
way to start thinking about where to price may be to set a price premium that is
two-thirds of the vertical distance between the market average price and the "market wants" line—two-thirds of the premium that customers would expect to pay
for this level of quality. This accomplishes two things at once. First, the enterprise
is pricing at a premium above market average price for its superior quality, thereby
satisfying shareholders. Second, it remains below the "market wants" line so it is
pleasing customers and gaining market share at the same time that it is enjoying
attractive margins. We call this *double-win two* in the Market Value Process, since
the enterprise is simultaneously pleasing both constituencies. As the slope of the
"market wants" line changes over time in response to innovation in the marketplace, the enterprise can adjust its price to reflect the new two-thirds distance.

Exhibit 7.7. Customer Value Map: The Rule of Twenty and Two-Thirds.

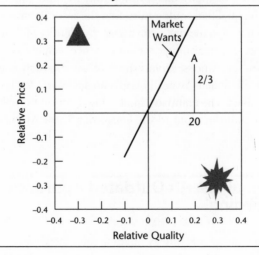

The rule of twenty and two-thirds should only be a starting point for your thinking. If an enterprise wants to gain share more rapidly, it should set its price at a lower level. In fact, the enterprise will be forced to do so if it has a competitor who is adopting a "Take No Prisoners" strategy.

Mapping Relative Customer Value for Buying Constellations

The process of making the purchase decision often involves a group of two or more people acting in collaboration. Marketers call this group a buying constellation. Buying constellations may occur in big-ticket consumer markets, such as collaboration among family members in buying a car. In business-to-business marketing, they may occur among managers in an enterprise having input into a decision to buy a mainframe computer. They may even take place among individuals in several enterprises, such as when doctors, patients, hospitals, and third-party reimbursement enterprises try to reach a consensus regarding which prescription drugs to use. The input for the Customer Value Map needs to reflect the influence of each member of the buying constellation.

Let's consider a few examples of two-person buying constellations. One of the two members may drive the buying decision with the other having modest input at best. In this case, the driver's assessments of relative quality and relative price are the ones to use in the Customer Value Map. Alternatively, the two participants may exert an equal influence. In this case, the assessments should reflect their consensus, which might be the average of their individual assessments. Finally, the nature of their collaboration may by quite different. For example, one may select the qualified competitors, and the second may make the choice among them. In such a case, the first determines the identity of Competitors A, B, C, and D, and the second determines the importance weights and performance ratings.

The number of possible variations of the interaction among participants in buying constellations is large. There is no substitute for thoughtfully diagnosing which one reflects the reality of the buying decision in each of your markets and making sure that the input to the Customer Value Map accurately models this buying decision.

Using SWOT Analysis: An Outdated Approach to Strategy Building

Much of what passes for strategy building today centers on an analysis of strengths versus weaknesses and opportunities versus threats (SWOT). This is an outdated approach to strategy building. It is much more powerful to package strengths and weaknesses into a Customer Value Map than to create a disconnected list in two columns on a pad of paper. Similarly, it is much more powerful to package opportunities and threats into a Scenario Map that depicts a cause-and-effect logic, as we did in Chapter Five, rather than simply listing them. Measuring and mapping provide insights that are orders of magnitude more powerful. If you measure and map strengths, weaknesses, opportunities, and threats, you will build strategies that outperform the ones built by competitors who work from lists.

Carried Value

 As a result of our work with relative price and relative quality, we can measure the customer value we are creating. As Exhibit 7.8 shows, we carry this forward to Step Seven, Integrated Customer Value Strategy, and Step Nine, Market Share and Sales, years one through five.

    If you have followed each of the steps we have discussed up to this point, you will have mapped the customer value that your enterprise offers in each market with a precision that few competitors achieve. This provides a strong foundation on which to build precision strategies that will enhance this value if it is already strong—or that will fix it if it is weak.

Exhibit 7.8. Carried Value: Prestrategy Customer Value.

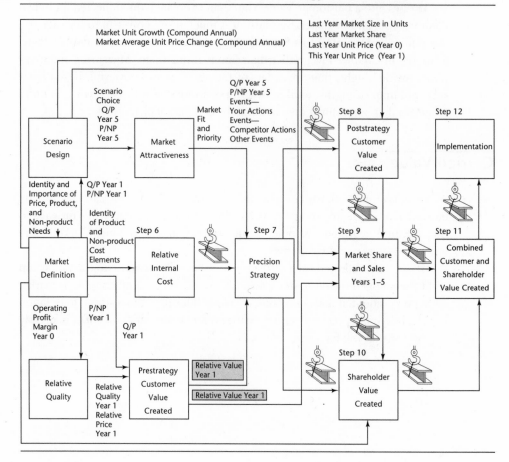

CHAPTER EIGHT

MANAGING INTERNAL COSTS

Once an enterprise knows the relative quality and price of its offering in each market, it needs to measure and map its internal cost, both product and non-product, relative to the competition. Product cost is the cost an enterprise incurs to offer product quality. Non-product cost is the cost needed to deliver non-product quality, such as information provided by consultative selling or the availability for purchase provided by a strong distribution system.

Knowing its relative product and non-product cost puts an enterprise's relative quality and relative price in perspective. If the enterprise is the high-cost competitor in either the product or non-product dimensions, it must ask itself whether this is necessary in order to offer superior product and non-product quality. There is a school of thought that says quality is "free," or even constitutes a savings, because the benefits of increasing quality outweigh the costs. The enterprise needs to decide whether this is the case in its particular situation. An enterprise's relative cost is also significant in relation to its relative price. If it is the high-cost competitor, its ability to fight a value war in which price is the value leverage factor is severely limited.

Using Price-Driven Costing, Not Cost-Driven Pricing

It is important for an enterprise to think through its situation in each market in the sequence of quality, price, and cost. First it should think about the quality it needs to achieve and second about the price it needs to set in order to gain the position it wants to have on the Customer Value Map. A good starting point is to shoot for a 20 percent quality advantage, which gives an enterprise a strong high-end position, and to price using the rule of twenty and two-thirds that we discussed in Chapter Seven. Then an enterprise needs to think about the cost position it must have in order to create value for shareholders at the same time that it creates value for customers. All too often, people think instead in the quality, cost, price sequence—determining the cost entailed to provide quality and adding a margin on top to arrive at price. Thinking this way can leave an enterprise whose costs are too high in a badly overpriced position on the Customer Value Map. On the other hand, if an enterprise's relative costs are very low, it can lead to underpricing the value proposition.

A December 14, 1992, *Fortune* article entitled "The Revolution at Compaq Computer" (excerpted in Exhibit 8.1) describes how Compaq's strategy had recently shifted to this quality, price, cost sequence. This is a perfect example of the importance of using price-driven costing rather than cost-driven pricing. An enterprise can no longer let its internal processes determine price. Instead, price must determine the processes. The implications for the time to complete key processes such as new-product development are profound. Price-driven costing doesn't work if it takes five to six years to complete the new-product development process. The picture from the Customer Value Map that determined price will have shifted too much in half a decade. To set a realistic price and cost structure, the enterprise must have a development cycle of three years or less. In many areas of the fast-moving microcomputer hardware and software markets, this cycle must be as short as twelve to eighteen months.

Exhibit 8.1. The Revolution at Compaq Computer.

Price-Driven Costing

Compaq has totally revamped how it prices its products. In the past, product designers totaled up the cost of the features they wanted on a machine, figured out which sole supplier would provide each part at what price, and added on a margin like 40%. This was the price to dealers who typically added another 15% markup.

Now the process is reversed. Managers first decide what they want the street price to be, based on competitive factors. Then they assume a dealer markup, subtract a Compaq gross profit margin—about 30% today—and instruct the departments of materials, engineering, manufacturing, and marketing to resolve among themselves how to allocate the remaining costs to make the product.

Source: Kirkpatrick, D. "The Revolution at Compaq Computer." *Fortune,* December 14, 1992, pp. 80–88.

Knowing Your Own Unit Costs

Before an enterprise can know its relative cost position, it must know its own unit costs, such as the cost of each instrument that Sportmed sells to the Progressive Market. At this point, the manufacturing members of Sportmed's cross-functional teams begin to play a key role. Marketing professionals, however, continue to be active players. Marketers must understand costs as well as prices. Recent books have asserted that it is a dangerous myth that marketers don't need to know the manufacturing cost of the offering their enterprise makes to the market.[1]

To know its true unit costs, an enterprise must accurately allocate its total enterprise costs to each market it serves. It should do this by measuring the actual costs that its activities in each market incur—a process known as activity-based costing. Activity-based costing has come into wide use in the 1990s as the power of the information it provides has become more widely recognized.[2] An enterprise should not allocate costs by using some across-the-board allocation approach that fails to measure what it actually costs to compete in each market. Exhibit 8.2 provides an example of activity-based costing. While this example covers product costs, the approach should be used to allocate non-product costs as well. The point is a simple one. Use actual, activity-based costs, not costs derived from inaccurate allocation approaches.

Gathering and Maintaining Competitive Cost Information

We have just seen how an enterprise develops its own cost information using activity-based costing. Now we turn to the issue of gathering cost information about competitors. Entire books have been written on this subject of competitor intelligence.[3] All affirm that this entails never-ending detective work. The sources of competitive cost information are many—annual reports, trade journals, movement of employees among companies—but each source is incomplete. The detective work necessary to gather this information from many sources will be strenuous, but it will be well worth the effort.

The detective work, however, doesn't have to be perfect. The important principle in gathering competitor intelligence is that an educated guess, based on available information and intuition, is always better than no guess at all. Making educated guesses allows an enterprise to measure and map its relative cost position, as we will soon see. The insights that the enterprise can gain with educated guesses are too valuable to forego just because the information is imprecise.

Exhibit 8.2. Using Activity-Based Cost Allocation.

Inventory Control Department

	Receive Parts	Receive Material	Disburse Material	Total
Staff	10	6	4	
Total cost	$500,000	$300,000	$200,000	
Units of activity	25,000 shipments	12,000 shipments	20,000 production runs	
Unit activity cost	$20.00	$25.00	$10.00	

Business 1: 100 Units Produced

	Receive Parts	Receive Material	Disburse Material
Units of activity	150 shipments	80 shipments	60 production runs
Unit activity cost	$20.00	$25.00	$10.00
Unit cost	$30.00	$20.00	$6.00

$56.00

(150 × $20/100)

Old System
(Direct Labor)

$25.00

Assume that the inventory control department, one small part of total manufacturing overhead, employs twenty people. Ten of these work in receiving parts and cost $500,000 in total. The activity they perform is receiving parts shipments, and they receive 25,000 shipments over the course of a year. This means the unit activity cost, the cost per shipment received, is $20.00.

Now assume Business 1, serving Market 1, produces 100 units per year and, in doing so, receives 150 shipments. Its actual receiving cost for each unit it produces is $30.00 (150 shipments × $20.00 per shipment/100 units). A similar analysis of receiving material and disbursing material shows an actual, activity-based unit cost of $56.00 for the total inventory control activity in Market 1. This is dramatically higher than the cost of $25.00 shown by an older, inaccurate, across-the-board allocation approach based on direct labor. When this accurate, activity-based approach is extended beyond the inventory control department to all the costs incurred in Market 1, we then know our unit total cost in Market 1.

Note: Exhibit 8.2 was inspired by the excellent overview of activity-based costing by Robin Cooper and Robert S. Kaplan in "Measure Costs Right: Make the Right Decisions." *Harvard Business Review,* Sept.–Oct. 1988, pp. 96–103.

Precision will grow as the effort continues, and many insights are sufficiently robust that they emerge in broad strokes even if the cost information is imprecise. Even imprecise information will give the enterprise a handle on what pricing its competitors can withstand and what pricing they cannot withstand because of their disadvantage in relative cost.

Measuring and Mapping Your Relative Cost Position

Once an enterprise has measured its own unit costs in each of its markets and gathered competitive cost information, it can begin to measure and map its unit cost position relative to that competition. To do this, it divides costs into two groups—product costs and non-product costs. Product costs are the costs an enterprise incurs to offer its product quality. These include research and development, purchases, direct labor, and manufacturing overhead, of which the inventory control example from Exhibit 8.2 is a part. Non-product costs are the costs it incurs to offer its non-product quality. Among these costs are marketing and customer service, including distribution. All other costs, such as general corporate overhead, are assigned to product or non-product cost using the activity-based principle.

Now we will investigate how an enterprise can establish a neutral cost line, measure its relative product and non-product cost, and map its relative cost position in a way that gives the enterprise insights as powerful as those it got from mapping the customer value it creates.

Establishing a Neutral Cost Line

We need to establish a neutral cost line for a market, just as we established a neutral value line—the "market wants" line—on the Customer Value Map. By way of definition, when we say total cost, we mean total cost per unit produced. Similarly, we use the terms *product cost* and *non-product cost* on a per-unit-produced basis. Exhibit 8.3 describes the principles underlying the neutral cost line. It is the line along which an enterprise's advantage or disadvantage in product cost is exactly offset by a countervailing advantage or disadvantage in non-product cost. This means that along the neutral cost line, an enterprise's total cost equals the average of the four key competitors, including itself. For example, consider a market where competitive average product costs are twice as important and loom twice as large as non-product costs. In this case, an enterprise's 10 percent advantage in product cost would neutralize a 20 percent disadvantage in its non-product cost. The implications of this are profound. Assume that an enterprise runs a tight ship on the product side and establishes a 10 percent advantage in product cost. This means the enterprise can operate at a 20 percent disadvantage in non-product cost by investing heavily in marketing, distribution, sales, and customer service and still have a unit total cost that is equal to the competitive average.

Once we understand this fundamental proposition, we can map the information we just developed in a new and powerful way. Exhibit 8.4 shows how we

Exhibit 8.3.

If market average product cost is twice the non-product cost, a 10 percent product cost advantage neutralizes a 20 percent non-product cost disadvantage.

	Market Average Unit Cost	Percent of Total Cost	Competitor A Above/Below Average	Dollar Advantage/ Disadvantage
Product	$20	67%	−10%	$2 advantage
Non-product	$10	33%	+20%	$2 disadvantage
Total	$30	100%	0%	neutral

Exhibit 8.3 describes how to draw a neutral cost line by using an example in which the market average product cost is twice the market average non-product cost. The example shows that in this market, a 10 percent product cost advantage neutralizes a 20 percent non-product cost disadvantage.

In this particular example, the market average non-product cost for the four competitors is $10 per unit produced. The average product cost of the four competitors is $20, twice the non-product cost. We discussed how to assemble this information in the section "Gathering and Maintaining Competitive Cost Information." Now assume that Competitor A has a 20 percent non-product cost disadvantage caused by a heavy investment in marketing, distribution, sales, and customer service. This is a $2 disadvantage (20 percent of $10). This non-product disadvantage can be neutralized by running a tight ship on the product side and establishing a 10 percent product cost advantage. This is a $2 advantage (10 percent of $20). The non-product disadvantage is exactly offset by the product advantage, and competitor A's total cost is identical with the market average total cost of $30. Aggressive management of product cost has funded a potentially important investment in non-product cost.

We can immediately see that this neutralizing principle applies any time the two elements, product and non-product, have an advantage/disadvantage relationship inversely proportional to their respective importance in the total cost structure. For example, if product cost is three times as important as non-product cost, a 10 percent product cost advantage neutralizes a 30 percent non-product cost disadvantage.

---

can map the neutral cost line and draw conclusions about good and bad positioning. The chart shows relative unit non-product cost along the horizontal dimension and unit relative product cost along the vertical dimension. A competitor located at the center of the chart has both product costs and non-product costs that are equal to the market average. Now we can draw a neutral cost line for a market in which product costs are twice as important as non-product costs. Any competitor located on the neutral cost line will have a total cost that is equal to the market average total cost. Any competitor positioned above the line will have a total cost that is higher than market average and will therefore have a relative cost disadvantage. Any competitor positioned below the line will have a total cost that is lower than market average and will therefore have a relative cost advantage.

The payoff for this kind of precise thinking about cost is great. Now we can draw some important parallels between this Neutral Cost Line Map and the

Exhibit 8.4. Neutral Cost Line Map.

We can map the Neutral Cost Line and draw conclusions about good and bad positioning.

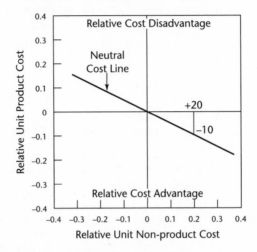

To draw the neutral cost line for a market in which product costs are twice as important as non-product costs, we go out 20 percent to the right, the "above-average" direction for non-product costs, and we go down 10 percent, the "below-average" direction for product costs. This is simply the graphical representation of the offsetting $2 non-product disadvantage and $2 product advantage we discussed in Exhibit 8.3.

Customer Value Map. In both, it is good to be "below the line." Competitors below the "market wants" line on the Value Map are offering a superior relative value. Competitors below the "neutral cost" line on the Neutral Cost Line Map have a superior relative cost. In both, the slope of the line has an important meaning. The steeper the upward slope of the "market wants" line, the more quality-sensitive the market, as we have already seen. The steeper the downward slope of the "neutral cost" line, the more important non-product cost is in the market average cost picture. Each map has a Bermuda Triangle quadrant and a Take No Prisoners quadrant. In the Customer Value Map, the Bermuda Triangle is the upper left one: below-average quality for above-average price. In the Neutral Cost Line Map it is the upper right one: above average in both product cost and non-product cost. In the Customer Value Map, the Take No Prisoners position is the lower right quadrant: above-average quality for below-average price. In the Neutral Cost Line Map it is the lower left one: below average in both product cost and non-product cost.

Measuring Relative Cost

Now that we have established these parallels, we can return to the Sportmed example and measure the relative cost position of Sportmed and its competitors. We can see the measurement of relative cost in the Progressive Market in Exhibit 8.5. This chart shows that relative total cost is a weighted average of relative product cost and relative non-product cost. The weights are the market average product/non-product cost structure.

Exhibit 8.5. Relative Unit Total Costs: Sportmed.

Relative total cost per unit produced is a weighted average of relative unit product cost and relative unit non-product cost. The weights are the market average product/non-product cost structure.

	Cost as a Percent of Competitor A				
	A	B	C	D	Average
Unit Product Cost	100	88	93	102	96
Unit Non-product Cost	100	70	75	50	74

	Market Average as Percent of Total	Cost as a Percent of Market Average			
		A	B	C	D
Unit Product Cost	69	104	92	97	107
Unit Non-product Cost	31	136	95	102	68
Unit Total Cost	100	114	93	99	95

In the top half of the chart, Sportmed took its relative product cost and non-product cost as 100 per unit produced. Then it assessed each competitor's costs as a percent of Sportmed's. The process is completely analogous to the way we calculated relative price earlier. Next it calculated the market average, 96 for product and 74 for non-product. Do not try to add these numbers to get a total cost score, because they are "horizontal" percentages (relative to A), not "vertical" percentages (relative to total cost).

In the bottom half of the chart, Sportmed expressed competitive costs as a percent of market average. For example, the 104 score for Sportmed shows that its score of 100, above, is 104 percent of the market average score of 96. Then it calculated its relative total cost as a weighted average of the two components, with the weights being the market average of each component as a percent of the total cost structure—69 percent for product and 31 percent for non-product. We discussed how to assemble this information in the section "Gathering and Maintaining Competitive Cost Information." The weighted result for Competitor A, Sportmed, was 114 as shown in the highlighted bottom row.

This process was similar to but simpler than measuring relative quality, since here there are only two components, rather than eight, to weigh.

Sportmed's relative unit total cost of 114 showed it was 14 percent above the market average in this important measure. Competitor B's relative unit total cost of 93 showed that it was 7 percent below average.

You may wonder at this point why the measurement in Exhibit 8.5 is necessary. You might simply want to assess directly each competitor's product and non-product cost per unit produced in dollars and then add the two amounts to get the total. There are three reasons for using the approach shown in Exhibit 8.5. First, it is often difficult to assess directly the dollar costs of competitors. Often, it is easier for an enterprise to assess competitor costs relative to its own and to assess the market average product/non-product cost structure—69/31 in this case. Exhibit 8.5 allows measurement of relative total cost through this set of assessments, which are more easily made. Second, in addition to using a simpler set of assessments, Exhibit 8.5 clearly shows how an enterprise's costs relate to the costs of each competitor and to the market average in a precise and comprehensive way that simple addition cannot. Third, Exhibit 8.5 creates a clear analogy to the measurement of perceived quality we saw in Chapter Six, in which product and non-product quality elements are weighted by importance just as product and non-product cost elements are here. This analogy reinforces the learning of both the quality and the cost measurements.

We can now summarize everyone's relative product and non-product cost in Exhibit 8.6.

Mapping Relative Cost

Now we are ready to take the powerful step of mapping each competitor's relative cost in the Progressive Market on the Cost Map, Exhibit 8.7. The slope of the "neutral cost" line is determined by moving out 0.69 to the right and 0.31 down. This reflects the proposition that in a market where product cost and non-product cost are 69 percent and 31 percent of the story, respectively, a 69 percent disadvantage in non-product cost (a move to the right) will be neutralized by a 31 percent advantage in product cost (a move down).

Sportmed, Competitor A, is positioned on the Cost Map at a 36 percent disadvantage in non-product cost (thirty-six units to the right) and a 4 percent

Exhibit 8.6. Relative Internal Cost Positions: Progressive Market.

	Competitor A	Competitor B	Competitor C	Competitor D
Relative Product Cost	+4%	−8%	−3%	+7%
Relative Non-product Cost	+36%	−5%	+2%	−32%
Relative Total Cost	+14%	−7%	−1%	−5%

Exhibit 8.7. Cost Map: Progressive Market.

A's relative unit total cost is 14 percent above the competitive average caused by a disadvantage of 4 percent in product cost and 36 percent in non-product cost.

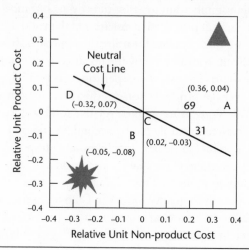

disadvantage in product cost (four units up). This positions Sportmed above the "neutral cost" line and places it in the cost disadvantage area. In fact, Sportmed's above-average position in both product and non-product cost places Sportmed in the Bermuda Triangle, the upper right corner of the Cost Map. Before criticizing Sportmed too harshly for this, we should remember that the Progressive Market is a high-slope one in which quality is more important than cost. So Sportmed may have been justified in incurring a cost penalty if it believed this was necessary to establish the 23 percent relative quality advantage it enjoyed in the Progressive Market. And in fact, Sportmed decided its 36 percent penalty in non-product cost was necessary to establish its non-product quality. Sportmed provided information to the customer through consultative selling by its own somewhat expensive sales force, which it regarded as a key to its quality edge in meeting this customer need. Its competitors, by contrast, relied on distributors to do this. Sportmed did, however, decide that its 4 percent penalty in product cost was not necessary to establish its product quality. Consequently, Sportmed made it a priority to streamline its product cost structure.

Each of the other competitors is positioned below the "neutral cost" line, which places each in the relative cost advantage area. In fact, Competitor B is in the Take No Prisoners quadrant with a below-average position in both product and non-product cost. We remember from its Position Map in Chapter Six that

Competitor B had a low-end quality position with a relative quality score of minus 9 percent, so it must compete on price. B's location in the favorable Take No Prisoners terrain on the Cost Map shows that B is indeed very well positioned to compete aggressively on price.

Now, let's see how an enterprise in an altogether different business area responded to the challenge of reducing relative cost.

Reducing Relative Cost at Dell

The best way for an enterprise to reduce relative cost is to understand and streamline, or rebuild, the processes it uses to create product and non-product quality.[4] Even large corporations typically have just six to eight key processes. Product quality processes include new-product development and order fulfillment. Non-product quality processes include customer acquisition and customer service.

Dell Computer, based in Austin, Texas, is one of the lowest-cost competitors per unit produced in the microcomputer industry. Its order fulfillment process was described by *Fortune* in an April 18, 1994, article entitled "Mr. Cozzette Buys a Computer."[5] Compaq Computer, Dell's archrival in Houston, is restructuring its entire logistics operation in hopes of achieving similar build-to-order manufacturing flexibility. This is sometimes called "mass customizing" to evoke the powerful image of using mass production techniques to fulfill customized orders.[6] Let's look at Dell's "mass customizing" order fulfillment process as described by *Fortune*:

> *Wednesday, 10:49 A.M.* Dave Cozzette, an accountant at Rothfos Corporation, a twenty-employee coffee broker, calls in his order for a Dell Dimension PC.
>
> *12:50 P.M.* Dell's financial services unit verifies the charge with Cozzette's credit card company and the details of his $2,700.22 order print on the production floor across the street at Dell's factory. The factory simultaneously prints the information sheet—called a traveler—which lists the sixty items that Cozzette's computer must include, from cables to software. The order is branded with a serial number that will identify the PC for its lifetime, regardless of who owns it.
>
> *1:00 P.M.* The assembly process starts with the installation of an Intel 486 DX2 chip—the brains of Cozzette's computer—onto the machine's main circuit board, known as the motherboard. Simultaneously, another worker readies the floppy drives and hard disk for installation later.

1:55 P.M. A worker applies a sticker bearing the nascent PC's serial number to the chassis and then lays in the motherboard, fastening it with screws.

2:01 P.M. Another worker inserts Cozzette's fax modem, a device that can send documents created on the PC to fax machines or other computers via telephone lines.

2:10 P.M. The floppy disk drive that was prepared earlier is installed, along with a tape backup unit. It will let Cozzette make up-to-date duplicates of his hard disk files in the event his machine has a breakdown.

2:20 P.M. The power supply, a transformer that converts electrical current for use in the PC, goes into the unit, and the PC's faceplate is added with the Dell logo subtly displayed.

2:26 P.M. A worker scans the computer's bar code to update Dell's inventory. The components that have been installed in Cozzette's PC are now listed as removed from the company's storage facility in another area of the plant.

2:27 P.M. The PC gets its first quality inspection. The traveler is checked to make sure Dell has installed every component the computer should have. A test diskette is created that will keep track of which software Cozzette has ordered and which components will need to be tested.

2:28 P.M. The PC powers up for the first time during a "quick test" that checks memory, video circuits, and floppy and hard disk functions.

2:40 P.M. A worker slides on the PC's hood. At this point, assembly is complete.

2:45 P.M. to 7:45 P.M. Cozzette's computer sits on a rack for an extended test called "burn in." Only 2 percent of PCs fail this test. Finally, the test diskette uses the network to download the programs Cozzette has ordered, such as Microsoft Windows.

8:20 P.M. A worker shoots a 25,000-volt charge into the PC's power supply. If the PC handles the jolt without going haywire, it earns a Federal Communications Commission Class B certification that it is safe to use in homes and offices.

8:32 P.M. During the PC's final test, the system is hooked up to a monitor and keyboard and operated without its test diskette, just as Cozzette will use it.

8:35 P.M. The PC goes through a "wipe-down"—a cosmetic inspection that includes scrubbing off grubby fingerprints.

8:37 P.M. The computer is put in a box with its keyboard, manuals, and warranty papers. Cozzette's address is slapped on.

9:25 P.M. An Airborne Express worker loads the PC onto a truck. If Cozzette had called Dell a few hours earlier, his PC would have made it onto the truck before the 7:00 P.M. deadline for next-day delivery. Instead, he'll get it on Friday.

Friday, 10:31 A.M. Airborne drops off the package at Cozzette's office. He plugs in his PC, and Dell's greeting software offers its congratulations.

At this point you should stop to consider the amazingly short amount of time it took to describe Dell's order fulfillment process in rich detail. This reflects the superbly streamlined process that Dell has developed, which is the envy of its competitors. And Dell's core competence in cost is not limited to product cost. Dell practically invented telemarketing as a customer acquisition process—a key process in non-product cost—for the microcomputer industry. Such low product and non-product cost put Dell in an enviable position on the Cost Map. As a competitor with a core competence of low cost, Dell is a standard setter.

Developing a New Manufacturing Strategy

An enterprise needs to build a lean cost structure that supports its pricing and its quality. But customers want different pricing and quality in the Progressive and Traditional Markets. Consequently, the enterprise will need to structure its costs differently in the two markets.

The Progressives are the early adopters who attach great importance to high quality. They are the customers who respond to innovation by paying up for it and thereby creating high-slope, quality-sensitive markets. The critical capabilities required by a manufacturer in this market are flexibility and innovativeness. The cost structures of competitors in this market will be shaped by their varying degrees of success in acquiring these capabilities but will be different from those in the Traditional Market.

The Traditionals attach great importance to price. They are the late adopters who are unwilling to pay up for innovation and quality and therefore create low-slope, price-sensitive markets. The critical capability required by manufacturers in this market is to be an efficient operator, as Dell Computer is. Again, the cost structures of competitors in this market will vary with their varying success in becoming efficient operators but will be different from those in the Progressive Market.

The key issue is what manufacturing strategy responds best to these differing need profiles and their propensity to shift over time. Let's trace the development of a new manufacturing strategy that does this.[7]

During the 1970s, manufacturing strategy shifted from the mass production of the Henry Ford era to "focused factories." This shift was based on the idea that no one plant can be expected to respond to both the Progressive and Traditional need profiles equally well. The focused-factory concept argues for splitting production for the Progressives and Traditionals into separate factories. The Progressive factory would employ highly skilled workers, general-purpose tooling, and little automation. It would be located close to research and development and, to reduce the risk of obsolescence, would produce small batches. The Traditional factory ought to be highly automated, located in areas where labor or material costs are low, employ less skilled workers, and, in order to minimize changeover costs, schedule production around long runs. Both factories would use lean manufacturing approaches, as Dell does, to streamline their manufacturing flows.

The problem is that neither the focused nor the lean approaches to manufacturing strategy pay much attention to strategic flexibility, which we know from our scenario work is highly desirable in turbulent times. In fact, both of these approaches work against flexibility. The focused approach to manufacturing strategy led top managers to focus their companies' operations around specific competitive priorities that tended to make them vulnerable to strategic shifts, such as the one that triggered Compaq's strategy rebuilding, described in Chapter One. And lean manufacturing drives companies to become similar to one another, edging toward a one-size-fits-all approach and sacrificing competitive differentiation.

A third and preferred approach, the new manufacturing strategy, is to decide which critical capabilities an enterprise needs in order to compete successfully. This takes us back to the core competence discussion in Chapter Five regarding market fit. Critical capabilities are simply the core competencies of quality and cost viewed with a higher-resolution microscope. Sportmed, for example, succeeds in the business area of sports medicine instruments by using microprocessor-based technology to develop multifunctional instruments. Then, *within* this critical capability, it can change the *tradeoff* between innovativeness and cost to serve the Progressives and the Traditionals. Viewed this way, the critical-capabilities approach to manufacturing strategy is a synthesis of the best aspects of the lean and the focused approaches. Choosing and putting in place the right capabilities leads to lean manufacturing, through which an enterprise makes its offering simultaneously better and cheaper. Differentiating within the critical capability leads to focus, which helps the enterprise produce distinctly different offerings for the Progressives and the Traditionals.

An important insight, extending beyond the manufacturing arena, is that critical technologies can be non-product as well as product. Dell's expertise in telemarketing microcomputers is an excellent example of a non-product critical capability.

The most desirable critical capabilities on which an enterprise builds its new manufacturing strategy have two characteristics. First, they should be ones that customers value. Second, they should be hard for competitors to duplicate. Becoming the lowest-cost manufacturer by moving offshore is easily copied by competitors. Being a world leader in low-cost microprocessor-based multifunctional instruments is not.

Looking at Reasons for Relative Cost Differences Among Competitors

There are strategic, tactical, and execution reasons for relative cost differences among competitors.

There are several strategic reasons for differences in product cost. Competitors may make different decisions for insourcing or outsourcing key components to gain a cost advantage. Dell Computer outsources virtually everything, while Digital Equipment Corporation does just the opposite. This causes major differences between them in the purchase part of their total product cost. Some competitors may deliberately decide to be the high-cost competitor in research and development with the expectation that this will pay off in a flow of innovative new products that boost product quality. Similarly, some competitors may decide to incur above-average non-product costs in marketing and customer service with the expectation that this will pay off in non-product quality. As we have just seen, this is the case with Sportmed. Total costs may be affected by competitor market shares. The high-share competitor is often the low-cost competitor because of the effects of scale and experience. Sometimes, however, a low-share competitor can also be the low-cost competitor in a market if that competitor's total costs are shared among several other markets.

There are several tactical reasons for misperceptions of differences in costs among competitors. An enterprise may misallocate its own costs among markets if it does not use activity-based costing. Also, an enterprise may simply lack a sound knowledge of its competitors' costs because it has not done a sufficiently thorough job of competitor detective work.

Finally, there are execution reasons for cost differences. For example, an enterprise may not have done as thorough a job as its competitors of implementing the lean manufacturing practices we just discussed.

Comparing Your Relative Cost and Relative Price

We can gain significant insights by examining the Customer Value Map and Cost Map side by side. Doing this tells us how much latitude a competitor has

in repositioning itself on the Customer Value Map. We can visualize this latitude by examining Exhibit 8.8. The chart questions whether Competitor A can
adopt a "Take No Prisoners" strategy and, if not, whether A cares. On the right
we see the Customer Value Map for the Progressive Market that we examined in Chapter Seven. If Sportmed were to adopt a "Take No Prisoners" strategy, it would lower its price and move straight down to position A1. The
problem is that Sportmed's disadvantageous cost position in the Bermuda Triangle on the Cost Map on the left suggests that it would be in profit-margin
trouble if it made this move. Its latitude to move down is limited. Possibly,
Sportmed doesn't care. Right now this is a high-slope, quality-sensitive market,
and Sportmed remembered from its Scenario Map that quality continued to
be half or more of the future buying decision in all scenarios. The value leverage factor is quality, not price. Sportmed will create customer value more
quickly by moving to the right, to A2 on the Customer Value Map, than it
will by moving down.

From this brief discussion, you can see clearly the importance of linking relative value and relative cost. We urge you not to look at a Customer Value Map
or Cost Map in isolation but to try always to look at the two side by side. Linking
customer value thinking and relative cost thinking moves us toward integrated customer value strategies to improve both. We discuss how to build these strategies
in Chapter Nine.

Exhibit 8.8. Comparing Relative Cost and Relative Price.

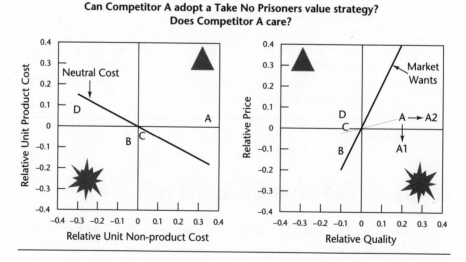

Can Competitor A adopt a Take No Prisoners value strategy?
Does Competitor A care?

Carried Value

We will carry forward the relative cost information and priorities among product and non-product cost elements we have just developed to Step Seven of the Market Value Process: creating an integrated customer value strategy. As Exhibit 8.9 shows, we have replaced all of the girder icons leading to Step Seven with the carried value from earlier steps.

This means that we have now completed our diagnosis of how well Sportmed is currently meeting customers' price, product, and non-product needs. In Chapter Nine we will turn our attention to building precision strategies that bridge the gap between Sportmed's current performance and its desired performance in quality, price, and cost.

Exhibit 8.9. Carried Value: Relative Internal Cost.

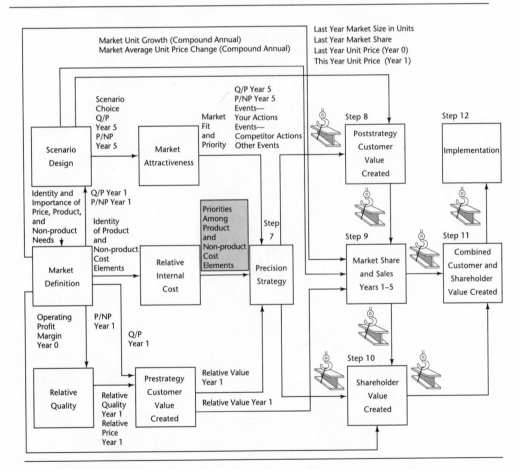

PART THREE

THE BRIDGE

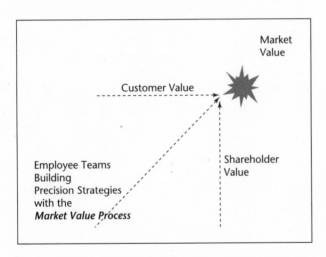

Market
Value

Customer Value

Employee Teams
Building
Precision Strategies
with the
Market Value Process

Shareholder
Value

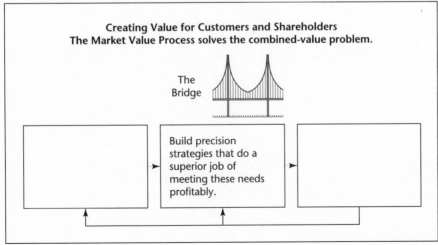

Creating Value for Customers and Shareholders
The Market Value Process solves the combined-value problem.

The
Bridge

Build precision
strategies that do a
superior job of
meeting these needs
profitably.

CHAPTER NINE

BUILDING PROFITABLE PRECISION STRATEGIES

O nce an enterprise knows the relative quality, price, and cost of its offering in each market, it can begin to build precision strategies to improve its position in all three areas. In building these strategies, the enterprise needs to consider the issues of sequence and emphasis.

An enterprise should always develop strategy in the following order: quality, price, and cost. This is because the customer makes the buying decision in this sequence. The customer asks first, "What product and non-product benefits am I getting?" and then, "How much am I paying to get them?" If the customer is entering into a long-term relationship with an enterprise, the question about its relative internal cost arises: "Can this supplier stay in business and prosper at these prices?" By mirroring the buying sequence in the strategy-building sequence, the enterprise aligns its thinking with the customer's thinking. This helps it to ensure that it is benefits driven.

Just because quality is always first in sequence doesn't mean it's always first in emphasis. Emphasis is how much time, energy, and resources the enterprise invests in developing strategy in quality, in price, and in cost. In quality-sensitive markets, the customer says, "How much is quality worth to me? It's worth a lot." Consequently, in these markets, an enterprise invests most of its efforts in building high quality. Here, quality is first in both sequence and emphasis. In price-sensitive markets, however, the customer says, "How much is quality worth to me? It's not worth very much." Quality is still considered first. Even in price-sensitive markets, quality counts for something—just not a lot. In these markets, an enterprise places emphasis on building a low cost structure.

It's important to note that in making the emphasis decision, the enterprise must consider both the quality-versus-price sensitivity of its markets today and the quality-versus-price sensitivity its scenarios envision for the future. If something is important either today or in the future, the enterprise can't afford to ignore it.

Funding Strategies, Not Projects

Before we begin to discuss strategy, you need to understand the importance of funding strategies, not projects. For example, an enterprise's quality strategy may call for a project that will increase the sophistication of the benefits the enterprise offers to meet a key product need such as advanced features. It may be necessary to couple this with a project that will increase the enterprise's customer service staff; this will help meet the non-product need for increased information and support so that customers can benefit fully from these new advanced features.

All too often, however, the financial analysis and approval process is conducted by someone who doesn't know the strategy. As a result, one of these projects may be approved and one turned down, even though one doesn't make sense without the other. The enterprise needs to make sure that the projects that comprise a strategy are evaluated and accepted or rejected as a package.

Building a Strategy to Support Each Objective

Before beginning to build precision strategies in detail, we need to recall our preliminary discussion of this subject in Chapter Two as it applied to our investment banker. There we accomplished three tasks. We identified alternative objectives that might be set in each market, built an integrated customer value strategy to attain each objective, and measured the combined customer and shareholder value created by each strategy. The rest of this strategy-building chapter shows how Sportmed accomplished the first and second of these tasks. We will look at the third in Chapter Thirteen.

Sportmed invested the time to build integrated customer value strategies to support three different objectives. The objectives were to gain, to hold, and to lose share in each of its Progressive, Traditional, and Commercial Markets. This was a total of nine strategies. The strategies supporting the gain, hold, and lose share objectives typically require significant, moderate, or few additional resources, respectively, as we see in Exhibit 9.1.

Exhibit 9.1.

Strategies supporting gain, hold, and lose share objectives typically require significant, moderate, and few human and financial resources, respectively.

	Resources Required to Attain Different Objectives		
	Gain Share	Hold Share	Lose Share
Progressive	Significant	Moderate	Few
Traditional	Significant	Moderate	Few
Commercial	Significant	Moderate	Few

We are now ready to see how Sportmed built one of these nine strategies. The strategy we will look at is the one supporting the "hold share" objective in the Progressive Market. We tackle the Progressive Market first because our carried value from Chapter Five reminds us that Sportmed gave this market top priority in its market attractiveness assessment.

Integrating the Quality Strategy

Sportmed began to build the strategy supporting the hold share objective by thinking about what the strategy should emphasize. The Customer Value Map showed that today's Progressive Market is a quality-sensitive market. Sportmed recalled that the scenario it chose for strategy development, the conventional wisdom "Business as Usual" scenario, indicated that this would continue to be true over this scenario horizon. Consequently, quality was first in emphasis as well as sequence, and Sportmed would invest most of its effort on quality.

If we were examining the price-sensitive Traditional Market, the situation would be quite different. There, the appropriate strategy would emphasize the importance of low price and of building a low product and non-product cost structure to support this low price.

In building a quality strategy, we need to examine each of the product and non-product needs that comprise quality. This will allow us to attach a priority for strategy development to each of these needs. To assign priorities, we must know three things about each need. The first is its importance to customers. This second is whether it represents a pull-ahead opportunity. The third is whether it offers high or low potential for Sportmed and its competitors to differentiate their offerings on that particular need. We will see next how each of these three—importance, pull-ahead opportunity, and differentiation potential—flows directly from the customer's buying decision that we depicted in Exhibit 6.1. Because it is first in emphasis, we will develop this quality strategy in some detail.

Looking for the Customer's Important Needs

Sportmed carried forward from Exhibit 6.1 the importance customers in the Progressive Market attached to each need and displayed this in Exhibit 9.2. Of the eight customer needs, Sportmed highlighted the four most important. Notice that two of these are product needs and two are non-product needs. This gives an early indication that balanced importance must be attached to these two categories of needs.

Pulling Ahead by Dealing from Strength

A new issue to consider is whether a customer need represents a pull-ahead opportunity. The competitive performance ratings in Exhibit 9.2 show each competitor's performance as a percent of the market average. The 1.10 score for Competitor A (Sportmed) on advanced features means that A is performing 10 percent above average in meeting this need and has thereby pulled ahead of the competitive average. Interestingly, when a manager examines the Position Map in Exhibit 6.4 for the first time, the initial reaction is usually to give priority to fixing weaknesses. The first thought is to improve performance on the two needs, multifunctions and ease of use, where Sportmed's performance is below average. This is because managers are trained to be problem solvers, and their mental model is to find problems and fix them.[1]

Exhibit 9.2.

Consider first, in your quality strategy, the needs that are most important to customers.

Product Needs	Importance Weight	Competitive Performance Ratings			
		A	B	C	D
Advanced Features	14	1.10	0.83	0.97	1.10
Multifunctions	12	0.77	1.08	1.08	1.08
Accuracy	14	1.29	0.77	0.90	1.03
Ease of Use	10	0.92	1.08	1.08	0.92
Total Product Needs	50				
Non-product Needs					
Ongoing Education	13	1.28	0.80	0.80	1.12
Service	10	1.64	0.91	0.91	0.55
Reputation	12	1.33	0.74	0.89	1.04
Consultative Selling	15	1.45	1.09	0.91	0.55
Total Non-product Needs	50				

In fact, it is better to give first priority to enhancing strengths—that is, to pulling further ahead on the six needs where Sportmed is already performing above market average. We can see these six highlighted pull-ahead opportunities, identified by numbers greater than one, in Exhibit 9.3. This exhibit is identical to Exhibit 9.2, but now we focus on performance rather than importance. The message of Exhibit 9.3 is, in building the quality strategy, to consider second those needs where an enterprise has a pull-ahead opportunity and can increase quality and differentiation from the competition simultaneously.[2] Catch-up moves raise the enterprise closer to the rest of the competitors in the pack, increasing the enterprise's quality but reducing its differentiation from the pack. Such a move delivers a win in quality but a loss in differentiation. A pull-ahead move, on the other hand, creates a double win. Pull-ahead moves improve quality, just as the catch-up moves do. But pull-ahead moves also pull an enterprise ahead of the pack, thereby increasing, rather than decreasing, its differentiation from the other competitors. We call this *double-win three* in the Market Value Process. The double win that a pull-ahead move provides is the reason why, in building a quality strategy, you are better off enhancing strengths than fixing weaknesses. The only caveat is not to allow weaknesses to become so glaringly deficient that they disqualify the enterprise from competition.

Exhibit 9.3.

Consider second, in your quality strategy, the needs where you have a pull-ahead opportunity and can increase differentiation as well as quality.

		Competitive Performance Ratings			
Product Needs	Importance Weight	A	B	C	D
Advanced Features	14	1.10	0.83	0.97	1.10
Multifunctions	12	0.77	1.08	1.08	1.08
Accuracy	14	1.29	0.77	0.90	1.03
Ease of Use	10	0.92	1.08	1.08	0.92
Total Product Needs	50				
Non-product Needs					
Ongoing Education	13	1.28	0.80	0.80	1.12
Service	10	1.64	0.91	0.91	0.55
Reputation	12	1.33	0.74	0.89	1.04
Consultative Selling	15	1.45	1.09	0.91	0.55
Total Non-product Needs	50				

This mental model of enhancing strengths before fixing weaknesses often seems counterintuitive at first. It may help to think of an example in a career development setting. Suppose a young person comes to a manager for career advice. One thing the manager might say is "Know your strengths and weaknesses, then work hard to fix your weaknesses and turn them into strengths." An entirely different piece of advice might be "Know your strengths and weaknesses, work hard to build your strengths further, but don't allow your weaknesses to be so glaring that they become career knockouts." Which is the better piece of advice? In our view, the second one. Our personal strengths are core competencies that each of us usually acquires in the very early stages of life. They are not easy to change. Advising someone to play catch-up in a career setting is, in effect, advising someone to deal from weakness. It is better to deal from strength and not allow the weaknesses to be fatal to success. The same concept is a good mental model for building integrated customer value strategies. We devoted most of Chapter Five to the concept of winning by leading from strength. There we measured market attractiveness by assessing the fit between a competitor's core competence—quality or cost—and the value leverage factor in the market.

Peter Drucker made this point with his usual incisiveness in an October 21, 1993, article in *The Wall Street Journal* entitled "The Five Deadly Business Sins," excerpted in Exhibit 9.4.[3] It would be difficult to state the case for pull-ahead moves more persuasively.

We can depict the six pull-ahead moves available to Sportmed in Exhibit 9.5, the Customer Need Satisfaction Map for the Progressive Market. It shows that Competitor A has six pull-ahead opportunities and two catch-up challenges. This chart displays graphically the numbers we saw in Exhibit 9.3. It shows the importance weights along the horizontal dimension and the relative performance scores along the vertical dimension. Any customer need that is positioned above

Exhibit 9.4. Giving Opportunities Priority Over Problems.

The last of the deadly sins is feeding problems and starving opportunities. For many years I have been asking new clients to tell me who their best-performing people are. And then I ask: "What are they assigned to?" Almost without exception, the performers are assigned to problems—to the old business that is sinking faster than had been forecast; to the old product that is being outflanked by a competitor's new offering; to the old technology—e.g., analog switches, when the market has already switched to digital. Then I ask: "And who takes care of the opportunities?" Almost invariably, the opportunities are left to fend for themselves.

All one can get by problem solving is damage containment. Only opportunities produce results and growth. And opportunities are every bit as difficult and demanding as problems are. First draw up a list of the opportunities facing the business and make sure each is adequately staffed (and adequately supported). Only then should you draw up a list of the problems and worry about staffing them.

Exhibit 9.5. Customer Need Satisfaction Map: Progressive Market.

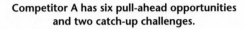

Competitor A has six pull-ahead opportunities and two catch-up challenges.

P1 Advanced Features
P2 Multifunctions
P3 Accuracy
P4 Ease of Use

N1 Ongoing Education
N2 Service
N3 Reputation
N4 Consultative Selling

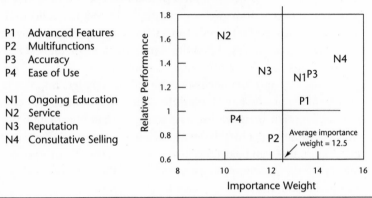

the horizontal line, which is the market average performance, shows that Competitor A is performing above average in meeting this need. This positioning represents a pull-ahead opportunity. Any of the customer needs to the right of the vertical line is of above average importance to the customers. Consequently, the chart depicts nicely both the importance and the pull-ahead issues.

Assessing the Potential for Differentiation

Another new issue is whether a customer need offers a high or low potential for an enterprise and its competitors to differentiate their offerings on that particular need. The enterprise has to make a judgment call regarding whether any competitor in the market would find it easy or difficult to differentiate from the competition in meeting a given product or non-product need. If competitors can't differentiate, the pull-ahead and catch-up issues won't exist. Everyone will be stuck at parity.

A clue to making this call can be found in examining the model of the customers' buying decision, Exhibit 6.1. Suppose customers give competitors widely different performance ratings on meeting a need. This automatically means that differentiation potential is high, since competitors have in fact achieved it.

Suppose, on the other hand, that customers give competitors identical performance ratings of nine on meeting a need. This is a red flag that raises the question of whether the potential for differentiation is low since competitors have not in fact achieved differentiation. For example, in the IBM-compatible mainframe market, it is, almost by definition of the word "compatible," difficult to differentiate on product needs. Another example is the pharmaceutical industry where the chemical properties of generic drugs are, by law, virtually the equivalent of branded prescription products. Some product needs like these, which are both important and which offer a pull-ahead opportunity, may have a low potential for differentiation. Sometimes product needs are collectively more important than non-product needs but at the same time have low differentiation potential. Consequently, differentiation in the area of highest importance, what we call "differentiation at the core," is difficult.

While non-product needs may be collectively less important than product needs, they typically have high differentiation potential.[4] An enterprise can always differentiate on needs like customer service or information provided through consultative selling. This "differentiation at the margin," the area of lower collective importance, can be decisive if the customer sees no price or product differentiation among the competitors. It can make the difference between winning or losing the value war.

Sportmed highlighted two needs it thought had especially high differentiation potential in Exhibit 9.6. This chart reminds an enterprise to consider third in its quality strategy the needs that may have low importance but may be highly differentiable and therefore can be "tiebreakers" in a close buying decision.

Exhibit 9.6.

Consider third, in your quality strategy, the needs that may have low importance but may be highly differentiable and therefore can be "tiebreakers" in a close buying decision.

		Competitive Performance Ratings			
Product Needs	Importance Weight	A	B	C	D
Advanced Features	14	1.10	0.83	0.97	1.10
Multifunctions	12	0.77	1.08	1.08	1.08
Accuracy	14	1.29	0.77	0.90	1.03
Ease of Use	10	0.92	1.08	1.08	0.92
Total Product Needs	50				
Non-product Needs					
Ongoing Education	13	1.28	0.80	0.80	1.12
Service	10	1.64	0.91	0.91	0.55
Reputation	12	1.33	0.74	0.89	1.04
Consultative Selling	15	1.45	1.09	0.91	0.55
Total Non-product Needs	50				

Although it highlighted only these two factors, Sportmed felt that all the product and non-product needs offered a high differentiation potential.

Setting Priorities for Integrating the Quality Strategy

We have now examined three issues relating to each product and non-product need—importance, pull-ahead opportunity, and differentiation potential. We have seen how each flows directly from the customer's buying decision in Exhibit 6.1. One of the distinctive characteristics of the Market Value Process is how it builds strategies directly from the way the customer makes the buying decision. This comes into sharp focus now, as we use these three issues as criteria for attaching priority to product and non-product needs in building a quality strategy.

An enterprise should give first priority to a need where all three of the following hold true: (1) the need is important, (2) it represents a pull-ahead opportunity, and (3) it offers high differentiation potential. The enterprise should give second priority to a need where two of these three criteria hold true. It should give third priority to a need where one or none of the criteria holds true.

Sportmed examined the needs in the Progressive Market against these criteria in Exhibit 9.7. Sportmed assigned top priority to meeting the following needs, which met all three criteria: advanced features, accuracy, ongoing education, and consultative selling.

Exhibit 9.7. Quality Strategy: Progressive Market.

Your quality strategy should give first priority to needs that meet all three criteria.

Product Needs	Importance Weight	Pull-Ahead Opportunity	Differentiation Potential
Advanced Features	14	Yes	High
Multifunction	12	No	High
Accuracy	14	Yes	High
Ease of Use	10	No	High
Total Product Needs	50		
Non-product Needs			
Ongoing Education	13	Yes	High
Service	10	Yes	High
Reputation	12	Yes	High
Consultative Selling	15	Yes	High
Total Non-product Needs	50		

Integrating the Price Strategy

Since Sportmed was developing strategy in support of a hold share objective in the Progressive Market, its price strategy was to price its quality at a level that represented a neutral value. We saw in Chapter Two that competitors positioned on the "market wants" line are offering neutral value and are positioned to hold market share. Consequently, as we see in Exhibit 9.8, Sportmed increased its price from 5 percent above market average to the "market wants" line.

Sportmed recalled that one of its earlier insights was that it was selling the same line of instruments to each of its Progressive, Traditional, and Commercial Markets. Its pricing of this "one size fits all" offering represented a superior value to the Progressives but an inferior value in the other two markets. Raising the price on this "one size fits all" line of offerings would worsen an already bad situation in the Traditional and Commercial Markets. Sportmed saw, with renewed clarity, the necessity of developing separate lines of low-end instruments to offer to these two markets.

Integrating the Cost Strategy

Sportmed placed less emphasis on its internal cost strategy than it did on its quality strategy because the Progressive Market was quality, rather than price, sensi-

Exhibit 9.8. Price Strategy: Progressive Market.

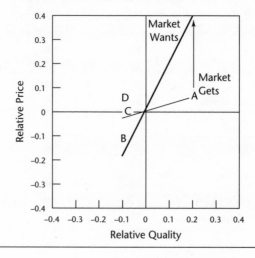

Sportmed's strategy increases price from 5 percent above market average to the "market wants" line.

tive. In the future, Sportmed envisioned that this would continue to be the case. We saw in the Scenario Map that quality, in year five, will continue to be half or more of the buying decision in all scenarios. Consequently, Sportmed did not feel a critical need to cut costs to the bone in order to reduce price. Instead, value leverage lay in improving product and non-product quality of the line of instruments it was currently offering, thereby moving to the right on the Customer Value Map, as we saw in Exhibit 8.8.

Sportmed felt that its disadvantage in non-product cost was necessary to provide superior non-product quality in ongoing education and information provided by consultative selling. We saw in Chapter Eight that a key cause of Sportmed's 36 percent non-product cost disadvantage was that it sold through its own sales force rather than through distributors, as its competitors did. This sales force, however, was precisely the source of Sportmed's quality advantage in these key areas of non-product quality. Consequently, Sportmed regarded this expense as a marketing investment in non-product quality and decided not to reduce it.

Sportmed, however, was concerned that it was not able to fund this marketing investment and its resulting disadvantage in non-product cost by running a tighter manufacturing ship than the competition and creating an advantage in product cost. Sportmed did not feel that its 4 percent disadvantage in product cost was required to deliver superior product quality, and it took steps to correct this disadvantage. Sportmed visualized this cost strategy in Exhibit 9.9. The message is to fix the problems in purchases, P1, and in manufacturing overhead, P3. This chart is similar in appearance to the Customer Need Satisfaction Map, Exhibit 9.5, but now the good direction is a downward move to cut cost

Exhibit 9.9. Cost Strategy: Progressive Market.

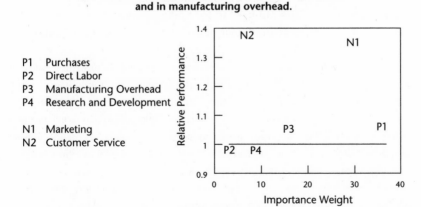

rather than an upward move to increase quality. Sportmed outlined its steps to reduce cost as part of its integrated customer value strategy, the topic to which we will turn next.

Mapping the Final Integrated Customer Value Strategy

Sportmed combined its quality, price, and cost strategies into the final integrated customer value strategy for the hold share objective. We depict this strategy on the Integrated Strategy Map, Exhibit 9.10.

Note the precision with which the strategy is stated on a single page. What makes this precision possible is the careful work we have done in each step of the Market Value Process to this point. Everything has been prepared to fit concisely into place in the quality-price-cost thought sequence. The great benefit of having one-page strategy statements is that people read them rather than putting them in a book that goes on a shelf. Integrated customer value strategies should not be complex or wordy.

One-page strategies make the preparation of multiple strategies realistic. If strategies run on page after page, the process of creating multiple strategies will collapse under its own weight. As the information in the upper left corner of Exhibit 9.10 suggests, a strategy should be outlined in broad strokes for each market, using multiple objectives and scenarios. Remember that Sportmed had earlier failed to build precision strategies for its different markets. This led to the "one size fits all" line of instruments that caused it to lose, rather than win, customers in the Traditional and Commercial Markets. Now, Sportmed took the time to build strategies in each market for each of three objectives—gain, hold, and lose share—giving it a total of nine strategies. Such a menu of multiple strategies would be unthinkable with strategy statements longer than one page. The biggest reason most enterprises fail to plan for multiple markets, scenarios, and objectives is that their strategy statements lack the conciseness of the Integrated Strategy Map.

In Exhibit 9.10, specifying the scenario under which the strategy is being built serves several purposes. It reminds an enterprise of the items listed in the upper right corner—the identity of its competitors, the emphasis of the strategy, and the future slope of the "market wants" line in year five, all of which are carried value from our scenario work. Remember that scenarios force an external view of strategy development because their events describe innovations by competitors as well as an enterprise's own innovations. Consequently, the Scenario Map strongly influences the actions in the Integrated Strategy Map, which is the purpose of preparing the Scenario Map in the first place.

Exhibit 9.10. Integrated Strategy Map: Progressive Market.

 Advanced features, accuracy, ongoing education, consultative selling, purchases, and manufacturing overhead are top-priority items.

Market: Progressive   Competitors: B, C, D
Scenario: "Business as Usual"   Strategy Emphasis: Quality
Objective: Hold Market Share   Future Slope: High: Q/P = 65/35

Quality Strategy	*Priority*	
P1	Advanced Features	1	Invest heavily in current and new models of all instruments
P2	Multifunctions	3	Link current and new models using electronic media
P3	Accuracy	1	Invest in software that interprets results
P4	Ease of Use	3	Develop user interface that is easy to use
	Summary		Emphasize advanced features and accuracy
N1	Ongoing Education	1	Increase funding for seminars and resident programs
N2	Service	2	Continue to improve service response time
N3	Reputation	2	Maintain quality of advertising and promotion; provide donations to schools
N4	Consultative Selling	1	Develop sales aids, proof sources, and financial models
	Summary		Emphasize ongoing education and consultative selling

Price Strategy	Increase from 5 percent above market average to "market wants" line

Cost Strategy	
P1	Purchases	Continue to select JIT/TQC suppliers; explore strategic off-shore alliances
P2	Direct Labor	Enhance productivity by providing cross training
P3	Manufacturing Overhead	Increase productivity by job consolidation (for example, buyer-planner)
P4	Research & Development	Increase R&D spending 2 percent above current level as percent of sales
	Summary	Emphasize purchases and manufacturing overhead
N1	Marketing	Develop managers with global focus; increase promotion and advertising
N2	Customer Service	Continue present level of support (customer call back, 800 number, customer visits)
	Summary	Make sure high quality requires our 36 percent non-product cost disadvantage

Operating Profit Margin (When Strategy Is in Place)	15%

P = Product; N = Non-product; Q/P = Quality/Price

Notice that the layout of the rest of the page follows a quality-price-cost sequence and thereby directs the preparer's thinking in the same sequence that the customer uses in making the buying decision.

There are two levels of priority at work in Exhibit 9.10. The first is the priority among the broad categories shown in bold type—quality, price, and cost. We have seen that in this Progressive Market, the priority is quality. The second is the priority among individual needs. The work we did earlier in this chapter provides this focus. Sportmed highlighted its top-priority quality action items—advanced features, accuracy, ongoing education, and consultative selling—and paid especially close attention to these. Sportmed also highlighted its top-priority cost action items—purchases and manufacturing overhead—and paid close attention to these as well. On the right side of the chart, Sportmed summarized, in a few words for each, what it proposed to do for each product and non-product quality need, its price, and each area of product and non-product cost. These are the actions needed to build precision strategies that win customers and shareholders.

It is critically important to end the Integrated Strategy Map with an assessment of the operating profit margin—the earnings before interest and taxes—that the strategy is anticipated to deliver once it has been put in place. This action links customer value to shareholder value by showing a key financial payoff opportunity that customer value opens: profit margin. Sportmed highlighted its 15 percent assessment in the bottom left corner. An enterprise can do this with greater confidence the more clearly and concisely it summarizes the strategy on the Integrated Strategy Map.

Now let's see how one of the world's largest enterprises can state one of its strategies with the same kind of precision.

Building Strategy Through External Actions: Disney Acquires Capital Cities/ABC

In an August 1, 1995, article entitled "All Ears—Disney's Deal for ABC Makes Show Business a Whole New World," *The Wall Street Journal* described Disney's blockbuster acquisition of ABC.[5]

An enterprise can build precision strategies to improve product and non-product quality through external as well as internal means. Sometimes an enterprise has the building blocks for meeting product needs in hand but lacks the building blocks for meeting non-product needs. We have seen that a key non-product need is availability provided by a strong distribution system. Disney's availability through distribution was probably average, not weak, but it represented a pull-ahead opportunity. Beyond this, availability was important and highly differentiable. This made it a priority-one item for strategy-building actions—strengthening it either with internal actions or by acquisition. By acquiring ABC, Disney brought in-house a powerful distribution system for its famous product line.

The Disney-ABC agreement represents a major about-face for Disney and its charismatic and hard-driving chairman, Michael Eisner. As recently as two years ago, Mr. Eisner said Disney would remain a "content" business, providing movies and other entertainment rather than bothering with the means of distribution—the TV stations, radio stations, and other outlets. He said Disney didn't need to make an acquisition like a television network.

With this background, let's take a wide-angle view of the quality strategy, need by need, that the acquisition reflected. The list shows that Disney has great product quality. The acquisition provided non-product quality in the form of availability through distribution that Disney got from the Capital Cities/ABC acquisition.

Product Needs: Content (Provided by Disney)

P1—Film and Music. Walt Disney Pictures has the most famous film library in the world, with titles ranging from *Snow White* to *The Lion King*. Other entries include Touchstone Pictures, Miramax Films, and Hollywood Records.

P2—TV Shows. These are natural accompaniments to film and music and include the Disney Channel, Walt Disney Television, and Touchstone Television.

P3—Theme Parks. These range from the original Disneyland and Walt Disney World to interests in Tokyo Disneyland and Disneyland Paris.

P4—Consumer Products. This awesome content spins off many consumer products through the licensing of cartoon characters, the Disney Store, and the Disney Gallery.

Non-product Needs: Distribution (Provided by ABC)

N1—Television Network. The gilt-edged ABC Network provides a host of shows through which Disney content can be distributed.

N2—Broadcast (Television and Radio Stations). Broadcast capabilities include ten television stations, twenty-one radio stations, radio networks serving 3,400 stations, a controlling interest in ESPN and ESPN2, and part ownership of the Arts and Entertainment channel.

N3—Cable and International. These facilities include a half interest in Tele-Muchen, a German TV production and distribution company; one-third interest in Hamster Productions, a French independent television company; one-third interest in Eurosport, a London-based pan-European sports-programming service; and interests in cable programming in Japan, Germany, and Scandinavia.

N4—Publications. These include Fairchild Publications, parent of *Woman's Wear Daily;* the *Fort Worth Star-Telegram; Kansas City Star;* and many weekly newspapers.

This new strategy (the adding of Capital Cities/ABC's non-product quality to Disney's product quality) responds to dramatic changes in the world since the two years following Eisner's assessment that content alone would ensure Disney's future. For one thing, networks are increasingly producing their own shows, threatening the TV-production business of Disney and others. Indeed, Mr. Eisner says ABC is an attractive acquisition for its programming as much as for its top-rated network.

Moreover, Disney was in danger of being left behind as the entertainment industry's consolidation continued unabated. Beverage giant Seagram had recently snapped up control of Disney's rival MCA and has been considering other entertainment purchases. Viacom, having digested both Paramount Communications and Blockbuster Entertainment, was rumored to be weighing a return to the acquisition trail. News Corporation had been aggressively expanding overseas. General Electric Company, parent of the NBC network, had already had talks with both Turner Broadcasting System and Time Warner. And while GE hadn't been in active discussions recently, it could come under pressure to try it again.

"This just confirms the trend that the direction the business is going is to larger, vertically integrated companies," says money manager Gordon Crawford at Capital Research Group, one of the largest institutional shareholders of both Capital Cities and Disney.

For now, top management of Disney and ABC are focusing on the future vision for the combination of what they called "the premier family entertainment communication companies in the country." They promise nearly limitless synergies, such as more Disney-produced shows on ABC, promotion on the Disney Channel during Disney-produced Saturday morning cartoon shows, and the use of Disney's syndication muscle to sell programs owned and produced by ABC. Globally, they said, the ESPN sports cable channel could be packaged along with the Disney Channel.

"The synergies are under every rock we turn over," Mr. Eisner said. "I am totally optimistic that one and one will add up to four here."

It is difficult to imagine a merger producing a stronger combination of the product and non-product building blocks of a precision strategy.

Communicating Your Superior Value to the Marketplace

After building strategies that enhance customer value, the enterprise needs to communicate this enhanced value to the marketplace. Remember that quality and value exist only if perceived, and perceptions must be created. It is the job of marketing communication to create these perceptions.

We have made the case for the merits of a one-page strategy statement. We make the case for an even more concise marketing communication statement. It must be extremely brief and hard-hitting.

Happily, the same guidelines apply to marketing communication that apply to strategy building. Communication should focus on the superior way the enterprise meets customer needs that are important, needs where the enterprise is pulling ahead of the competition, and needs that have a high differentiation potential. Consequently, customer needs that are priority one for strategy building are also priority one for marketing communication. The marketing communication team needs to review the top-priority items from the Integrated Strategy Map and turn the proposed action steps for each into a short, high-impact message.

An excellent example from a recent workshop we conducted came from a strategy for pediatric antibiotics. A team of managers was building a strategy for two markets defined by the age of the targeted pediatric patient: zero to four years and ten to fourteen years.

The two top-priority needs in each market were accurate dose (making sure the child took the right amount of medication at the right time) and ease of administration (persuading the child to take the medication at all). For the zero to four market, the action step was to package the medication as a piece of candy. The team communicated this in the message: "Finally . . . proven once a day efficacy without the fight." Notice how this message artfully combines both needs—accuracy and ease—into a single, memorable phrase. For the ten to fourteen market, the action step was to deliver the medication through a transdermal patch. The team devised the message: "We've patched the compliance leak in antibiotic therapy and guarantee success." Again, notice the clever way the team packaged both the accuracy and ease needs into a single, memorable phrase. The team concluded its work with a brief statement of the medium through which they would communicate these messages. Exhibit 9.11 summarizes their highly creative work.

For Sportmed, as well as pediatric antibiotics, priorities from the Integrated Strategy Map automatically become the priorities for the marketing communication campaign. We saw in Exhibit 9.10 that the top priorities in the Progressive Market are advanced features, accuracy, ongoing education, and consultative selling.

Exhibit 9.11. Marketing Communication Campaign: Pediatric Antibiotics.

Market:	Pediatric antibiotics, ages zero to four
Message:	Finally . . . proven once a day efficacy without the fight
Medium:	Journal ads—pediatric journals
	Direct mail to top prescription-writing pediatricians
	Booth at national pediatric convention
Market:	Pediatric antibiotics, ages ten to fourteen
Message:	We've patched the compliance leak in antibiotic therapy and guarantee treatment success.
Medium:	Journal ads—family practitioner journals
	Direct mail to top prescription-writing family practitioners
	Attendance at family practitioner convention

Exhibit 9.12. Marketing Communication Campaign: Sports Medicine Instruments.

Market:	Progressive practitioner
Message:	Leading-edge software boosts diagnostic precision
Medium:	Journal ads—sports medicine journals
	Direct mail to top prescription-writing practitioners
	Booth at national sports medicine convention

The challenge is to develop a message that communicates not two but four needs. The action steps for the two product needs are to introduce new models of all instruments with software that interprets results. Sportmed devised the message: "Leading-edge software boosts diagnostic precision." This message does a solid job of communicating, in a single phrase, features, accuracy, education, and consultative selling. This message becomes the foundation for Sportmed's media campaign. We summarize the result in Exhibit 9.12.

It is beyond the scope of this book to pursue marketing communication programs in depth. The key point to remember, however, is that a communication campaign in each market grows directly out of the enterprise's Integrated Strategy Map.

Carried Value

Exhibit 9.13 shows the result of our work in this chapter. Sportmed carried forward to Poststrategy Value Created the quality, price, and cost actions summarized

on the Integrated Strategy Map. Sportmed carried forward to Shareholder Value Created a key link between customer value and shareholder value: the operating profit margin that the strategy was anticipated to deliver once it had been put in place. Now that we have built the bridge—the strategies—we are ready to test the result: the degree to which our strategies have solved the combined-value problem.

Exhibit 9.13. Carried Value: Precision Strategies.

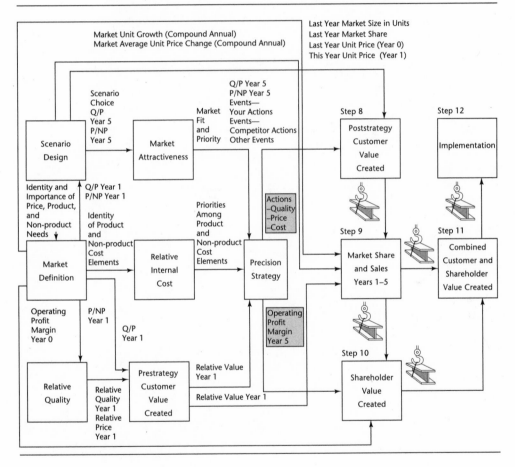

PART FOUR

THE PAYOFF

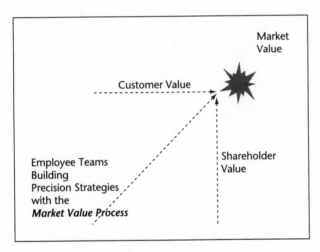

Market
Value

Customer Value

Employee Teams
Building
Precision Strategies
with the
Market Value Process

Shareholder
Value

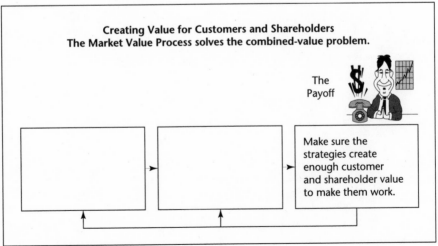

Creating Value for Customers and Shareholders
The Market Value Process solves the combined-value problem.

The
Payoff

Make sure the
strategies create
enough customer
and shareholder value
to make them work.

PART FOUR

THE PAYOFF

CHAPTER TEN

MAPPING POSTSTRATEGY CUSTOMER VALUE

You are now ready to envision, measure, and map the poststrategy customer value that your enterprise's precision strategy will create. This is a pivotal step in the Market Value Process because both the market evolution from the scenario work and the market share evolution from the strategy work converge at this point. An enterprise should measure poststrategy customer value at the end of the strategy period. During this period it has implemented the quality, price, and cost actions that form the integrated customer value strategies. As we saw earlier, Sportmed used a five-year time frame for its strategy period.

Since no one knows what will happen during a particular time frame, there are many uncertainties involved in mapping poststrategy value, and the enterprise must cope with them. The scenarios the enterprise has written help it to foresee competitor actions. The integrated strategy the enterprise just built is the blueprint for its own actions. Together, competitor actions and the enterprise's own actions are the source of the customer's importance weights and relative performance ratings that determine poststrategy customer value. Mapping poststrategy value is an essential ingredient to envisioning the market share and revenue growth a strategy is likely to deliver, as we will see in Chapter Eleven. The purpose of Chapter Ten is to show how to create this poststrategy Customer Value Map.

There is an inherent danger in making relative performance assessments for the key competitors for year five. This danger is the tendency to overfocus on the actions an enterprise is taking and underfocus on competitor actions. All too often an enterprise assumes the competition is standing still while the enterprise itself is putting its strategy in place. The importance of focusing on competitor actions seems obvious. Why do people lose sight of these actions? One answer is that people become so absorbed in the challenge of developing their own strategy that they forget the competition. The Market Value Process forces an enterprise to focus on competitors in assessing both importance weights and performance ratings in year five. We will examine each of these tasks next.

Assessing Importance Weights

The scenario design step in Chapter Four forces a competitor focus in envisioning market evolution. The carried-value chart at the end of Chapter Four included the quality/price sensitivity and the product/non-product sensitivity in year five. We remember that the driving force behind these sensitivities is the product and non-product innovation that an enterprise and its competitors deliver during the strategy period. A high rate of innovation creates a market in which customers attach high importance to quality. A low rate of innovation creates a market in which they attach high importance to price. The focus of the innovation on the product or non-product areas will affect the product/non-product sensitivity balance.

The degree of innovation directed at individual product and non-product needs will influence the importance customers attach to them. Needs that are the recipient of exciting innovation through the latest technology are likely to increase in importance to customers. This is especially true when customers are not yet aware, or are only subliminally aware, of the need. An excellent example is the importance customers came to attach to the ease of use provided by the graphical user interface Apple Computer introduced in the early 1980s.

Innovation impacts performance ratings as well as importance weights, as we see next.

Envisioning Performance Ratings

We wrote our scenarios to be specific not only about the amount and split of product and non-product innovation but also about which competitors were the innovation leaders. Specifically, the scenarios Sportmed wrote in Chapter Four centered around the magnitude and timing of an innovation by Competitor B and

Sportmed's response to it. The innovation leaders are likely to be the competitors with high performance ratings in year five in meeting customer needs, both product and non-product. The reader will remember from our Intel example in Chapter Four that the high-innovation competitor gains a double win in the value war. The first win is the increase in quality sensitivity in the market that innovation produces. The second win is a leading position in performance ratings for the importance-heightened quality.

Customers in year five will continue to assess competitive performance in meeting each need on a scale of zero to ten from worst to best. However, the standard against which customers measure performance has changed profoundly. The new standard is the new state of product and non-product technology that the innovation leader's Integrated Strategy Map delivers. Let's think again about our microprocessor example in Chapter Four. Intel delivered a major new innovation in that market every three years. To keep a performance rating of ten in meeting product and non-product needs in this rapidly changing market would mean being the innovation leader or keeping pace with the leader, stride for stride. Standing pat with yesterday's innovation will cause a performance rating of ten in year one to drop to five or six or worse in year five. This might not be high enough to cross the performance threshold to be a qualified competitor in the business area, however low the obsolete technology is priced.

Now, we need to depict the combination of market evolution and market share evolution over the strategy period in a Year-Five Value Map.

Mapping Poststrategy Customer Value Created

Sportmed's planning team in the Progressive Market outlined, in broad strokes, its own innovation and its competitors' innovation in its scenarios. The team fleshed out Sportmed's own innovation significantly in its integrated customer value strategies where it detailed Sportmed's quality, price, and cost actions. Now the team is ready to bring together, in the Year-Five Customer Value Map, the quality/price and product/non-product sensitivities and competitor innovations from its Scenario Map and Sportmed's own actions from its Integrated Strategy Map.

We can see the result in Exhibit 10.1, the Customer Value Map for year five in the Progressive Market. This reflects the "Business as Usual" scenario under which innovation continues at past levels and therefore quality/price and product/non-product sensitivities remain unchanged at 65/35 and 50/50, respectively. Consequently, the market remains a high-slope, quality-sensitive one. The "Business as Usual" scenario envisioned that Competitor B introduced a

Exhibit 10.1. Customer Value Map: Progressive Market—Year Five.

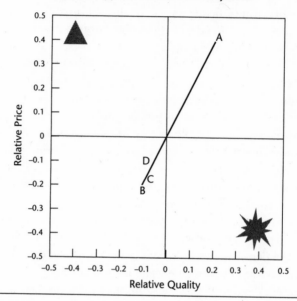

A is offering a neutral relative value, which is just enough value to support the hold share objective.

highly innovative but not frame-breaking offering, and each competitor responded in a stride-for-stride way that left competitor performance ratings as well as importance weights unchanged between year one and year five. The end result is that everyone's relative quality is also unchanged. Remember, however, that the ten rating for accuracy, P3, that Sportmed receives is the result of measurement against a different standard for accuracy than existed five years earlier. The same holds true for each product and non-product need.

While importance weights and performance ratings don't change, a major change has taken place in Sportmed's price relative to the market average. This Customer Value Map reflects the strategy in support of the hold share objective that Sportmed developed in Chapter Nine. We saw that Sportmed raised its price enough to move vertically upward to the "market wants" line, which represents a neutral-value, hold share position. This means that Sportmed is creating just enough customer value, which in this case is a neutral value, to achieve the hold share objective that the strategy supports. All competitors are now lined up along the "market wants" line in hold share positions, so the "market wants" and "market gets" lines coincide.

Meeting a Subliminal Need: Consumers Didn't Know They Needed Television

The Sportmed example centers on building strategies for meeting product and non-product needs that customers have identified. The Market Value Process can also help an enterprise build strategies to meet a need that customers have not yet identified. An example of this would be Apple Computer building a strategy to meet the unmet need for a graphical user interface for microcomputers—a need that key competitors like IBM, as well as customers, were unaware existed. The Market Value Process can't put an idea into an inventor's head. The inventor has to come up with an idea, as the Apple inventors did. Once that idea is there, however, the Market Value Process provides the concepts and tools to assess the idea's likelihood of success in the marketplace.

The invention of television is an excellent historic example of leading customers where they want to go but don't know it yet. We see in the poststrategy Customer Value Map in Exhibit 10.2 how the inventor who initially commer-

Exhibit 10.2. Customer Value Map: Television—Innovator Market.

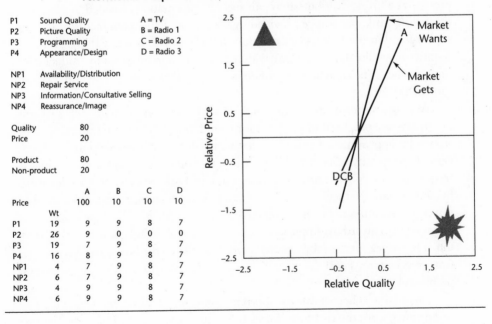

Television is a superior value, even at ten times the price of radio.

		A	B	C	D
P1	Sound Quality	A = TV			
P2	Picture Quality	B = Radio 1			
P3	Programming	C = Radio 2			
P4	Appearance/Design	D = Radio 3			

NP1	Availability/Distribution
NP2	Repair Service
NP3	Information/Consultative Selling
NP4	Reassurance/Image

Quality	80
Price	20

Product	80
Non-product	20

		A	B	C	D
Price		100	10	10	10
	Wt				
P1	19	9	9	8	7
P2	26	9	0	0	0
P3	19	7	9	8	7
P4	16	8	9	8	7
NP1	4	7	9	8	7
NP2	6	7	9	8	7
NP3	4	9	9	8	7
NP4	6	9	9	8	7

cialized television might have depicted his idea. Let's examine this Customer Value Map in some detail. Clearly, the assessments must be the inventor's own, since the result of market research with potential customers would probably have been "We've gotten along with radio for fifty years, we're very happy with radio, and we can't see how we would ever need television." The inventor, however, had a mental model for success that he depicted on this Customer Value Map. He knew he would be selling to a psychographic market—consisting of the "Innovators"— that was quality sensitive. He was convinced, once this market saw a television in operation, it would perceive that the picture offered a major quality advantage over radio. The combination of making an extremely high-quality offering to an extremely quality-sensitive market would allow the Innovator to charge a price ten times higher than radio and still offer a superior value in the Innovator Market. These initial sales to the Innovators would allow the inventor to get into higher-volume production, to lower costs as volume increased, lower prices, increase quality further, and ultimately move into the mainstream market. Once an inventor conceives an idea, the inventor can use the Market Value Process in this way to build a strategy to implement it.

With these thoughts in mind, let's examine the mental model of the inventor in greater detail. He believed that the underlying product needs were sound quality, picture quality, programming available, and the appearance and design of the television set. He believed the non-product needs were availability for purchase provided by strong distribution, repair service, information provided by consultative selling, and reassurance provided by the image of the manufacturer. The inventor felt that the Innovators, a group that is eager to try new things, is more sensitive to quality than price and, within quality, is more sensitive to product than non-product. The specific assessments were a Q/P ratio of 80/20 and a P/NP ratio of 80/20.

Among product needs, picture quality was the most important, with a weight of twenty-six compared to nineteen for sound, nineteen for programming, and sixteen for appearance. These four product needs together accounted for 80 percent of the quality story. The design and appearance of a consumer product is frequently one of the four key product needs. Early television consoles were bought, in part, for their attractiveness as a piece of furniture. The importance of this need continues today. In its June 6, 1994, issue, *Business Week* gave one of its annual design awards to Apple Computer's "personal digital assistant," the Newton. The judges felt the subtly curved lines that created the Newton's "Ferrari" effect were key to its early sales, which were otherwise limited by performance problems.[1]

Among the collectively less important non-product needs, repair service and reassurance were the two most important with a six weight. The two least important were availability and information with a weight of four. The non-product needs accounted for only 20 percent of the quality story for the Innovators.

The competitors were the new television manufacturer, Competitor A, and the three leading radio manufacturers, Competitors B, C, and D. The inventor decided to price his new invention at ten times the price of radio, correctly believing that the quality-sensitive Innovators would be willing to "pay up" for picture quality. In rating competitive performance, the key is picture quality—nine for television and zero for the radio competitors since they offered no picture. The inventor believed that performance ratings on the remaining product and non-product needs would be reasonably close.

The net result of this set of assessments is a position below the "market wants" line on the Customer Value Map, indicating a superior relative value. Assuming the validity of the assessments, a strategy built around this idea has a good chance of working in the marketplace. All new-product decisions an enterprise makes should be pretested with this kind of thought process during the concept investigation phase.

You may object that inventors do not use a mental model like this to flesh out their creative insights. It is worth remembering here the *National Geographic* observation about Thomas Edison and Alexander Graham Bell mentioned in Chapter Two. Bell could not replicate Edison's "invention factory" because his approach to invention was different. Edison tried to identify a commercial need and then look for a way to meet it. Bell was more likely to be struck by a physical phenomenon and then look for a way to use it. The implication is that the best inventors develop a mental model that measures and maps the customer's buying decision through a process very similar to that of the poststrategy Customer Value Map.

Carried Value

 As shown in Exhibit 10.3, we will carry forward Sportmed's year-five relative value to Step Nine in the Market Value Process. We will combine the four inputs to this step, depicted by the four input arrows, into a new way to envision market share and revenue growth.

Exhibit 10.3. Carried Value: Poststrategy Customer Value.

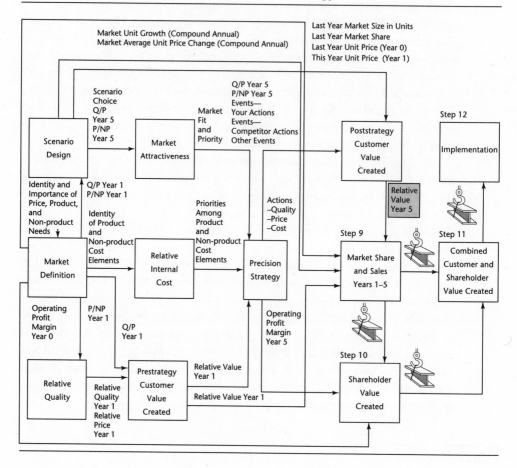

CHAPTER ELEVEN

ENVISIONING REVENUE GROWTH

At this point, the Market Value Process opens a new way to envision the revenue growth a strategy can deliver. We call this unique approach the *value-based revenue outlook*. Building a value-based revenue outlook entails a two-step thought process. This first step is to use scenarios to envision market growth. The second step is to envision the enterprise's market share growth by measuring and mapping the change between the prestrategy and poststrategy value the enterprise offers its customers.

This new way is far superior to the traditional approach. The traditional approach is the *history-based sales outlook*. It entailed projecting an enterprise's historic sales into the future through extrapolation or forecasting techniques. This is unsound because it rests on the often dangerous assumption that the past is a good guide for the future. As we saw in Chapter Four, the future may be full of discontinuities. In addition, the traditional approach makes the mistake of envisioning sales directly rather than through the two components of sales: market growth and market share growth. Now we will see how to put this new way into practice.

Two key inputs to a value-based sales outlook are the enterprise's future price, expressed as dollars per unit sold, and its future market share. We are now ready to show how to compare prestrategy and poststrategy Customer Value Maps to arrive at these key inputs. Let's turn first to unit price.

Assessing Unit Price Change

To arrive at its unit price for the strategy period, the enterprise draws on carried value from its work with scenario design and strategy building. The enterprise developed its integrated customer value strategy in Chapter Nine. As one part of this, the enterprise built its product and non-product quality strategies. The enterprise designed scenarios in Chapter Four in which it looked at the product and non-product innovation it might expect from its key competitors. These two pieces of work provided the basis for the Year-Five Customer Value Map in the last chapter. This Customer Value Map reflects the relative customer value each competitor is offering after everyone's strategy has been put in place. In the comparisons we are about to make, we will use an example different from Sportmed in order to demonstrate a move from inferior value to superior value. We will return to the Sportmed example in the next chapter.

Exhibit 11.1 shows the Price Map, a combination of Year-One and Year-Five Customer Value Maps. These Value Maps provide the basis for envisioning an enterprise's relative price evolution. Note the positioning of the enterprise, Competitor A, in years one and five. Focus on the vertical distance at which A is

Exhibit 11.1. Price Map: Progressive Market.

Your year-one and year-five Customer Value Maps provide the basis for envisioning your relative price evolution.

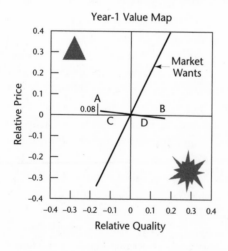

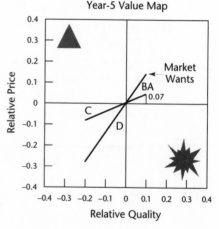

	Year 1	Year 2	Year 3	Year 4	Year 5
Relative Price, Competitor A	108	108	107	107	107

positioned above or below the zero relative price line in each Value Map. In year one, Competitor A is 0.08 above this line, offering a relative price that is 108 percent of the market average. In year five, Competitor A's position is 0.07 above this line, a relative price of 107 percent. At the bottom of the chart, the enterprise shows these two end points together with its year-to-year timetable for moving from one end point to the other.

Once an enterprise has determined relative price for each year, it measures its unit price outlook, as shown in Exhibit 11.2. This chart shows many items of carried value from prior steps converging to help make this measurement. Making this measurement is a big step because unit price is one of the two components an enterprise needs in order to envision its value-based sales outlook.

Exhibit 11.2. Measuring the Unit Price Component of Your Customer Value Strategy.

	Year Zero	Year One	Year Two	Year Three	Year Four	Year Five
1. Your Unit Price Today (Market Definition Map)		$12.00				
2. Your Relative Price Today (Value Map, Year One)		108				
3. Market Average Unit Price Today: (1)/(2)		$11.11				
4. Market Average Unit Price Change (Scenario Map)			+10%	+10%	+10%	+10%
5. Market Average Unit Price Outlook: (3) × (4)			$12.22	$13.44	$14.79	$16.27
6. Your Relative Price Strategy (Value Map, Years One and Five)		108	108	107	107	107
7. Your Unit Price Last Year (Market Definition Map)	$10.00					
8. Your Unit Price Outlook: (5) × (6)			$13.20	$14.39	$15.82	$17.41

From its market definition work, the enterprise carries forward its own unit price in each market in year one, this year (item 1 on the chart) and year zero, last year (item 7). We just saw that an enterprise can read its relative price today (item 2) from the Customer Value Map. Today's market average unit price (item 3) is simply the enterprise's price divided by its relative price. One of the items of carried value from the Scenario Map was the annual change in market average unit price (item 4). Applying this to today's market average unit price (item 3) gives the market average unit price outlook for five years (item 5). We just saw how to combine an enterprise's year one and year five Value Maps in the Price Map to know its relative price for each year. Applying this to the market average unit price outlook gives the enterprise's own year-to-year unit price outlook (item 8).

Foreseeing Market Share Evolution

Next, the enterprise is ready to envision its market share evolution over the five-year strategy period. To do this, it needs to do some additional creative thinking as it makes a different comparison between the Year-One and Year-Five Customer Value Maps. Exhibit 11.3 shows this different comparison of the same two Customer Value Maps we used in Exhibit 11.1.

This Market Share Map turns the enterprise's focus toward the perpendicular distance between the position of Competitor A, which is the enterprise itself, and the "market wants" line. We know that the length of this line is the measure of the relative value that Competitor A offers to customers. Any position above the "market wants" line represents an inferior customer value, which is a prescription for losing market share. This is the position in which Competitor A finds itself in year one. The longer the perpendicular line, the more rapidly Competitor A will be losing share. Any position below the line represents a superior customer value, a prescription for gaining share. This is the position that Competitor A's integrated customer value strategy has enabled it to attain in year five. The longer the perpendicular line, the more rapidly Competitor A will be gaining share.

Exhibit 11.3. Market Share Map: Progressive Market.

Your year-one and year-five Customer Value Maps provide the basis for envisioning your market share evolution.

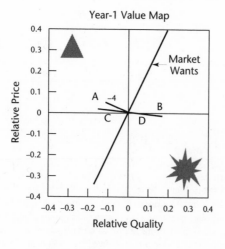

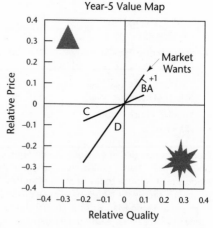

	Year 1	Year 2	Year 3	Year 4	Year 5
Market Share Change, Competitor A	−8	−5	−3	−1	2

Now is the time for some creative thinking. The enterprise needs to examine the length of the two lines in relation to each other. Note that the length of the year-one line, marked as −4, is four times the length of the year-five line, marked as +1. This means that Competitor A is losing share four times as rapidly in year one as it is gaining share in year five. Next, the enterprise needs to bring some judgment to bear in order to change this relative measure to an absolute measure. What absolute share change would be consistent with this relative change? One possible answer would be a share loss of eight points in year one and a share gain of two points in year five. These beginning and ending assessments would be consistent with the four-to-one ratio, with the intervening years estimated as shown at the bottom of Exhibit 11.3.

Other assessments, however, are also internally consistent. One would be a twelve-point share loss in year one coupled with a three-point share gain in year five. Another would be a four-point share loss in year one coupled with a one-point share gain in year five. Both continue to maintain the four-to-one ratio. How is the enterprise to know which of these assessments best fits the situation depicted by the Market Share Map? The answer is that it needs to make some judgments based on the absolute length of the perpendicular lines. The judgment it makes in this case is that the absolute length of the line in the Year-One Value Map is consistent with an eight-point share loss. The enterprise judges that a twelve-point loss would mean an even deeper positioning in the Bermuda Triangle than that shown on the Market Share Map. The enterprise also judges that this positioning is too deep in the Bermuda Triangle to hold share loss to four points.

Clearly, these assessments require judgments. Crucially, however, the judgments must be consistent with both the relative and the absolute length of the perpendicular lines, which are critical outputs from the Market Value Process. This provides a new way to envision market share that was not open to the enterprise until it understood how to read the Customer Value Map.

It is important to think deeply about market share change in the years between the end points because these years reflect the enterprise's estimate of how quickly its integrated customer value strategy can be put in place. Exhibit 11.3 reflects improvements in annual share change in equal increments of two to three share points per year (−8 percent, −5 percent, −3 percent, −1 percent, +2 percent). This, in turn, reflects an assessment that the strategy will be put in place and its benefits felt in equal increments over the five-year period. The enterprise must ask itself if this rate of implementation is fast enough. Many books have been written in recent years about time-based competition.[1] If other competitors move more quickly than Competitor A, its strategy for returning to year-zero dollar sales by year five will be jeopardized. Conversely, if A can move more quickly than Exhibit 11.3 predicts, the sales turnaround picture in Exhibit 11.4 would brighten considerably.

Exhibit 11.4. Measuring the Sales Your
Integrated Customer Value Strategy Generates.

	Year Zero	Year One	Year Two	Year Three	Year Four	Year Five
1. Market Unit Growth (Scenario Map)		+10%	+10%	+10%	+10%	+10%
2. Market Unit Size (Market Definition Map)	10,000					
3. Market Unit Size Outlook: (1) × (2)		11,000	12,100	13,310	14,641	16,105
4. Market Share Change (Value Map, Years One and Five)		−8%	−5%	−3%	−1%	+2%
5. Your Market Share (Market Definition Map)	25%					
6. Your Market Share Outlook: (4) + (5)		17%	12%	9%	8%	10%
7. Your Unit Sales Outlook: (3) × (6)	2,500	1,870	1,452	1,198	1,171	1,611
8. Your Unit Price Outlook (From Exhibit 11.2)	$10.00	$12.00	$13.20	$14.39	$15.82	$17.41
9. Your Dollar Sales Outlook: (7) × (8)	$25,000	$22,440	$19,166	$17,238	$18,530	$28,039

One of the items of carried value from the Scenario Map was the annual market unit growth (item 1). The enterprise was able to know, once it had completed its market definition, last year's size of the market in units (item 2). Applying this growth, which the enterprise got from a scenario, not a forecast, to last year's size gives the market unit size outlook for years one through five (item 3). Market Share Map analysis, Exhibit 11.3, shows the year-to-year market share change (item 4). The enterprise knows its last year's market share (item 5) from its market definition work. Adding year-to-year share gains to this beginning market share gives the market share outlook (item 6). Applying the share outlook to the market size outlook gives the enterprise's year-to-year sales outlook in units (item 7). Multiplying this by the enterprise's unit price outlook, which it just finished in Exhibit 11.2, gives its dollar sales outlook for years one through five.

Envisioning Sales Through a Value-Based Revenue Outlook

Once an enterprise has envisioned its unit price change and market share evolution, it can determine its value-based sales outlook in Exhibit 11.4. This exhibit pulls everything together to show how to measure the sales a precision strategy can deliver. Again, we see many items of carried value from earlier steps of the Market Value Process coming into play. The highlighted sales outlook in the bottom line is a key link between customer value and shareholder value, as we will see in the next chapter.

Now, let's look at Netscape as an example of how coming quickly to market with a high poststrategy customer value impacts an enterprise's market share and sales.

Springing the Web Trap at Netscape

On January 18, 1996, *The Wall Street Journal* carried an article entitled "Web Trap: Internet's Popularity Threatens to Swamp the On-Line Services."[2] One of the chief causes is a slick Web "browser," created by the wildly successful start-up, Netscape, which makes the Internet's World Wide Web easily accessible to casual computer users.

The article pointed out that people like Anthony Thompson, an electrician in Queens, are sending a shock to commercial on-line services.

Mr. Thompson has subscribed to most major services, from the hot America Online (AOL) to General Electric's fading GEnie. But lately he has dropped all but one of his on-line accounts—and will likely be dropping the remaining one soon. Instead of paying a brand-name commercial service, he uses a much smaller—and much cheaper—"access provider" to surf the vast seas of the Internet.

"Most everything I can find on the on-line services, I can find using an Internet service provider," Mr. Thompson says. "For me, the need for an on-line service is diminishing."

For years the commercial services such as America Online, CompuServe, and Prodigy toiled on the cyberspace frontier, trying to hook customers on the idea of using their personal computers to get electronic mail, chat up friends, and download information. Now the services risk getting crushed by the craze they helped create, as the Internet and its snazzy World Wide Web area outgrow even the most buoyant forecasts.

Subscriber defection is just one of the myriad challenges besetting the commercial services. Media companies that had used them to set up a newsstand in cyberspace are now bypassing them to go directly to the Internet. This has forced the on-line services into a bidding war for "content," even as they cut monthly prices to keep growing. Rates may fall even more as cable systems and telephone companies enter the Internet-access business.

As a result, services such as AOL are in a bad crunch: the cost of signing up new users and new "content" is rising, yet the monthly fees they charge to cover that cost are falling.

The rise of Internet "turns the model of the on-line services industry upside down," says Scott Kurnit, who quit as the number two executive at Prodigy last year to run the new Internet services of News Corporation and MCI Communications. Forrester Research analyst William Bluestein adds, "Their whole proprietary model has been shattered." On-line firms had better develop Internet skills fast, he says, "or else they'll get blown out of the water."

To survive, the big on-line services are rewriting their strategies to embrace the very force that threatens their existence—the multimedia World Wide Web. Some are starting Internet-only services that will compete with themselves. They are also spending hundreds of millions to buy Web software firms. Microsoft Corporation put up an estimated $130 million to acquire Vermeer Technologies, Inc.

The on-line services also are rushing to create "programming" themselves, even offering some new fare free on the Web, despite the risk that this will convince more subscribers that they don't need a commercial service.

"I was gung ho about America Online, but then I saw the Web and realized there's a real world out there. AOL is its own worst enemy," says subscriber Peter Kesselman of Valencia, California. He had spent $70 a month on his AOL account but now spends $20 for unlimited Internet access. He canceled his AOL account this week. "AOL is like the Internet on training wheels."

This couldn't have happened if the Internet had remained impossibly difficult for casual computer users to access. The Internet started in 1969 as an obtuse medium for scientists and academics. It took almost twenty-five years to spill over into the world of business and consumers, with the advent of the World Wide Web in 1991. Then, Netscape came along.

In 1994, a meeting took place between Silicon Valley legend Jim Clark, founder of workstation-maker Silicon Graphics, and Mark Andreesen, a recent graduate of the University of Illinois who created Mosaic, the hottest software on the Net. A meeting of the men created a meeting of minds. The two formed Mosaic Communications, subsequently rechristened Netscape, to create a state-of-the-art Web browser. Clark brought in Jim Barksdale, former CEO of $2.3 billion McCaw Cellular, to become Netscape's CEO. The three proved to be a winning combination. Their Netscape Navigator's slick interface provided ease of access to the once forbidding Internet terrain. Suddenly, the customers of the on-line services could get direct, high-quality, low-price access to the World Wide Web—an irresistible proposition for many of them. This value proposition rocketed Netscape to market leadership. By early 1996, Netscape held an 85 percent share of the browser market.

You know by now that customer value opens the possibility for shareholder value. On Wall Street, the momentum shift from on-line firms to the Web is dramatic. For much of 1994–95, shares of AOL sizzled. Then Netscape went public on August 9, 1995. Its stock price doubled on the first day of trading. Even after this doubling, its stock has soared over 100 percent between August 9 and the January 18, 1996, the date of *The Wall Street Journal* article. AOL shares during that time went up a meager 10 percent. In the same period a year before, AOL had climbed 60 percent.

Carried Value

 We carry forward the enterprise's sales growth to Step Ten, Shareholder Value Created. We also carry forward its year-five market share and sales to Step Eleven, Combined Customer and Shareholder Value Created. The reader can trace this flow in Exhibit 11.5. At this point, we are ready to see the ultimate financial payoff of customer value—the shareholder value that precision strategies create. In Chapter Twelve we shift from a customer-value focus to a shareholder-value focus. It's important to note that we could not have made this shift until we forged the link between customer value and shareholder value that we have just finished putting in place. This link is the revenue growth we have envisioned with the help of the value-based sales outlook process.

Exhibit 11.5. Carried Value: Market Share and Sales.

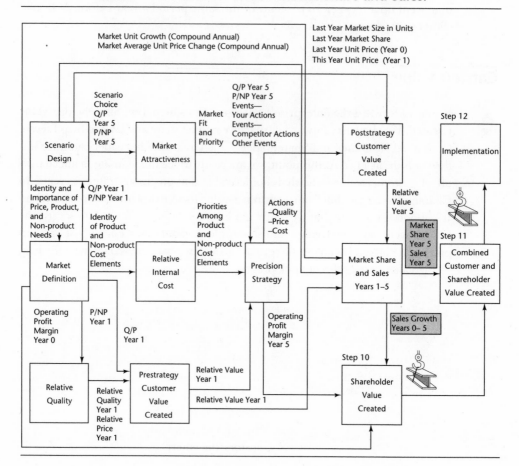

CHAPTER TWELVE

MAPPING SHAREHOLDER VALUE

An enterprise must always work to create value for both customers and shareholders. Creating value for one constituency doesn't automatically lead to value for the other. The enterprise needs to please customers in a way that delivers the revenue growth and profit margins that will please shareholders. Offering superior customer value is key to generating revenue growth, as we saw in the last chapter. A good relative cost position built into each integrated customer value strategy is key to attaining good operating profit margins. Nevertheless, despite these comforting indicators, the enterprise must always specifically check to make sure that its revenue growth and profit margins are large enough to create value for shareholders as well as customers.

Financial professionals on the enterprise's cross-functional strategy-building teams play a key role in measuring shareholder value created. We saw in Chapter Eight that when manufacturing managers begin to assume a key role in determining relative costs, marketing people should not become passive participants in the Market Value Process. Similarly, neither marketing nor manufacturing professionals should become inactive during the shareholder value part of the process. Both marketing and manufacturing have a critical role to play in assessing the validity of the inputs to shareholder value creation that come from their areas of expertise. Managers from all functions, not just financial managers, should have a grasp of the principles of creating shareholder value.

Shareholder value has two parts. The first is the increase in value of the business, measured between the beginning and end of the five-year strategy period, that an enterprise's precision strategies bring about. The second consists of the year-to-year cash consequences, during the strategy period, of putting these strategies in place. Creating shareholder value is a strategic necessity. So it is a strategic necessity that the sum of these two parts be positive.

You have already examined the principles of customer value creation. You have also learned how to measure and map customer value created. Now you are ready to learn the principles of shareholder value creation. Then you will be able to measure and map the value your strategy creates for shareholders.

First, however, we will see an example of the often disastrous result when an enterprise doesn't insist that sales growth be accompanied by profit margin.

Going from Glory to Jeopardy at Borland

On June 2, 1994, *The Wall Street Journal* carried a front-page article entitled "His Way: How 'Barbarian' Style of Philippe Kahn Led Borland International from Glory to Jeopardy."[1] It is worth quoting at some length. The article described how Kahn, self-proclaimed "barbarian" of the software industry, finished a triumphal autobiography in 1992. In the manuscript he reveled in his image as an industry renegade, espousing "a management style for the nineties" that "rejects the conventional comfort and wisdom of America's Fortune 500."

In retrospect, a measure of convention might have benefited Mr. Kahn. At a time when he was stunt flying at trade shows and building a $100 million corporate headquarters, he was committing blunders that left his company, Borland International, Inc., in tatters.

Born in France, Mr. Kahn arrived in the United States a decade ago at the age of thirty-one with only pocket money, and he proceeded to build a tiny mail-order software firm into an empire. At his peak, he was widely considered the only person with enough business acumen and software knowledge to match wits with William Gates III, the powerful chief executive of Microsoft Corporation. In 1991, enthusiastic stock pickers anointed Borland the "next Microsoft."

Mr. Kahn's downfall, critics say, began when he started taking the comparison with Mr. Gates too seriously and using unconventional, even reckless means to attempt to make it true. He greatly increased the sales of his company by his 1991 acquisition of Ashton-Tate, Inc., famous for its dBase database software. He failed, however, to install proper management to ensure a smooth transition. As a result, the company was devastatingly late in developing a version of dBase for

Windows, Microsoft's state-of-the-art operating system for microcomputers. In 1992, he launched a key new spreadsheet version that was supposed to steal customers from Microsoft, but instead it merely confused most potential buyers. And he began building the $100 million headquarters "campus" just as cash was growing tight.

The destruction has been dramatic. The company's market capitalization has been reduced by $2 billion since January 1992, when its stock hit a high of $86 a share. Borland closed below $9 in early June 1994, the time of the story.

In one of Mr. Kahn's characteristic rejections of convention, his key strategy was to slash prices, selling programs at as little as a quarter of his rivals' prices. The tactic boosted sales but leveled profits. Even at the best of times, Borland had profit-margin problems, earning just a dime on every dollar of sales, less than half of what Microsoft took in. We saw in Chapter Seven that competing on price requires an enterprise to have a core competence in low internal cost. Mr. Kahn was unconcerned with the profit consequences of this lack of competence. Profits "personally have never driven me," Mr. Kahn says, adding that "we arrived later than the other guys, so we always had to compete against an entrenched leader."

Slick marketing helped in addition to price cutting. Borland was the first big software supplier to offer competitive "upgrades" at discount prices. The deal was simple. If you owned a Lotus spreadsheet, you could buy the latest version of Borland's spreadsheet for as little as a tenth of the list price; the tactic became standard industry practice. Borland's sales grew rapidly, increasing to $226 million in the fiscal year ending March 1991, up from $91 million two years earlier.

Microsoft dropped two bombshells in 1992, acquiring its own database company and then introducing a new database for the Windows operating system at a super-low price of $99. This move forced Mr. Kahn to slash prices on his own Windows database. Borland's database sold impressively, but because of its low price, "it didn't give the lift it otherwise would have," says David Heller, an investment banker and Borland director for ten years. "You can argue our pricing strategy came back and bit us. Live by the sword, die by the sword."

By 1992, Mr. Kahn's marketing touch seemed to be fading. That fall Borland introduced a much-delayed version of its Quattro Pro spreadsheet. To one-up his rivals, Mr. Kahn sold versions for the MS-DOS and Windows operating systems in a single box. This confused customers so much, however, that the promotion had to be canceled.

Borland's troubles grew deeper in 1993. This was the crucial year for Borland to enter the Windows market big time, and the company flubbed it. At Mr. Kahn's urging, Borland embraced a pioneering approach to software programming called "object-oriented" programming, which appealed to Mr. Kahn's technical aesthetics but made poor business sense. Having to use the new programming code at the same time as it attempted to shift to Windows caused Borland to miss delivery dates by a wide margin.

The combination of brutal price competition and late introduction of new products devastated profit margins. Borland's last profitable year was the year ending March 31, 1991. Over the next three years the company lost a total of $420 million. To raise enough cash to keep the company afloat, Mr. Kahn sold his Quattro Pro spreadsheet to Novell in March 1994. In June, he began a worldwide promotion tour for Borland's new dBase for Windows. The new dBase, however, fell short of expectations, and Borland faced a struggle for survival. In January 1995, Mr. Kahn resigned from the company.

Borland is a classic example of the consequences shareholders face when an enterprise fails to insist that sales growth be accompanied by profit margins.

Examining Four Principles of Shareholder Value Creation

Creating shareholder value is a surprisingly simple yet robust proposition. It rests on four principles, summarized in Exhibit 12.1. We will now examine each of these in turn.

Understanding the Time Value of Money

The first principle is the concept of the time value of money and the idea of present value. If a person is offered the choice between receiving a dollar today and a dollar a year from now, that person will always prefer to have a dollar today. This

Exhibit 12.1. Four Principles Underlying Shareholder Value Creation.

Principle One: The time value of money and the idea of present value

Principle Two: The cash consequences of ownership
- Year-to-year net cash flow
- The difference between beginning and ending value of the operation

Principle Three: The income statement and balance sheet cash flows
- Cash from the income statement minus cash put back into the balance sheet

Principle Four: The idea of a perpetual annuity
- Beginning perpetual annuity
- Taking the operation to a new plateau over the strategy period
- Ending perpetual annuity

is true because of the existence of interest rates. If interest rates are 10 percent, $1.00 today is worth $1.10 a year from now, not $1.00. Similarly, $1.00 a year from now is worth $0.91 today. This is why an enterprise cannot add dollars across time. It must bring dollars from different years in the future to the same point in time, usually the present, before it can add them.

Separating Cash Flow and Value Increase

Since shareholder value focuses on the cash that shareholders receive from owning a share of stock, an enterprise needs to understand the cash consequences of ownership. Suppose an investor buys a small apartment building, holds it for five years, and then sells it. How does the investor know whether the transaction has been financially successful? The investor must consider the sum total of the two parts of ownership. The first is the year-to-year cash flow—rent received minus mortgage payments, property taxes, and maintenance. The second is the increase in the value of the apartment building—the difference between the price the investor pays for the apartment building and the price for which the investor sells it five years later. If the sum of the present value of cash flow and the increase in value is positive, the transaction is a financial success.

Including Income Statement and Balance Sheet Cash Flows

In measuring year-to-year cash flow, an enterprise should include cash flow from both the income statement and the balance sheet. Year-to-year cash flow is the cash an enterprise takes out of the income statement minus the cash it has to put back into the balance sheet to support the sales growth of the business. The cash an enterprise has to put back into the balance sheet is the net working capital plus the net fixed capital it needs to support each dollar of sales increase. Net working capital is what the enterprise's customers owe it plus the enterprise's inventory minus what it owes its suppliers and employees. Net fixed capital is the plant and equipment the enterprise needs to expand its operation minus its depreciation, which reduces its taxes.

Measuring Value Increase with a Perpetual Annuity

The final principle for creating shareholder value is the idea of a perpetual annuity. The enterprise can't measure the beginning and ending value of an operation as easily as it can for a project such as an apartment building. This is because the enterprise is not buying and selling the operation at the beginning and ending of the strategy period. Instead, the enterprise uses the idea of a beginning and an ending perpetual annuity. The enterprise assumes the beginning, or prestrategy, value of an operation is a perpetual annual cash flow in the amount of the beginning level of after-tax operating income. The enterprise also assumes the ending, or poststrategy, value of an operation is a perpetual annual cash flow, beginning at the end of the strategy period, in the amount of the ending level of after-tax operating income.[2] The increase in the value of the operation is the difference between the present value of these two perpetual annuities.

Return to the Integrated Strategy Map, Exhibit 9.10, for a moment. We can see that one purpose of the strategy is to create the higher operating profit margins required to increase the level of operating income between the beginning and the end of the strategy period. The level of operating income at the end of the strategy period—in Sportmed's case, 15 percent—is of towering importance in determining the ending perpetual annuity and thereby in determining the amount of shareholder value created.

Looking at Four Ways to Create Shareholder Value

We have noted that shareholder value has two parts: (1) the increase in value of the business brought about by an enterprise's precision strategies and (2) the year-to-year cash consequences of putting these strategies in place. The sum of these two parts must be greater than zero; otherwise, the strategy producing them is destroying, not creating, shareholder value. In some situations, however, it is common for one of these two parts to be negative. This is not a problem as long as it is more than offset by a positive contribution from the other part. Exhibit 12.2, the Shareholder Value Map, shows this graphically. It shows four ways to create $1 million of shareholder value. The importance of this chart, as we will see, is that it relates patterns of creating shareholder value to differing objectives that an enterprise may seek to satisfy—gaining, holding, or losing market share—during the process of creating customer value.

Growing Moderately

First, a business can be growing moderately, possibly growing as fast as the market, and thereby holding market share. It is positioned on the "market wants" line of the Customer Value Map. In this case, it may be generating $1 million of shareholder value created (SVC) by getting a positive contribution from each of the two parts—year-to-year net cash flow (NCF) and the increase in value (Inc Val) between the beginning and the end of the strategy period. This is a very common pattern for a mature business.

Exhibit 12.2. Shareholder Value Map.

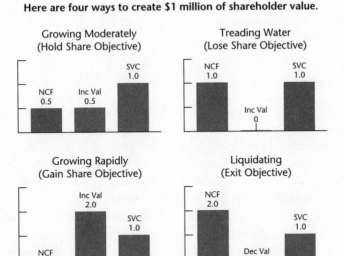

Here are four ways to create $1 million of shareholder value.

Growing Moderately
(Hold Share Objective)

Treading Water
(Lose Share Objective)

Growing Rapidly
(Gain Share Objective)

Liquidating
(Exit Objective)

NCF = Net Cash Flow, Inc Val = Increase in Value, SVC = Shareholder Value Created

Growing Rapidly

Next, a business may be growing rapidly, growing faster than the market, and thereby gaining market share. It is positioned below the "market wants" line, maybe even in "Take No Prisoners" territory on the Customer Value Map. In this case, it may be generating $1 million of shareholder value by running a $1 million negative net cash flow but more than offsetting this by a $2 million increase between beginning and ending value. This is a common pattern in start-up businesses that require venture capital financing. It is also a common pattern in new-product launches that require financial support from the parent company. In rapidly growing businesses, the assessment of value increase is of even greater than usual importance in the shareholder value picture. Consequently, it is crucial to consider carefully the year-five operating profit margin from the Integrated Strategy Map, Exhibit 9.10. The year-five operating profit margin influences heavily the ending perpetual annuity that determines the value increase.

Treading Water

A business may also create $1 million of shareholder value by treading water. Perhaps its sales are remaining constant in a market that is growing, so it is losing market share. It is positioned above the "market wants" line, possibly even in the Bermuda Triangle on the Customer Value Map. In this case, it does not require fixed or working capital to support sales growth, since there is no sales growth to support. Consequently, it may be generating $1 million of value in year-to-year net cash flow but not increasing the value of the business.

Exiting the Market

Finally, the business may generate $2 million of cash by selling all its inventory, collecting all accounts receivable, selling its plant and equipment, and liquidating. It is left with a $2 million pile of cash on the table but gives up 100 percent of the $1 million value the business had at the outset. The net effect, again, is to create $1 million in shareholder value. This pattern may also represent not a liquidation but the outright sale of the business to a third party.

Large enterprises use each of these four ways to create shareholder value. In some markets the enterprise is growing rapidly and gaining share; in some it is growing moderately and holding share; in some it is treading water and losing share; and in some it is in the process of withdrawing.

Measuring Shareholder Value Created

You are now ready to examine the six inputs that determine the amount of shareholder value created by your enterprise's precision value strategies. We see these inputs in Exhibit 12.3. The first two of these inputs, sales growth and operating profit margin (earnings before interest and taxes divided by sales), are carried value

Exhibit 12.3. Inputs to Measuring Shareholder Value Created: Progressive Market.

	Year 0	Year 1	Year 2	Year 3	Year 4	Year 5	Carried Value From Step Number
Sales	63.20	69.50	76.40	84.10	92.50	101.80	9
Operating Profit Margin	0.07	0.08	0.09	0.09	0.12	0.15	1,7
Net Fixed Capital		0.10	0.10	0.10	0.10	0.10	
Net Working Capital		0.30	0.30	0.30	0.30	0.30	
Tax Rate	0.43	0.43	0.43	0.43	0.43	0.43	
Cost of Capital	0.13	0.13	0.13	0.13	0.13	0.13	

Year 0 = Last Year, Year 1 = This Year

from earlier steps of the Market Value Process. Sales growth and operating profit margin represent the financial payoff of customer value, and together, they are the link that integrates customer value and shareholder value.

We saw how to use the Market Value Process to envision an enterprise's sales growth in Chapter Eleven. We summarized the enterprise's strategy work in Chapter Nine. At the bottom of the Integrated Strategy Map, Exhibit 9.10, the enterprise assessed the operating profit margin that it felt the strategy would deliver once the strategy had been put in place. We saw that Sportmed felt this would be 15 percent in year five in the Progressive Market. Earlier in the process, when it finished its market definition work in Chapter Three, Sportmed noted that its current operating margin in this market was 7 percent. Sportmed felt that its integrated customer value strategy would gradually increase this to the 15 percent level over the strategy period, and it showed this in the highlighted second row of Exhibit 12.3. Sportmed knew this would be a key assessment in the measurement of shareholder value created that it was about to make.

We highlight this operating profit margin to emphasize the importance of the timing of the margin increases. We saw in Chapter Eleven that it was important to think deeply about market share change between year one and year five because the timing of this change reflects the enterprise's estimate of how quickly its integrated customer value strategy can be put in place. The same is true for operating profit margin. If the timing for the margin gains shown in Exhibit 12.3 can be accelerated, the favorable impact on shareholder value created will be enormous. Sportmed realized that it needed to make a concerted effort to accelerate the timing for putting its strategy in place.

The last four inputs in Exhibit 12.3 reflect the financial situation of the business. They are the net fixed capital (capital expenditures minus depreciation) required to support each dollar of sales increase, the net working capital required to support each dollar of sales increase, the tax rate, and the cost of capital, which is the interest rate an enterprise uses to bring all cash flows to their present value. Sportmed's financial organization, as part of the team effort, provided the information that the Progressive Market planning team displayed in the last four rows of Exhibit 12.3.

Of the six inputs to measuring shareholder value created shown in Exhibit 12.3, the most important is operating profit margin. We have emphasized the importance of Sportmed's assessment that its strategy would deliver a 15 percent margin in Year 5. If the operating profit margin had remained at Sportmed's Year 0 level of 7 percent throughout the strategy period, a Shareholder Value Map would show that the strategy was destroying, rather than creating, value for shareholders. Small, rapidly growing businesses may have profit margins that are low, or even negative, during a part of the strategy period. These temporarily low or negative margins necessary to grow a business rapidly can ultimately pay off for shareholders as shown in the "Growing Rapidly" example in Exhibit 12.2. But, they will do so only if these margins can be brought up to an acceptable level by the end of the strategy period. If, at the end of the strategy period, a strategy's return on capital is less than the cost of capital, it will destroy value for shareholders.[3]

Mapping Shareholder Value Created

Sportmed used the principles in this chapter to calculate the shareholder value created by the hold share strategy we saw Sportmed build in Chapter Nine. We see the result in Exhibit 12.4, the Shareholder Value Map for the Progressive Market.

Sportmed saw that the pattern of the heights of the three bars was similar to the classic pattern for a business that was growing moderately and holding market share. Of the total created shareholder value of $23.80 million, there were

Exhibit 12.4. Shareholder Value Map: Progressive Market.

The sales growth and operating profit margins, provided by Competitor A's integrated customer value strategy, create value for shareholders.

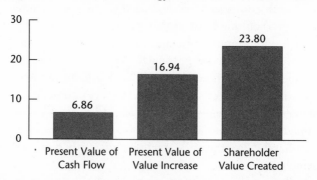

Sportmed measured the year-to-year cash flow that the strategy generated, brought each year's cash flow back to its present value, and arrived at a value creation of $6.86 million from the present value of year-to-year cash flow.

Sportmed calculated the poststrategy value of the business to be $66.95 million, based on the ending perpetual annuity generated by its year-five operating income after tax. The present value was $36.34 million. It calculated the prestrategy value of the business to be $19.40 million, based on the perpetual annuity generated by its year-zero (last year) operating income after tax. The difference between the beginning and ending value was $16.94 million. This is the present value of value increase.

positive contributions by each of the two parts—$6.86 million net cash flow and $16.94 million in increase in value. This means that about 70 percent of the shareholder value created in the Progressive Market comes from the time period beyond the next five years, because the ending annuity determines the increase in value. This is not unusual for mature businesses that are holding market share. A recent study showed that projected performance for the next five years accounted for only 20 percent of the current stock price of the Dow Jones Thirty Industrials Average. Fully 80 percent of the value of the stock prices of these companies came from their ending value five years in the future.[4]

Carried Value

Exhibit 12.5 shows how Sportmed carried forward the $23.80 million in shareholder value created in the Progressive Market, depicted by the "$$ SVC" sign within the frame, into Step Eleven, Combined Customer and Shareholder Value Created. At this stage of the Market Value Process we have measured and mapped both the customer value and the shareholder value that a precision strategy delivers. In the next chapter we will see what conclusions we can draw from this combined value.

Exhibit 12.5. Carried Value: Shareholder Value Creation.

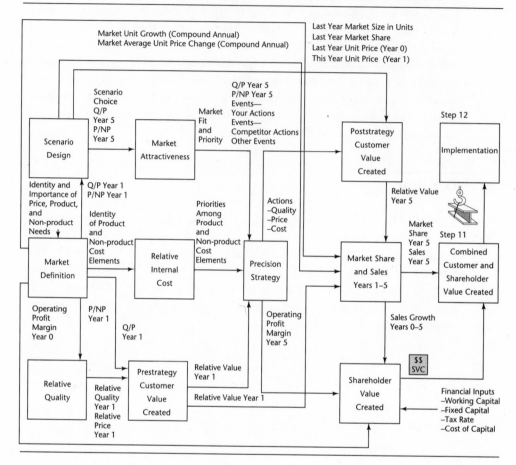

CHAPTER THIRTEEN

SELECTING STRATEGIES, SETTING OBJECTIVES, AND ALLOCATING RESOURCES

The enterprise has now measured and mapped the customer value and the shareholder value each of its strategies creates. This is a feat that few, if any, of its competitors have ever accomplished. This achievement gives the information the enterprise needs in order to make three major decisions. These are to select the best strategies from those it built in Chapter Nine, to set objectives, and to allocate resources. An enterprise can't do these things at the onset without going through the diagnosis, the bridge, and the payoff steps of the Market Value Process. If it tried, it would simply be flying by the seat of its pants. The "right" strategies and objectives in each market are those that create the best combination of customer and shareholder value; until the enterprise has followed the steps of the Market Value Process, it doesn't know which strategies and objectives offer the best combined value and thus provide the best solution to the combined-value problem. But once the enterprise has completed Steps One through Ten, it is in a position to make the right choices among strategies, objectives, and resource allocation priorities. Management *of* objectives—that is, choosing the best ones—always comes before managing *by* objectives in the thought process. Until the enterprise chooses its best objectives with the Market Value Process, it can't know the right ones by which to manage.

Some people are uncomfortable with the concept of a "best" combination of customer and shareholder value. These people hold the view that an enterprise is in business for its shareholders and is interested in customers only as a vehicle to enrich shareholders. The danger in this thinking is that it can imply that customers "won't notice" if an enterprise moves to increase profit margins by cutting costs in a way that cuts quality. In Chapter Two we described the disaster that overtook Schlitz when it acted on the "won't notice" premise. An enterprise does indeed need the "best" combination of customer and shareholder value. A view that edges toward the thought that shareholder value reigns supreme and customer value is ancillary is fraught with danger for shareholders. With this in mind, we are ready to move through the thought process for determining the "best" combination of customer and shareholder value.

Exhibit 13.1 shows the scope of the work an enterprise needs to do to build integrated customer value strategies. Chapter Nine focused on building a strategy to support a hold share objective under the "Business as Usual" scenario in the Progressive Market, the shaded area in Exhibit 13.1. As an enterprise becomes engrossed in building a single strategy, it cannot lose sight of the fact that it needs to build a number of strategies from which it will select the best. The three-dimensional view shown in Exhibit 13.1 reminds the enterprise of the dimensions along which these strategies range.

Sportmed began its thinking about the global sports medicine instruments "business area" in Chapter Three by defining its three markets as Progressive, Traditional, and Commercial. It saw that these three sets of customers had quite different price, product, and non-product needs and that it would need different strategies to meet these differing needs. We depict this range of markets along the

Exhibit 13.1.

We can develop an integrated customer value strategy for each objective under each scenario for each market.

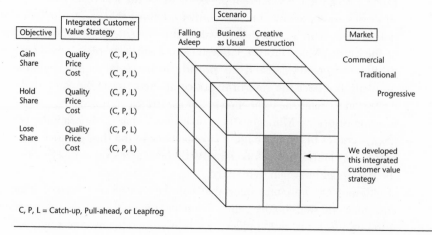

C, P, L = Catch-up, Pull-ahead, or Leapfrog

right side of the chart. Chapter Four examined how these needs would evolve over time in response to different levels of product and non-product innovation that competitors might offer in these markets. Sportmed chose one of these scenarios, "Business as Usual," on which to base its strategy but reminded itself that it must have summary strategies in mind for the other scenarios. By doing this, Sportmed will be ready to change to the right strategy more quickly than its competitors can in the event that one of the other scenarios actually materializes. In addition, Sportmed can take actions that will assist the most favorable scenario to materialize. We depict this range of scenarios along the top of the chart.

Sportmed assessed the attractiveness of each of its markets in Chapter Five and measured and mapped its quality, price, and cost position in each market in Chapters Six, Seven, and Eight. In Chapter Nine the cross-functional teams examined how to improve quality, price, and cost in each market through different integrated customer value strategies they built to support the three different objectives of gain share, hold share, and lose share. We depict this range of objectives along the left side of the chart. Sportmed needed to build a strategy for each objective before it could know which objective was best, based on the combined customer and shareholder value its supporting strategy created.

To handle this array of strategies, an enterprise needs a process that is very compact, and compactness is a key characteristic of the Market Value Process. Remember the compactness of the one-page Integrated Strategy Map in Chapter Nine? The strategies took only a dozen words or so to outline the necessary catch-up, pull-ahead, and leapfrog actions in each product and non-product need. Massively long strategy statements are usually unnecessary at best; at their worst, they are bound into large books that are put on the shelf and quickly forgotten. It is usually true in the marketplace that broad, streamlined thinking will dominate narrow, deep thinking that doesn't cover the necessary ground. The Market Value Process encourages this broad, streamlined thinking. Good strategies are usually simple, not complicated; they are clear and robust and can be expressed in a few words rather than many. The reality that an enterprise can build strategies in a streamlined way makes it possible for the enterprise to perform the critical action of ranging broadly over many strategies in order to find the right one.

Using the Investment Attractiveness Thought Process

The Market Value Process concludes in this chapter with a compact, powerful tool to choose the best objective and supporting strategy in each market and to assign priorities to these markets for investment of resources. This tool is called the

Customer and Shareholder Value Map. We considered this map briefly in Chapter Two and now begin a much fuller consideration of it.

Exhibit 13.2 shows the thought process for determining how attractive a strategy is for investment. It shows us that the Investment Attractiveness of a strategy depends on its risk-reward profile, which we call the *Customer Value Index,* combined with the shareholder value it creates. The Customer Value Index profiles the risk and reward of a strategy because it combines the market share and sales reward, flowing from an enterprise's position on the Customer Value Map, with the risk an enterprise takes to arrive at this position. In this sense, the Customer Value Index is really a risk-adjusted Customer Value Map. It helps the enterprise answer such questions as "What is the reward of a trip from a Bermuda Triangle position to a Take No Prisoners position, and how risky is that trip?"

Moving left in Exhibit 13.2, "Business Attractiveness" consists of the reward—market share and sales in year five—that the enterprise receives from attaining its desired position on the Customer Value Map. We saw how to measure this reward in Chapter Eleven, when we constructed the value-based sales outlook. "Strategic Fit" measures the risk posed by the new customers and the new technology an enterprise faces as it moves to its desired position on the Customer Value Map.

Exhibit 13.2.

The Investment Attractiveness of a strategy depends on its risk-reward profile (the Customer Value Index) and the shareholder value it creates.

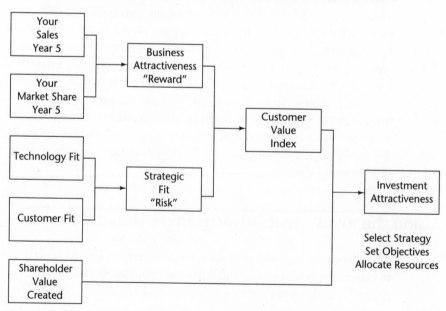

Exhibit 13.3. Investment Attractiveness Input Information.

This is the Investment Attractiveness input information for three objectives for each business under the "Business as Usual" scenario.

Business	Progressive			Traditional			Commercial		
Objective	GS	HS	LS	GS	HS	LS	GS	HS	LS
Sales ($MM)—Year 5	119	102	72	13	8	5	29	19	8
Market Share (%)—Year 5	43	34	24	17	9	6	38	25	16
Technology Risk (C, R, N)	N	R	C	C	C	C	R	C	C
Customer Risk (C, R, N)	N	R	C	N	C	C	R	C	C
Shareholder Value Created ($MM)	29	24	9	5	4	2	7	5	2

GS, HS, LS = Objectives to Gain, Hold, or Lose Market Share
C, R, N = Current, Related, New

We will see how to measure Strategic Fit in this chapter.

Because of the groundwork it has laid by this point, the enterprise already has most of the information it needs to assess Investment Attractiveness. Altogether, it needs only five items of information for each market. These items are depicted in the column of five blocks on the left side of Exhibit 13.2, and Exhibit 13.3 shows them in a table. The enterprise has already developed three of these. Sales and market share in year five are items of carried value from Chapter Eleven. Shareholder value created is the carried value from Chapter Twelve. Sportmed developed these inputs for the hold share objective in the Progressive Market. It used the same process to develop this information for all three objectives—gain, hold, and lose share in each of its three markets.

Assessing Reward: Market Share and Sales

We can see the Business Attractiveness of Sportmed's nine strategies in Exhibit 13.4. Business Attractiveness is the reward—market share and sales in year five—that customers give an enterprise for its position on the Customer Value Map. The chart depicts the year-five sales and market share that each strategy delivers. The stronger the position of a strategy on the Customer Value Map in a sizable market, the more likely a strategy is to be located in the favorable upper right corner—the area of high Business Attractiveness.

Four of Sportmed's nine strategies, including the strategy supporting the gain share objective in the Progressive Market—P(G)—and the strategy supporting the hold share objective in the Progressive Market—P(H)—fall in the high Business

Exhibit 13.4. Business Attractiveness Assessments.

Business Attractiveness, or reward, results from the relative value your offering delivers to customers.

Year-5 Market Share	Year-5 Sales		
	Low $10MM	Medium $30MM	High
Strong 30%	Medium —Invest Selectively	High —Invest C(G)	High —Invest P(G), P(H)
Competitive 10%	Low —Avoid C(L)	Medium —Invest Selectively T(G), C(H)	High —Invest P(L)
Weak	Low —Avoid T(H), T(L)	Low —Avoid	Medium —Invest Selectively

P, T, C = Progressive, Traditional, or Commercial Business
G, H, L = Objective to Gain, Hold, or Lose Market Share

Attractiveness area. Two of the strategies fall along the diagonal of medium Business Attractiveness, and three fall into the lower left corner—the area of low Business Attractiveness. Remember, however, that Business Attractiveness, or reward, is only half of the story of the Customer Value Index. Next, the enterprise needs to consider the other half—Strategic Fit, or the measurement of risk.

Assessing Risk: Newness in Customers and Technology

A much-debated management issue is how to reflect the element of risk in the return an enterprise expects from a strategy. In general, the enterprise should expect that higher return will be accompanied by higher risk. A move from the

Bermuda Triangle to Take No Prisoners terrain on the Value Map offers the rewards of high year-five market share and sales. The move, however, may require
that the enterprise accept the risk of stretching toward unfamiliar customers or
technology. Then the enterprise faces the problem of how best to reflect the risk
this stretch entails.

We can see the Strategic Fit, or risk, of Sportmed's nine strategies in the "Business as Usual" Scenario in Exhibit 13.5. This exhibit tells us that Strategic Fit, or
risk, is the degree of "newness" in customers an enterprise must win and the technology it must undertake to establish its customer value position. This chart depicts
whether a strategy entails winning a customer base that is current, related, or new
and whether it entails undertaking a technology that is current, related, or new.

Five of Sportmed's strategies fall in the upper right corner, the area of high
Strategic Fit, or low risk. They entail dealing with a customer/technology picture

Exhibit 13.5. Strategic Fit Assessments.

**Strategic Fit, or risk, is the degree of "newness" in customers you must win
and the technology you must undertake to establish your customer value position.**

	Customer Base		
Technology/Product	New	Related	Current
Current	Medium —Invest Selectively T(G)	High —Invest	High —Invest P(L), T(H), T(L) C(H), C(L)
Related	Low —Avoid	Medium —Invest Selectively P(H), C(G)	High —Invest
New	Low —Avoid P(G)	Low —Avoid	Medium —Invest Selectively

P, T, C = Progressive, Traditional, or Commercial Businesses
G, H, L = Objective to Gain, Hold, or Lose Market Share

that is current along at least one dimension and no worse than related along the other. Three of Sportmed's strategies—including hold share strategy for the Progressive Market, P(H)—fall along the diagonal of medium Strategic Fit. Strategies in support of a gain share objective sometimes fall in the lower left corner. This means a low Strategic Fit due to the higher risk inherent in the stretch they entail along both the customer and the technology dimensions. We see that this applies to the strategy supporting the gain share objective in the Progressive Market, P(G). In this strategy, Sportmed had to reach a new customer base, small-volume practitioners, who were substantially different from Sportmed's current customer base of high-volume practitioners. In this strategy, Sportmed also had to use a new laser technology in its instruments.

Strategies should encompass the right amount of risk. The Market Value Process does not discourage risk in a strategy to achieve a favorable position on the Customer Value Map. Moderate risk along both the customer and the technology dimensions or the high risk of a long stretch along one dimension coupled with low risk along the other does not position a strategy in the low—avoid area. The high risk of a long stretch along both dimensions at once, however, should be a signal for the management of an enterprise to stop and think twice before moving ahead.

There are many different approaches to measuring risk. This two-dimensional approach was developed several decades ago, and its robust simplicity has stood the test of time well.[1] There are more sophisticated approaches to measuring risk, but their complexity is also greater, and we will not introduce them here. We favor a more fundamental measure of risk based on management judgment, because it is easier to understand and therefore easier to use. This simplified approach is more than equal to the task.

Combining Risk and Reward: The Customer Value Index

Exhibit 13.6 depicts the Customer Value Index, a powerful way to combine the risk and reward in a strategy. We just saw that we can think of the Customer Value Index as a risk-adjusted Customer Value Map because it combines the reward from reaching a desired position with the risk of getting there. Strategies that rank high on Business Attractiveness, or reward (year-five market share and sales), and rank high or medium on Strategic Fit (which means low or medium in risk) have a high Customer Value Index. Strategies that rank medium on Business Attractiveness and rank high or medium on Strategic Fit have a medium Customer Value Index. Strategies that rank low on Business Attractiveness or rank low on Strategic Fit (high in risk) have a low Customer Value Index.

Exhibit 13.6. Customer Value Index Assessments.

Your Customer Value Index combines the reward of your poststrategy position on the Customer Value Map with the risk of attaining it.

	Strategic Fit (Risk)		
Business Attractiveness (Reward)	Low	Medium	High
High	Low —Avoid P(G)	High —Invest P(H), C(G)	High —Invest P(L)
Medium	Low —Avoid	Medium —Invest Selectively T(G)	Medium —Invest Selectively C(H)
Low	Low —Avoid	Low —Avoid	Low —Avoid T(H), T(L), C(L)

P, T, C = Progressive, Traditional, or Commercial Businesses
G, H, L = Objective to Gain, Hold, or Lose Market Share

In the upper left corner of Exhibit 13.6, note that P(G) has a low Customer Value Index score. It has this low score because of its high risk along both the customer and technology dimensions we saw in Exhibit 13.5. Importantly, risk matters to customers as well as to the enterprise itself. Customers may be cautious about an enterprise's promise to deliver a high customer value in year five if the customer knows that the enterprise must take high technology or marketing risks in order to deliver on this promise. Such caution might be enough for a customer to exclude the enterprise's offerings from the customer's long-term plans.

The power of the Customer Value Index lies in its intuitive appeal. An enterprise would naturally want to undertake strategies that offer a high reward coupled with manageable risk. Next, it would choose those strategies offering a medium reward with manageable risk. The enterprise would think twice, however, about undertaking strategies characterized by either low reward or high risk. It might not reject these strategies, but it would take a second look at them before adopting them.

Mapping the Combined Customer and Shareholder Value That Strategies Create

Combining a strategy's reward and risk in the Customer Value Index provides a breakthrough. It allows an enterprise finally to see the Investment Attractiveness of each strategy in the Customer and Shareholder Value Map, Exhibit 13.7. This is the end result of the enterprise's work because it shows the combined risk-adjusted customer value and shareholder value that each strategy creates. The Customer Value Index, the result of marketing strategy, is shown along the horizontal dimension. Shareholder value created, the result of financial strategy, is shown along the vertical dimension. We have now carried the graphic on the title page through its first use as an interpretive chart in the Schlitz and Bowmar example in Chapter Two to its ultimate level of development in Exhibit 13.7.

The closer a strategy's position is to the upper right corner, the higher the combined customer and shareholder value that the strategy generates and the more attractive the strategy is for investment. The "best" combination of customer and shareholder value is located in the upper right corner, the one marked "invest—priority." Strategies in the bottom row are destroying rather than creating shareholder value and should be improved or rejected. Strategies in the left-hand column but above the bottom row are categorized invest—selectively. Strategies in this column are assigned a low Customer Value Index because they either offer small rewards or are risky—that is, they deliver a low combination of sales and market share in year five, or they carry a high combination of customer and technology risk. While an enterprise should think twice before undertaking them, this does not rule them out. There is room in an enterprise for a few strategies that offer small but safe rewards and a few strategies that are risky but offer big rewards. These strategies, however, should get a second look before they are approved.

Assigning Priorities to Strategies

Based on this Customer and Shareholder Value Map, Sportmed selected the strategy supporting the hold share objective in the Progressive Market, the strategy supporting the gain share objective in the Commercial Market, and the strategy

Exhibit 13.7. Customer and Shareholder Value Map:
Sports Medicine Instruments Business Area.

 Mapping combined value allows us to see which strategy will work best in each market and to set priority for investment among markets.

Customer Value Index (Marketing Strategy)

Shareholder Value Created (Financial Strategy)	Low	Medium	High
High	Invest —Selectively P(G)	Invest	Invest —Priority P(H)
10			
Medium	Invest —Selectively T(H), T(L) C(L)	Invest T(G), C(H)	Invest C(G), P(L)
0			
Low	Withdraw	Improve Financial Performance or Withdraw	Improve Financial Performance or Withdraw

Strategies P(H), T(G), and C(G) offer the greatest investment attractiveness for the Progressive, Traditional, and Commercial Markets, respectively.

supporting the gain share objective in the Traditional Market. Sportmed selected these because they created higher combined customer and shareholder value than did the strategies supporting other objectives in those markets.

The conclusion to hold rather than gain share in the Progressive Market initially surprised Sportmed. This was a market where the fit was good between the value leverage factor, quality, and Sportmed's core competence, which was also quality. Beyond this, Sportmed saw from the bottom row of Exhibit 13.3 that the strategy supporting the gain share objective promised $29 million in shareholder value created compared to $24 million for the strategy supporting the hold share objective.

From its work with the Market Value Process, however, Sportmed remembered that the choice of the hold share posture resulted from the risk associated with the gain share posture. Sportmed remembered from its work with scenarios that Competitor B was poised to come to market with possibly frame-breaking technology under the Creative Destruction scenario. Sportmed decided to wait to see the result of this pioneering effort while keeping up the pressure on its own research and development effort so that it could respond quickly and hold share if the new technology proved successful. This R&D effort was at the heart of Sportmed's strategy in Exhibit 9.10 to stay ahead on the top-priority items of advanced features and accuracy so that it could respond quickly to Competitor B's initiative.

Assigning Priorities to Markets

Based also on the Customer and Shareholder Value Map, Sportmed assigned first priority for investment to the Progressive Market, second priority to the Commercial Market, and third priority to the Traditional Market. It gave top priority to the Progressive Market because its best strategy in that market created more combined value than its best strategy in the Commercial or Traditional Markets did. This confirmed the preliminary work Sportmed had done on market fit and priority in Chapter Five. It gave second priority to the Commercial Market because its best strategy in that market created more combined value than its best strategy in the Traditional Market did.

Consequently, Sportmed invested heavily in continuing the forward momentum of its R&D effort in the Progressive Market. Were Sportmed to run short on human and financial resources, the first market it would abandon would be the Traditional Market; the second would be the Commercial Market.

Next, since marketing strategy appears along one side of the Customer and Shareholder Value Map and financial strategy along the other, we will examine the appropriate relationship between marketing and finance.

Ending the War Between Marketing and Finance

Marketers and finance people are often at war. Finance accuses marketing of giving the store away with price cuts, unnecessary product features, and overkill on customer service. Marketing accuses finance of failing to understand the necessity to beat the competition in meeting customer needs. When this happens in an enterprise, it reflects a failure to understand the need for a balanced focus on creating value for customers and shareholders. A strategy must be sound from both a marketing and a financial standpoint before it can attain a strong position on the Customer and Shareholder Value Map.

Marketing has grown greatly in scope during the past few decades, but it must grow further. At one time, marketing was viewed as the task of persuading customers to buy the product or service that the enterprise was currently offering. Since then, strategic marketing has come to be viewed much more broadly as the art of figuring out what people want, designing it, manufacturing it, and selling it at a competitive price. We saw in Chapter Eight that marketers must understand costs as well as prices. But the scope of marketing must grow even beyond this. Marketers must know the shareholder value that their strategies create. The superior marketing professional is able to measure and map shareholder value by using the Shareholder Value Map in Chapter Twelve. Only then can the marketing professional communicate successfully with financial professionals. This communication is key to creating combined value.

Just as marketing was once viewed as nothing but sales support, finance people were once seen as primarily accountants. The scope of the finance job was subsequently enlarged to include raising money, and the concept of the chief financial officer was born. Despite this, the focus of finance all too often remains on cost—the cost of operations and the cost of capital. It was a sign of admiration to call a financial person a "bottom-line" financial executive—one who kept costs low enough to ensure profit. Finance must grow beyond this cost focus. Today an enterprise needs a "top-line" financial officer. The successful financial person must understand how to use the concepts and tools in Chapter Eleven to develop a value-based sales outlook, the top line of the income statement, driven from the enterprise's position on the Customer Value Map. The double meaning of "top line" in this context is an excellent one. The superior financial professional is the one who understands how customer value drives the top line of the income statement. It is this top-line financial professional who will be able to communicate successfully with the marketing professional.

When an enterprise puts a bottom-line marketing executive and a top-line financial professional to work on cross-functional strategy-building teams like Sportmed's, then the war between marketing and finance will be over.

With this vision of the entire enterprise pulling together to solve the combined-value problem in mind, let's look at the process of creating combined value in the brutally competitive international commodity markets.

Displaying the Marvels of High Margins at Goodyear

The concepts and tools of the Market Value Process apply to commodity businesses with as much power as they do to high-technology enterprises. On May 2,

1994, *Fortune* carried a story entitled "The Marvels of High Margins: Goodyear Tire & Rubber."[2] The story reported that the tire business isn't a game of long passes and thrilling broken-field runs but of four-yard advances in clouds of gritty dust. Yet when a team is captained by an all-American like Goodyear Tire & Rubber's CEO Stanley Gault, it can be an exciting game nonetheless.

It can also be a winning game. Since Gault joined the team in 1991, after eleven brilliant seasons leading the Rubbermaid squad, Goodyear has gone from its first yearly loss in two generations, just before he joined, to 1993's championship earnings of $388 million, second highest in company history. That leaves the other giants in the international league far behind. Says competitor Hubertus von Gruenberg, chairman of Germany's Continental tire company, "Stan Gault is setting a world standard for profitability."

Gault has pursued a double mission during the past three years. His first goal was to shrink and restructure, selling off nonessential businesses, reducing the work force, and cutting costs. These were activities with low Investment Attractiveness. As the company was slimming down, Gault attacked the second and really creative task: putting some profitable growth on the board. His strategy: find and seize the industry's fastest-growing, highest-margin markets. If need be, create them.

In a commodity business, finding growth markets means looking for specialty niches. So Gault asked Goodyear's product development people to brew up a flood of new products distinctive enough to command a premium price. In the past two years, twenty-two creations have tumbled out of the factories, much more than in any previous two-year period in Goodyear's history.

Gault understood that while the automakers who buy about half of Goodyear's tires are sophisticated engineers who specify precisely what they want, the consumers who buy replacement tires can be lured by attractive features that intelligent marketing can divine. The former offered medium Investment Attractiveness, and the latter offered high Investment Attractiveness. For Goodyear developers, the new marketing savvy made all the difference. The marketers discovered not only what consumers wanted but what the tire should look like. To buy a high-traction tire, says Joe Gingo, vice president for worldwide tire technology, "the consumer has to look at the tire and say—*traction*."

Everyone knows about Goodyear's first new product success, the much advertised Aquatred, a tire with a furrow down the middle for wet traction. Premium priced, it accounts for 6 percent of Goodyear's volume and 8.5 percent of profits. Stiff-arming competitors crowding in with copycats, Goodyear has introduced the son of Aquatred, a tire boasting not one but *two* grooves, designed to provide wet traction combined with high performance when dry.

Other new-product winners, collectively more important than Aquatred, are much less well known. For the free-spending owners of sports cars, Goodyear has concocted complete sets in which each tire, slightly different, is designed for a specific wheel, so consumers buy them four at a time, not one by one. Tires for four-wheel-drive vehicles offer a jazzy appearance and three bands of tread in differing patterns and materials. The five replacement passenger-tire models introduced in 1992 and 1993, though only 14 percent of unit volume, account for 16.5 percent of revenues and a spectacular 20 percent of gross profits.

Not all Goodyear's players are stars. Its margin laggards are tires sold to automakers themselves. But Gault is widening the profits on them as well by concentrating on the high-margin, high-performance tires that manufacturers put on four-wheel-drive vehicles, vans, and pickups. Goodyear dominates this category, growing so fast that it has jumped from 10 percent of the market in 1987 to 23 percent today.

To boost his replacement-tire business further, Gault changed his retail distribution strategy. Goodyear had sold only through independent dealers whose business was stagnating. Says Gault, "Too many people were telling us that it was not convenient for them to purchase Goodyear products, because there wasn't an outlet where they preferred to shop." So he started selling through Sears, Wal-Mart, and other mass merchants. Of course, the independent dealers protested vehemently, but Goodyear is helping to reenergize them with lots of marketing and advertising support plus all those new products. Result: sales to dealers rose 2 percent in 1993, a flat year for the U.S. replacement auto tire market.

The result for combined customer and shareholder value created in these markets? We have seen the market share gains Goodyear's superior customer value delivered. For shareholders, the sales growth and profit margin increases propelled the stock from just over $5 a share in 1990 to $40 in mid 1994. *Fortune*'s story ended on this upbeat note. No doubt continuing this momentum will represent a stiff challenge. Strategies built with this kind of precision, however, stand an excellent chance of winning customers and shareholders, even in the most difficult markets.

Arriving at the End Result of the Market Value Process

The enterprise has now accomplished everything it set out to accomplish with the Market Value Process. It has seen that low growth and stock price are not problems but symptoms. They are symptoms of the combined-value problem. The enterprise has completed its journey through the diagnosis, bridge, and payoff thought process that provides the solution to the combined-value problem. It has built a family of precision strategies that will win customers and shareholders because the strategies create value for both constituencies. The enterprise has identified the best objective and supporting strategy in each market based on how well the supporting strategy achieved the goals of creating high combined customer and shareholder value. Finally, the enterprise has set priorities for investment in each of its markets based on the combined value it believes it can create for customers and shareholders in each. Importantly, the enterprise has avoided the dangerous assumption that customer value automatically leads to shareholder value or that shareholder value automatically delivers customer value. Instead it has checked to make sure that its precision strategies create high value for both constituencies. These strategies deliver high-quality offerings at low prices, thereby pleasing customers. The strategies deliver vigorous sales growth and high profit margins, thereby satisfying shareholders.

In the next, and last, chapter we will see how to implement the Market Value Process and the strategies it delivers.

CHAPTER FOURTEEN

IMPLEMENTING PRECISION STRATEGIES

We have broken new ground in thinking about customer and shareholder value by measuring and mapping how each must come into play to solve the combined-value problem. In this last chapter we will focus on the role of cross-functional employee teams in making this happen. Of course, we have seen Sportmed's teams at work from the beginning, but now we will look at their jobs in greater detail.

The key to implementing the Market Value Process and the strategies it generates is to empower employee teams to accomplish four tasks. The teams need to stay on top of shifting customer needs in the marketplace. Then they need to build precision strategies to meet these shifting needs. Next, they need to make sure the strategies create enough value for customers and shareholders to make the strategies work. Finally, they need to detail who must do what and by when in order to put the strategies in place. An enterprise can accomplish these four things by following the suggestions embodied in each subhead in this chapter.

Seeing the Big Picture

One of the things about the Market Value Process that makes it satisfying is its comprehensiveness. We can see the result of all the carried values of the enterprise's work in Exhibit 14.1. This chart shows all items of carried value that lead to the top shaded box on the far right: setting priority among strategies and priority among markets. Note that the three sections below this one show shareholder value and the result of customer value—market share and sales—joining to solve the combined-value problem. This is the graphic on the title page, but now it has become the culminating flowchart of the Market Value Process.

Seeing this big picture is the first step in implementing both the Market Value Process and the strategies it produces. By finishing this book, you have taken the first implementation step. The consistent feedback we receive from our private and public workshops is that it is exciting to see all the steps come together into a set of priorities among strategies in each market and a set of priorities among markets, as we saw in Chapter Thirteen. This sense of excitement creates momentum for the remaining steps.

Exhibit 14.1. Carried Value: Choice Among Strategies and Markets.

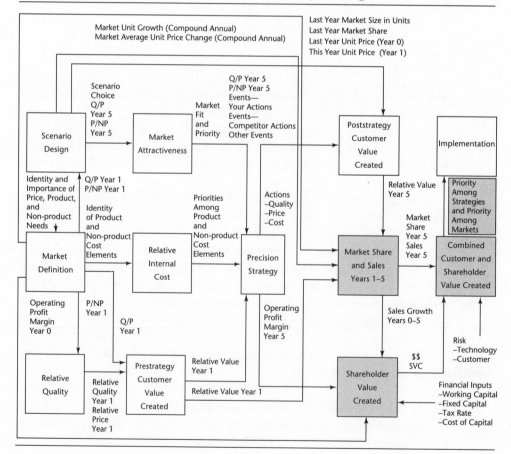

Training

Many organizations have publicly embraced the philosophy of offering customers and shareholders a superior value. Unfortunately, many have not followed through. Consequently, customer value and shareholder value have become empty slogans to employees, customers, and shareholders alike. This usually does not reflect bad faith on the part of management but rather a lack of concepts and tools for moving forward. In a real sense, this entire book has been about implementation and about providing the concepts and tools to make implementation happen. The Market Value Process is a blueprint for moving forward. Now that you know the steps, you are in a position to begin to train others to put these steps into practice.

Sportmed's top management group began its work with the Market Value Process with a training overview of the entire process. The overview gave this group a familiarity with the key maps in the Appendix. The Sportmed team had a high level of enthusiasm for this road map with its principles of focusing equally on customer value and shareholder value and not assuming that either one leads automatically to the other. Having a road map of the steps it needed to follow to reach its goal of combined-value creation gave Sportmed confidence from the outset that it would reach its destination.

It is important to avoid the temptation of working on one or two of the steps in depth to the exclusion of the others. Instead, begin by quickly working through the process from beginning to end in one of your enterprise's key markets to determine the best strategy for it. Then do it for another market and see which market has higher priority.

Creating a Culture Based on Delivering Value to Both Customers and Shareholders

The completion of initial training should mark the beginning of an enterprise's effort to create a combined-value culture.

During the 1980s and 1990s, a number of books have been written about the relationship between corporate culture and performance. There is a growing body of evidence that one of the keys to performance is a top management group that shares values concerning the importance of satisfying customer, employee, and shareholder needs, providing empirical support for the validity of the graphic on the title page.[1] Focusing on just one constituency doesn't get the job done.

Sportmed's management group satisfied all three constituencies by creating value for customers and shareholders through employee teams empowered to do what was necessary to create combined value. In learning the concepts and tools of the Market Value Process in Chapters Three through Thirteen, you must not lose sight of the reality that it was Sportmed's planning teams that were using these concepts and tools, step by step, to build the precision strategies they selected in Chapter Thirteen. The result was so successful precisely because of this balanced emphasis on employees, customers, and shareholders. The balanced focus provided by the book's graphic is so important that we show it again in Exhibit 14.2. None of the three dominates the picture, as advocates of one constituency or the other might suggest. All three need to fit in place. Since you have read Chapter Seven, the shell-burst icon has additional meaning for you. The icon shows that this balanced focus leads to a "Take No Prisoners" result in the competition for creating shareholder value, just as it did in the competition for creating customer value.

Just Starting

Immediately after completing initial training, Sportmed's thirty-person top management group, including the president, divided itself into cross-functional planning teams to build precision strategies in each of the markets it had defined. A group began to work its way through the Market Value Process in each of the Progressive, Traditional, and Commercial Markets. Sportmed empowered each group to make the key decisions in each of its markets, subject only to a peer review from members of other teams at the end of the planning process. Each team shared with the others the lessons learned as the process moved forward.

Exhibit 14.2.

Winning cultures have a balanced focus among customers, shareholders, and employees.

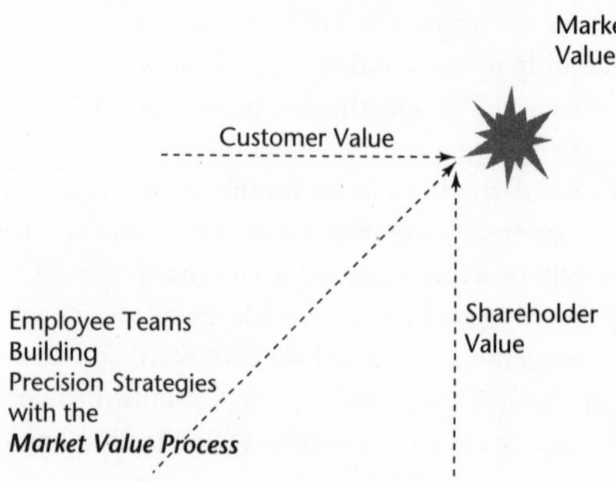

Market Value

Customer Value

Employee Teams Building Precision Strategies with the *Market Value Process*

Shareholder Value

Keeping It Simple

Implementing all twelve steps of the Market Value Process and the strategies that result makes it essential to keep things simple at each step. We have emphasized many times in the book that strategies can usually be expressed in fewer rather than many words and that simple measuring and mapping approaches often work better than more sophisticated ones that are more difficult to use. Broad, streamlined thinking will usually dominate narrow, deep thinking that doesn't cover the required ground. Each of the Sportmed teams came up with a precision strategy on a single page similar to the one we saw in Exhibit 9.10.

Expecting Full Results and Expecting It to Be Fun

Sportmed's management group worked through the entire process in each market in about sixty days. Each of the teams met individually on a weekly basis to keep the effort moving ahead. Because of the compact, user-friendly nature of the Market Value Process, Sportmed was able to do this while continuing to keep the company running smoothly. At the end of the sixty days, the groups assembled as a single body, and each team reviewed its work with its peers from the other teams. The flow of the presentations, using the charts in the Appendix, was identical to the flow you have followed in Chapters Three through Thirteen of this book. Everyone felt very confident with the result. At least as importantly, they felt that the process for arriving at the result had been the "event of the year," and this created momentum and consensus for moving ahead to implement the quality, price, and cost actions that comprised each precision strategy.

Encouraging Cross-Functional Involvement

The biggest successes with the Market Value Process come when there is strong cross-functional involvement in the strategy process, as was the case with Sportmed. This is true for two reasons. First, this involvement captures everyone's knowledge about how the customer makes the buying decision. The second reason is that broad involvement captures the highest-level expertise that the various functional areas will have in price, product and non-product quality, and product and non-product cost. This balance of knowledge of how customers buy and how best to offer customers the benefits they seek is key to building precision strategies that win customers and shareholders. In the Preface to this book we listed all the ways that different functional areas could put the Market Value Process into practice. Now is the time to seek this contribution from each function.

Making Sure the Builders Are the Implementers

Since the strategies were being built by the top group of operating managers at Sportmed, the same group was responsible for implementing them successfully. The feeling of ownership of strategies is key to their successful implementation. Involvement builds the commitment that leads to action.

Ownership of implementation for each action item should be spelled out on the Implementation Map, Exhibit 14.3. This is the Integrated Strategy Map from Chapter Nine with all the priorities shown, but here the description of each action has been replaced by the identity of the functional group or process team accountable for its implementation. Then the enterprise establishes a date when the strategy will be put in place and the operating profit margin in the bottom left corner of the Implementation Map will materialize. Finally, the enterprise works backward to set completion dates for each quality, price, and cost action and the intermediate milestones required to complete each of these actions.

Using the Nominal Group Technique to Generate Detailed Action Steps

Sportmed further detailed the actions assigned in Exhibit 14.3 by using a powerful process called the nominal group technique.[2] We will not spell out the actions themselves but simply give the reader the flavor of this process.

The nominal group technique (NGT) is a powerful process for helping the strategy-building team to make the transition to more detailed implementation thinking. It consists of six steps:

Step One: Put a question to the group such as "Who has to do what in order to put this strategy in place?" This provides the focus for everything that follows.

Step Two: In silence, each member generates individual ideas that come to mind. The member jots each of these five- or six-word ideas down on a list. While each idea should be expressed concisely, there is no limit to the number of ideas each member generates. This gives each member's creativity full rein, free from evaluation by others.

Step Three: Share each person's best idea in a round-robin fashion. No discussion of the ideas is allowed. Do this for a second round to capture everyone's second-best idea. Repeat for as many rounds as seems desirable. This way, the group sees the full scope of the members' thinking without premature evaluation.

Step Four: Spend three to ten minutes evaluating each of the two dozen or so ideas that result from Step Three. This brings the group's evaluative thinking into play so that everyone can see the pros and cons of each idea.

Exhibit 14.3. Implementation Map: Progressive Market.

Advanced features, accuracy, ongoing education, consultative selling, purchases, and manufacturing overhead are top-priority items.

Market: Progressive   Competitors: B, C, D
Scenario: "Business as Usual"   Strategy Emphasis: Quality
Objective: Hold Market Share   Future Slope: High: Q/P = 65/35

Quality Strategy		*Priority*	*Ownership for Implementation*
P1	Advanced Features	1	Research & Development
P2	Multifunctions	3	Research & Development
P3	Accuracy	1	Research & Development
P4	Ease of Use	3	Research & Development
	Summary		Emphasize advanced features and accuracy
N1	Ongoing Education	1	Marketing
N2	Service	2	Customer Service
N3	Reputation	·2	Marketing
N4	Consultative Selling	1	Sales
	Summary		Emphasize ongoing education and consultative selling

Price Strategy		Sales

Cost Strategy		
P1	Purchases	Manufacturing
P2	Direct Labor	Manufacturing
P3	Manufacturing Overhead	Manufacturing
P4	Research & Development	Research & Development
	Summary	Emphasize purchases and manufacturing overhead
N1	Marketing	Marketing
N2	Customer Service	Customer Service
	Summary	Make sure high quality requires our 36 percent non-product cost disadvantage

Operating Profit Margin (When Strategy Is in Place)	15%

Step Five: Vote on the ideas in a private process. Each member gives five points to the idea that the member feels to be the best, four to the second best, three to the third best, two to the fourth best, and one to the fifth best. The fifth-best idea is by no means a weak one, since it is fifth from a list of about two dozen. In this way, each member has an equal voice in evaluating, without peer pressure, the list of ideas that has been set forth and discussed.

Step Six: Add up the total points for each idea. The first winning idea is the one with the highest total points. The second winning idea is the one with the second highest total, and so on down. The group of highest-scoring ideas is a prioritized idea map of the group's thinking on the subject.

Human behavioral professionals would say that the NGT creates an excellent map of the group's thinking on the question posed in the first step. During Steps Two and Three—individual idea generation and round-robin idea sharing—members who are usually silent have as much chance to contribute as those who are usually more vocal. During Step Four, the group discussion of each idea, everyone's critical judgment, both positive and negative, comes to bear. In the private voting process, individual thinking again operates without peer interaction or pressure. The end result is a detailed implementation plan shaped by a combination of individual thinking and group participation. The group has high confidence in the end result since everyone has watched it unfold.

In a final level of action planning, each member of the cross-functional team leads a similar process within the member's own functional area to create a detailed functional implementation plan.

As a final thought on the NGT, no idea presented should be ignored, even if it receives no votes. Remember that it was one of the top ideas on some individual's list. It may be a brand-new idea whose merit is only beginning to emerge. The NGT is so powerful and comprehensive that the implementation team should not discard any part of its output.

Communicating Your Strategies the Same Way You Build Them

Sportmed set priorities for building its quality strategies based on whether a need was important to customers, whether the potential for competitors to differentiate their offering in providing this benefit was high, and whether Sportmed had an opportunity to pull ahead of the pack. There can be no better way for an enterprise to win customers than to convince them that this is just what its offering delivers. The enterprise must communicate to its customers that it understands their important needs, that it has better ways to meet them than the competitors do, and that it is out in front of the competition in doing this—and at a fair price. We saw how to begin this communication effort at the end of Chapter Nine. Communicating to customers this kind of superior value at the end of the trail that the enterprise has mapped and followed will propel the enterprise to leadership in its most attractive markets and reward its shareholders in the process.

Redoing the Process Each Time a Competitor Makes a Major Move or You Enter a New Market

If a competitor makes a major move such as introducing a new product, an enterprise must respond rapidly. Virtually every Information Age example we have used in this book requires frequent rethinking as the competitive situation changes. The best way to respond is to work through the Market Value Process to assess the impact of the response. A person familiar with the process can work through all twelve steps in two hours. Without doing this, an enterprise can't know the impact its countermoves will have on combined customer and shareholder value, and good decisions hinge on this knowledge. It is even more important to redo the process when entering new markets, as the following example demonstrates.

Keeping Implementation Rolling at Motorola

In an April 18, 1994, article entitled "Keeping Motorola on a Roll," *Fortune* described Motorola's past achievements and the challenges it faces in continuing them.[3] Motorola is superbly managed—but doubling in size every five years, it faces the curse of bigness.

Mention Motorola, the company that almost everyone loves to love, and the accolades fairly gush: titan of TQM, epitome of empowerment, tribune of training, icon of invention, prince of profits. A leader in the worldwide revolution in wireless communications, this manufacturer of cellular telephones, pagers, two-way radios, semiconductors, and other electronic gadgets has become that most unusual of creatures—a big company that sizzles.

At issue now is whether Motorola can keep getting better as it keeps getting bigger, whether this huge, decentralized, multinational corporation can avoid falling victim to the bureaucracy, complacency, and hubris that have afflicted so many other large American businesses.

Motorola's sales jumped 27 percent to a record $17 billion in 1993, propelling the company to the number twenty-three spot on the Fortune 500. Earnings surged 127 percent to $1 billion, and analysts envision this continuing in the future. Even in the skittish 1994 stock market, Motorola shares traded at all-time highs. Says Anthony Langham, a NatWest Securities analyst who has followed Motorola for twenty-six years, "This company is just on a tremendous roll. They're very, very good at everything they do."

Motorola's transformation from a slowly declining American electronics company to a world-beating, Baldrige Award–winning powerhouse has become the stuff of industrial legend. Management books and business school case studies have chronicled the company's fanatic pursuit of six-sigma (3.4 mistakes per million) quality, its high-profile battles with the Japanese, and its pioneering advances in self-directed work teams, training, and business process reengineering. Consultants marvel at the way Motorola decentralizes decision making, breaks down organizational boundaries, and promotes cooperation between labor and management. Calling the company an exemplar of the "high-performance workplace," Labor Secretary Robert Reich recently awarded Motorola—which has no unions—his prestigious Opportunity 2000 award.

With all this good news, we have to work hard to see clouds on the horizon. Perhaps there are two.

The first cloud is pressure on employees. Training is one of Motorola's enormous strengths. The company's Motorola University is one of the most renowned corporate training organizations in the country, so when it speaks, people listen. William Wiggenhorn, corporate director of training believes that in the immediate future, Motorola must help employees deal with the stress of working in a hothouse environment where sixty-hour-plus weeks are common: "We say, 'Take risks,' but we also say, 'Do it right the first time.' Well, that can drive you to your psychologist real quick." The answer, he says, is to allow people to make a mistake and learn from it but not to repeat it.

The second cloud is that the company must become more adept at marketing. Admits Gary Tooker, who became CEO when George Fisher abruptly decamped to take charge of Eastman Kodak, "A lot of the six-sigma approach has been internal, taking defects out and saving money. But the totality of what the customer expects and what will really satisfy him includes lots of other things."

As Motorola churns out more affordable, pocketable products, it edges nearer to its roots as a consumer electronics company, a role it largely abandoned when it sold its color TV business to Matsushita in 1974. In early 1994, Motorola unveiled Envoy, its first handheld "personal wireless communicator." Unlike competing products such as Apple's Newton MessagePad, this device has a built-in modem. You can use Envoy, which weighs just 1.7 pounds and will retail for about $1,500, to write and send a fax, fetch your E-mail, tie into the Internet and America Online, manage your appointments, track your expenses, and order flowers for your cousin's wedding.

With products like Envoy, Motorola enters the frenetically competitive world of personal computing. Says Ira Brodsky, president of Datacom Research (a

Wilmette, Illinois, consulting firm), "As they move into the computer market, giving long-winded speeches about microscopic measures of quality isn't going to matter much. Consumers expect these things to work. The company needs to focus on packaging and promotion. Motorola has a marketing weakness."

Perhaps, but the company is addressing the issue. Motorola has begun recruiting marketing experts from companies like General Electric, Black & Decker, Apple Computer, and even Mattel. An outfit that has long followed the Henry Ford dictum on customer preference—any color as long as it's black—now offers pagers in eight different hues. You can buy one at Wal-Mart in a see-through plastic package (they used to come in opaque cardboard boxes), complete with the Good Housekeeping seal. With a television and magazine ad campaign launched in 1993, Motorola is targeting baby boomers, especially women. The main theme: security. If Mom packs a pager, the baby-sitter can reach her in an emergency.

In light of its past achievements, few would bet against Motorola's success in competing in this new market, as long as it keeps on top of the consumer's shifting needs.

Staying on Top of the Markets

A market-driven enterprise has a balanced customer and competitor focus. Apart from responding to the competition, the cross-functional employee teams need to be intensely alert to changes in customer needs, and they need to update their strategies to meet these shifting needs with continuing precision. As needs shift, the teams may need to redefine markets, using the Market Value Process to rethink the entire situation. The success of the Market Value Process ultimately depends on this final set of tasks: staying on top of shifting needs, responding with precision strategies, making sure these strategies create value for both customers and shareholders, and spelling out detailed implementation actions.

AN OVERVIEW OF A PRECISION STRATEGY

To maximize the usefulness of this book, this Appendix collects the key maps in the Market Value Process. This accomplishes two things. First, it enables you to see, in a streamlined and totally integrated way, an overview of the Sportmed example. Second, you can use this collection of maps as the step-by-step master road map for building precision strategies for each market served by your own enterprise and for mapping the combined customer and shareholder value these strategies create.

The process begins by identifying customer needs. We distinguish between core product needs and surrounding non-product needs, because strategy builders often underestimate the importance of the latter. Exhibit 3.1 depicts these needs for the business area of sports medicine instruments. Frequently, an enterprise uses focus groups as a means to identify key product and non-product needs and customer visit programs to stay abreast of any changes in these needs. Sometimes the enterprise envisions needs that customers are only dimly aware of or not aware of at all.

A creative aspect of the process is to think imaginatively of approaches to market definition in the three categories depicted in the three columns of Exhibit 3.2. One part of this creativity is the ability to conceive of nontraditional definitions; such definitions can help you detect greater differences in needs among customer groups than conventional approaches to definition will. Underlying each

Exhibit 3.1. Customers' Product and Non-product Needs:
Sports Medicine Instruments.

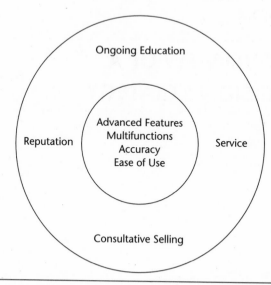

market in each approach is the same set of product and non-product needs we see in Exhibit 3.1.

While we have limited our discussion for Sportmed to two approaches in each category, there is actually no limit to the number of approaches an enterprise should consider in each. The more approaches considered, the better is the chance of finding a more creative one.

Having accomplished the creative step of identifying a number of choices, an enterprise now needs to make a judgment regarding which approach in each category discloses the greatest differences in importance that customers in each market attach to these common needs. The highlighted areas reflect these judgments.

Next, Exhibit 3.3 depicts, in three dimensions, the judgments made in Exhibit 3.2 regarding the "best" choice for the "who," "what," and "how" categories. Remember that the criterion for making this judgment is which choice discloses the greatest difference in price, product, and non-product needs between the two markets that underlie the approaches in each category. The value this "cube" adds to the information in Exhibit 3.2 is that it allows an enterprise to visualize the intersections among markets. As a consequence, each customer can be assigned simultaneously to one of the two markets in each approach along each dimension.

Exhibit 3.2. Alternative Approaches to Market Definition.

Business Area: Sports Medicine Instruments

"Whose price, product, and non-product needs are being met"	"What price, product, and non-product needs are being met"	"How price, product, and non-product needs are being met"
Approach: Age Market: Young Practitioners Market: Older Practitioners	Psychographics Progressive Traditional	Technology for Delivering Results Computer Display Printout
Approach: Specialty Market: Specialist—SM Market: Generalist—GP	Patient Diagnosis Muscle and Tendon Other	Testing Technology Nonmicroprocessor Based Microprocessor Based

Exhibit 3.3. Approaches That Reveal the Greatest Differences Along Each Dimension: Sportmed.

Business Area:
   Sports Medicine
   Instruments

Vertical Markets:
"Whose price, product, and non-product needs are being met"

Horizontal Markets:
"What price, product, and non-product needs are being met"

Diagonal Markets:
"How price, product, and non-product needs are being met"

Specialty Approach
Specialist Market | Generalist Market

Testing-Technology Approach
Microprocessor-Based Market

Nonmicroprocessor-Based Market

Psychographics Approach
Traditional Practitioner Market

Progressive Practitioner Market

It is important to realize, however, that it can be dangerous to define markets using approaches along the diagonal (front to back) dimension, alternative technology. This is true because the next step, after selecting the technology approach, is often to overfocus on only one of an enterprise's technology markets—its own—and to overlook others. It is risky to define markets in a way that encourages an enterprise to exclude competing technologies from its thought process.

An enterprise makes an informed judgment regarding the importance that customers in each market attach to their common set of price, product, and non-product needs. The scores of alternative approaches to market definition can be compared as shown in Exhibit 3.5, and the largest total difference score will indicate the best choice of approach to market definition. The "best" choice, in this case, is the psychographic one with a total difference score of 60, compared to 40 for the specialty approach.

Offerings tailored to the quality-sensitive Progressives and the price-sensitive Traditionals will be more distinctly different from each other than offerings tailored to SMs and GPs. Progressives and Traditionals will easily recognize which offering's benefit profile matches their need profile and move quickly to buy that offering. Offerings tailored for SMs and GPs, on the other hand, have a higher risk of being indistinct from each other and of more easily creating confusion among customers regarding which offering was tailored for which group. The result of this confusion would be lost sales.

Exhibit 3.5. Difference Scores of Alternative Approaches to Market Definition.

	Assessments Specialty Approach			Assessments Psychographics Approach	
	SM		GP	Progressive	Traditional
Price	40		60	35	65
Quality	60		40	65	35
Product	50		65	50	60
Non-product	50		35	50	40

	Measurements Specialty Differences			Measurements Psychographics Differences		
Price	40	20	60	35	30	65
Product	30	4	26	32.5	11.5	21
Non-product	30	16	14	32.5	18.5	14
Total Difference Score		40			60	

Exhibit 3.6. Market Definition Map:
Sports Medicine Instruments Business Area.

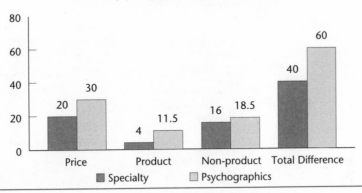

**Both the specialty and psychographics approaches are good,
but the psychographics approach is better.**

Exhibit 3.6 shows the picture painted by the numbers in Exhibit 3.5. This chart adds value by allowing us to compare, side by side and graphically, the price, product, and non-product buildup of the 60 and 40 scores for the psychographics and specialty approaches.

Once an enterprise has defined its markets by uncovering differences in price, product, and non-product needs, the next issue is to envision how these needs will evolve over time. The best way to do this is to determine the greatest uncertainty the market faces and then to describe different outcomes of this uncertainty using scenarios. Since the greatest uncertainty is often the timing, source, and magnitude of the next breakthrough in technology, tracking innovation is an important focus of scenario design. The degree of innovation determines the price-versus-quality sensitivity of each market. Exhibit 4.4 depicts a scenario space map that defines scenarios in the space created by innovation along the product and non-product dimensions. The sides of the chart show varying degrees of innovation in the four product and four non-product needs from Exhibit 3.1. The combinations of different levels of product and non-product innovation create scenarios, five of which are depicted in Exhibit 4.4.

Sportmed, our disguised example, decided to develop in detail the scenarios it had named "Business as Usual," "Falling Asleep," and "Creative Destruction." The three columns in Exhibit 4.5 depict these three scenarios. The third row of boxes from the bottom shows that quality is half or more of the buying

Exhibit 4.4. Scenario Space Map: Progressive Market.

Driver 1: Non-product Innovation
Education
Service
Reputation
Consultative Selling

Driver 2: Product Innovation Advanced Features Multifunctions Accuracy Ease of Use		Medium	High	Very High
	Very High	"Engineering Innovation" Scenario Q/P = 65/35 P/NP = 60/40		"Creative Destruction" Scenario Q/P = 80/20 P/NP = 50/50
	High		Conventional Wisdom "Business as Usual" Scenario Q/P = 65/35 P/NP = 50/50	
	Medium	"Falling Asleep" Scenario Q/P = 50/50 P/NP = 50/50		"Marketing Innovation" Scenario Q/P = 65/35 P/NP = 40/60

decision under all scenarios. The second row of boxes from the bottom highlights the logical conclusion that quality will be a critical component of a successful strategy under any scenario. The bottom row shows the specific outcomes envisioned under each scenario for market unit growth and market unit price.

Once an enterprise has defined its markets and envisioned their evolution, it must determine whether there is a good fit between its core competencies and the evolving price, product, and non-product needs of each market. Exhibit 5.2 provides a summary of such an assessment for the Progressive and Traditional Markets. The Progressive Market is attractive because there is a good fit between the value leverage factor in that market—quality—and Sportmed's core competence, which is also quality. The Traditional Market is unattractive because the fit is poor.

Having focused on markets, the enterprise now shifts its attention to market position and its consequence, market share. The starting point is to measure and

Exhibit 4.5. Scenario Map: Progressive Market.

Sportmed wrote three plays with three different end states and strategy implications.

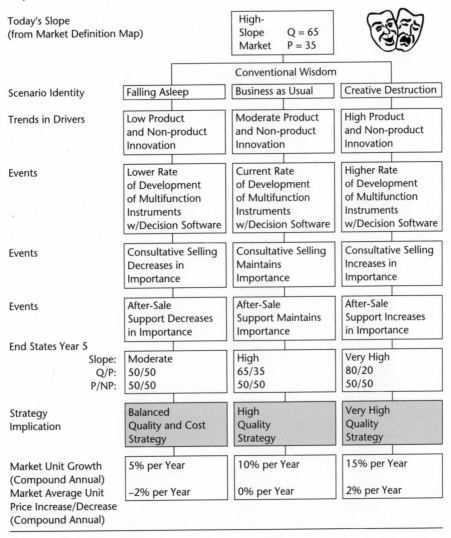

	Falling Asleep	Business as Usual	Creative Destruction
Today's Slope (from Market Definition Map)		High-Slope Market Q = 65 P = 35	
		Conventional Wisdom	
Scenario Identity	Falling Asleep	Business as Usual	Creative Destruction
Trends in Drivers	Low Product and Non-product Innovation	Moderate Product and Non-product Innovation	High Product and Non-product Innovation
Events	Lower Rate of Development of Multifunction Instruments w/Decision Software	Current Rate of Development of Multifunction Instruments w/Decision Software	Higher Rate of Development of Multifunction Instruments w/Decision Software
Events	Consultative Selling Decreases in Importance	Consultative Selling Maintains Importance	Consultative Selling Increases in Importance
Events	After-Sale Support Decreases in Importance	After-Sale Support Maintains Importance	After-Sale Support Increases in Importance
End States Year 5 Slope: Q/P: P/NP:	Moderate 50/50 50/50	High 65/35 50/50	Very High 80/20 50/50
Strategy Implication	Balanced Quality and Cost Strategy	High Quality Strategy	Very High Quality Strategy
Market Unit Growth (Compound Annual) Market Average Unit Price Increase/Decrease (Compound Annual)	5% per Year −2% per Year	10% per Year 0% per Year	15% per Year 2% per Year

map its customer-perceived quality relative to the competition in each market. To do this, the enterprise must assess the relative perceived benefits that its offering provides in each of the product and non-product needs the customer seeks to satisfy in making the buying decision. Exhibit 6.1 captures the judgments that customers make about the price, product, and non-product benefits that

Exhibit 5.2. Market Attractiveness Map: Sports Medicine Instruments Business Area.

The Progressive market is more attractive than the Traditional market.

Market/ Scenario	Q/P Year 5	Core Competence Required	Have It or Can Gain It	Attractiveness/ Priority
Progressive Practitioner/ "Business as Usual" Scenario	65/35	Quality	Have it	High Good fit between value leverage factor and core competence
Traditional Practitioner/ "Business as Usual" Scenario	35/65	Cost	Don't have it; unclear whether we can gain it	Low Poor fit between value leverage factor and core competence

Competitor A, Sportmed, and its three key competitors, B, C, and D, offer in the Progressive Market.

The Position Map in Exhibit 6.4 shows that Sportmed's relative perceived quality score of 23 percent, the bottom bar, exceeds the 20 percent goal in the Progressive Market. It is critical to have this quality edge in a quality-sensitive market. The eight pairs of bars show the buildup of the 23 percent score. In each pair, the top bar depicts Sportmed's performance on that need and the bottom bar depicts the importance weight of that need. Sportmed is performing above average on each product and non-product need from Exhibit 3.1 except P2, multifunctions, and P4, ease of use.

The quality and price scores from Exhibit 6.1 can be taken together to depict the relative customer value each seller is offering, as perceived by the customer. The Customer Value Map, Exhibit 7.4, positions each competitor based on its relative price and quality. Competitors positioned below the "market wants" line are offering a superior value because they offer a better quality-for-the-price trade-off than the market is prepared to accept. In this case, Competitor A, Sportmed, because of its high +23 percent relative quality and moderate +5 percent relative price premium in a quality-sensitive market, offers the best value to the customer. The Customer Value Map provides the foundation on which an enterprise can

Exhibit 6.1. Buying Decision: Progressive Market.

Customers make the buying decision by attaching an importance weight and a performance rating to each price, product, and non-product need.

Quality	65	A = Sportmed
Price	35	B = Competitor B
		C = Competitor C
Product	50	D = Competitor D
Non-product	50	

	Competitive Price per Unit (A = 100)			
	A	B	C	D
Price	100	85	95	100

Product Needs	Importance Weight	Competitive Performance Ratings			
		A	B	C	D
Advanced Features	14	8	6	7	8
Multifunctions	12	5	7	7	7
Accuracy	14	10	6	7	8
Ease of Use	10	6	7	7	6
Non-product Needs					
Ongoing Education	13	8	5	5	7
Service	10	9	5	5	3
Reputation	12	9	5	6	7
Consultative Selling	15	8	6	5	3

build precision strategies to improve its value proposition. It also suggests the moves that the competitors might make to improve their own value proposition.

Next the enterprise needs to measure its relative unit cost, which is the cost per instrument produced in Sportmed's case.

Exhibit 8.5 shows that relative unit total cost is a weighted average of relative unit product cost and relative unit non-product cost. The top half of the chart shows competitors' unit costs as a percentage of Sportmed's. In the bottom half of the chart, competitive costs are expressed as a percentage of market average. The bottom row shows that Sportmed has a unit total cost of 114, or 14 percent above the competitive average. This means that Sportmed will have difficulty competing on price in this market; this is one of the reasons that it is charging the +5 percent premium in relative price that we just saw on the Customer Value Map. Immediately above the 114 score we can see its components—a 36 percent disadvantage in unit non-product cost and a 4 percent disadvantage in unit product cost.

Exhibit 6.4. Position Map: Progressive Market—Competitor A.

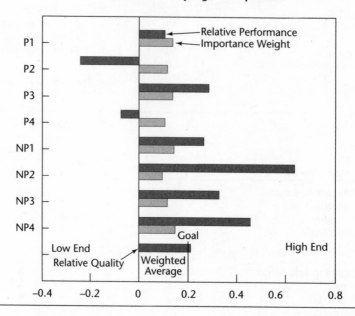

Competitor A has exceeded the 20 percent relative quality goal and attained a "very high-end" position.

Exhibit 7.4. Customer Value Map: Progressive Market.

Competitor A is offering a superior relative value.

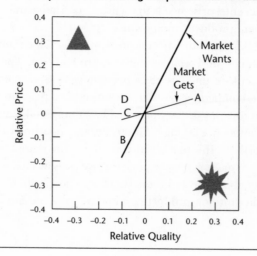

Exhibit 8.5. Relative Unit Total Costs: Sportmed.

Relative total cost per unit produced is a weighted average of relative unit product cost and relative unit non-product cost. The weights are the market average product/non-product cost structure.

		Cost as a Percent of Competitor A				
		A	B	C	D	Average
Unit Product Cost		100	88	93	102	96
Unit Non-product Cost		100	70	75	50	74

	Market Average as Percent of Total	Cost as a Percent of Market Average			
		A	B	C	D
Unit Product Cost	69	104	92	97	107
Unit Non-product Cost	31	136	95	102	68
Unit Total Cost	100	114	93	99	95

Similar to the Customer Value Map, the Cost Map in Exhibit 8.7 depicts each competitors' relative unit cost position in producing the product benefits and the non-product benefits. As is true for the Customer Value Map, the desirable positioning for a competitor on the Cost Map is to be "below the line." Sportmed, Competitor A, is positioned at a 36 percent disadvantage in non-product cost and a 4 percent disadvantage in product cost. This positions Sportmed above the neutral cost line in the cost disadvantage area.

Sportmed combined its quality, price, and cost strategies into a final integrated customer value strategy that is summarized in Exhibit 9.10. This precise, one-page summary is a very powerful encapsulation of the action steps Sportmed plans to take for each product and non-product quality need, its price, and each area of product and non-product cost in order to hold share in the quality-driven Progressive Market. Sportmed anticipates this strategy will deliver a 15 percent operating profit margin once it has been put in place.

We have made the case for the merits of a one-page strategy statement. We make the case for an even more concise marketing communication statement. It must be extremely brief and hard-hitting.

The challenge is to develop a message that communicates the four top-priority needs from Exhibit 9.10—advanced features, accuracy, ongoing education, and consultative selling. The action steps for the two product needs—advanced features and accuracy—are to introduce new models of all instruments with software that interprets results. Sportmed devised the message, "Leading-edge software boosts

Exhibit 8.7. Cost Map: Progressive Market.

A's relative unit total cost is 14 percent above the competitive average caused by a disadvantage of 4 percent in product cost and 36 percent in non-product cost.

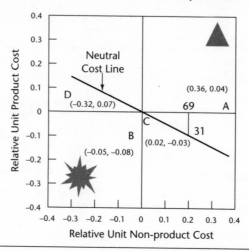

Relative Unit Non-product Cost

diagnostic precision." This message does a workmanlike job of communicating, in a single phrase, features, accuracy, education, and consultative selling. It becomes the foundation for Sportmed's media campaign. Exhibit 9.12 summarizes the result.

Exhibit 11.1 shows the Price Map, a combination of Year-One and Year-Five Customer Value Maps. These Value Maps provide the basis for envisioning an enterprise's relative price evolution. Note the positioning of the enterprise, Competitor A, in years one and five. Focus on the vertical distance at which A is positioned above or below the zero relative price line in each Value Map. In year one, Competitor A is 0.08 above this line, offering a relative price that is 108 percent of the market average. In year five, Competitor A's position is 0.07 above this line, a relative price of 107 percent. At the bottom of the chart the enterprise shows these two end points together with its year-to-year timetable for moving from one end point to the other.

In Exhibit 11.2, carried values from a number of earlier steps in the Market Value Process converge to help an enterprise envision its unit price evolution over the strategy period. Item six is the relative price evolution we just saw in Exhibit 11.1. The unique contribution of this approach to envisioning an enterprise's unit price evolution is that it is based on the enterprise's positioning on its

Exhibit 9.10. Integrated Strategy Map: Progressive Market.

 Advanced features, accuracy, ongoing education, consultative selling, purchases, and manufacturing overhead are top-priority items.

Market: Progressive	Competitors: B, C, D
Scenario: "Business as Usual"	Strategy Emphasis: Quality
Objective: Hold Market Share	Future Slope: High: Q/P = 65/35

	Quality Strategy	*Priority*	
P1	Advanced Features	1	Invest heavily in current and new models of all instruments
P2	Multifunctions	3	Link current and new models using electronic media
P3	Accuracy	1	Invest in software that interprets results
P4	Ease of Use	3	Develop user interface that is easy to use
	Summary		Emphasize advanced features and accuracy
N1	Ongoing Education	1	Increase funding for seminars and resident programs
N2	Service	2	Continue to improve service response time
N3	Reputation	2	Maintain quality of advertising and promotion; provide donations to schools
N4	Consultative Selling	1	Develop sales aids, proof sources, and financial models
	Summary		Emphasize ongoing education and consultative selling
	Price Strategy		Increase from 5 percent above market average to "market wants" line

	Cost Strategy	
P1	Purchases	Continue to select JIT/TQC suppliers; explore strategic off-shore alliances
P2	Direct Labor	Enhance productivity by providing cross training
P3	Manufacturing Overhead	Increase productivity by job consolidation (for example, buyer-planner)
P4	Research & Development	Increase R&D spending 2 percent above current level as percent of sales
	Summary	Emphasize purchases and manufacturing overhead
N1	Marketing	Develop managers with global focus; increase promotion and advertising
N2	Customer Service	Continue present level of support (customer call back, 800 number, customer visits)
	Summary	Make sure high quality requires our 36 percent non-product cost disadvantage
	Operating Profit Margin (When Strategy Is in Place)	15%

P = Product; N = Non-product; Q/P = Quality/Price

Exhibit 9.12. Marketing Communication Campaign: Sports Medicine Instruments.

Market:	Progressive practitioner
Message:	Leading-edge software boosts diagnostic precision
Medium:	Journal ads—sports medicine journals
	Direct mail to top prescription-writing practitioners
	Booth at national sports medicine convention

prestrategy and poststrategy Customer Value Maps. It thereby automatically reflects the enterprise's strategic objectives and reflects the logic of the enterprise's integrated customer value strategy.

The Market Share Map, a different combination of Year-One and Year-Five Customer Value Maps, helps an enterprise envision its market share evolution over the strategy period. This map shows that Competitor A's strategy will move it from a lose market share position in year one to a gain market share position in year five. The year-to-year timetable for moving from one position to the other appears at the bottom of Exhibit 11.3.

Exhibit 11.1. Price Map: Progressive Market.

Your year-one and year-five Customer Value Maps provide the basis for envisioning your relative price evolution.

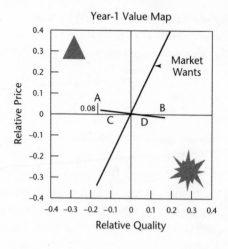

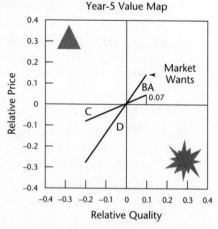

	Year 1	Year 2	Year 3	Year 4	Year 5
Relative Price, Competitor A	108	108	107	107	107

Exhibit 11.2. Measuring the Unit Price Component of Your Customer Value Strategy.

	Year Zero	Year One	Year Two	Year Three	Year Four	Year Five
1. Your Unit Price Today (Market Definition Map)		$12.00				
2. Your Relative Price Today (Value Map, Year One)		108				
3. Market Average Unit Price Today: (1)/(2)		$11.11				
4. Market Average Unit Price Change (Scenario Map)			+10%	+10%	+10%	+10%
5. Market Average Unit Price Outlook: (3) × (4)			$12.22	$13.44	$14.79	$16.27
6. Your Relative Price Strategy (Value Map, Years One and Five)		108	108	107	107	107
7. Your Unit Price Last Year (Market Definition Map)	$10.00					
8. Your Unit Price Outlook: (5) × (6)			$13.20	$14.39	$15.82	$17.41

Once an enterprise has made a market share judgment, it has all the ingredients to determine its sales outlook for the strategy period. Again, many items of carried value from earlier steps in the Market Value Process come into play. Item 4 in Exhibit 11.4 reflects the market share judgments we just saw in Exhibit 11.3. By following the steps outlined in Exhibit 11.4, the enterprise can envision its sales growth in a way that reflects key expectations regarding market unit growth, market unit size, market share change, and unit price change from earlier steps. This sales growth is one of the key factors that determine how much shareholder value a strategy creates.

The enterprise is now ready to examine the inputs that determine the amount of shareholder value created by its integrated customer value strategies (Exhibit 12.3). The first two inputs—sales growth and operating profit margin—are carried value from earlier steps in the Market Value Process. The highlighted 15 percent operating profit margin is carried from the Integrated Strategy Map, Exhibit 9.10. The last four inputs reflect the financial situation of the business. These include the net fixed capital and net working capital required to support each dollar of sales increase, the tax rate, and the cost of capital. These six inputs are all that the enterprise needs to calculate the shareholder value a strategy creates.

By using the inputs from Exhibit 12.3, Sportmed determined that shareholder value created by its hold share strategy in the Progressive Market is

---

Exhibit 11.3. Market Share Map: Progressive Market.

Your year-one and year-five Customer Value Maps provide the basis
for envisioning your market share evolution.

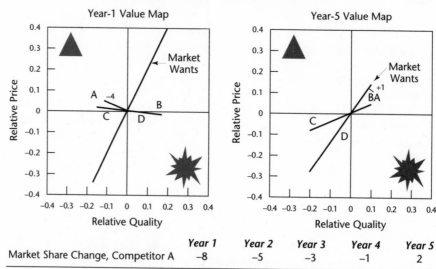

	Year 1	Year 2	Year 3	Year 4	Year 5
Market Share Change, Competitor A	−8	−5	−3	−1	2

Exhibit 11.4. Measuring the Sales Your
Integrated Customer Value Strategy Generates.

	Year Zero	Year One	Year Two	Year Three	Year Four	Year Five
1. Market Unit Growth (Scenario Map)		+10%	+10%	+10%	+10%	+10%
2. Market Unit Size (Market Definition Map)	10,000					
3. Market Unit Size Outlook: (1) × (2)		11,000	12,100	13,310	14,641	16,105
4. Market Share Change (Value Map, Years One and Five)		−8%	−5%	−3%	−1%	+2%
5. Your Market Share (Market Definition Map)	25%					
6. Your Market Share Outlook: (4) + (5)		17%	12%	9%	8%	10%
7. Your Unit Sales Outlook: (3) × (6)	2,500	1,870	1,452	1,198	1,171	1,611
8. Your Unit Price Outlook (From Exhibit 11.2)	$10.00	$12.00	$13.20	$14.39	$15.82	$17.41
9. Your Dollar Sales Outlook: (7) × (8)	$25,000	$22,440	$19,166	$17,238	$18,530	$28,039

Exhibit 12.3. Inputs to Measuring Shareholder Value Created: Progressive Market.

	Year 0	Year 1	Year 2	Year 3	Year 4	Year 5	Carried Value From Step Number
Sales	63.20	69.50	76.40	84.10	92.50	101.80	9
Operating Profit Margin	0.07	0.08	0.09	0.09	0.12	0.15	1,7
Net Fixed Capital		0.10	0.10	0.10	0.10	0.10	
Net Working Capital		0.30	0.30	0.30	0.30	0.30	
Tax Rate	0.43	0.43	0.43	0.43	0.43	0.43	
Cost of Capital	0.13	0.13	0.13	0.13	0.13	0.13	

Year 0 = Last Year, Year 1 = This Year

$23.80 million (Exhibit 12.4). The component parts are $6.86 million from the present value of cash flow and $16.94 from the present value of the value increase. This is fully described in Chapter Twelve.

Now that the enterprise has measured and mapped the customer value and shareholder value of each of its strategies, the next step is to select the best strategy. The best strategy in each market is the one that creates the best combination of customer and shareholder value. To have choices, the enterprise should build a number of strategies—usually one to support gain, hold, and lose share objectives for each market. To handle this array of strategies, the enterprise needs an evaluation process that is compact and efficient. The information needed to conduct such an evaluation process is summarized in Exhibit 13.3. In total, the enterprise needs five pieces of information, including sales, market share, and

Exhibit 12.4. Shareholder Value Map: Progressive Market.

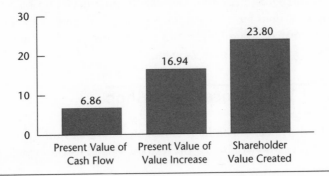

The sales growth and operating profit margins, provided by Competitor A's integrated customer value strategy, create value for shareholders.

Exhibit 13.3. Investment Attractiveness Input Information.

 This is the Investment Attractiveness input information for three objectives for each business under the "Business as Usual" scenario.

Business	Progressive			Traditional			Commercial		
Objective	GS	HS	LS	GS	HS	LS	GS	HS	LS
Sales ($MM)—Year 5	119	102	72	13	8	5	29	19	8
Market Share (%)—Year 5	43	34	24	17	9	6	38	25	16
Technology Risk (C, R, N)	N	R	C	C	C	C	R	C	C
Customer Risk (C, R, N)	N	R	C	N	C	C	R	C	C
Shareholder Value Created ($MM)	29	24	9	5	4	2	7	5	2

GS, HS, LS = Objectives to Gain, Hold, or Lose Market Share
C, R, N = Current, Related, New

shareholder value created, which it brings forward as carried values from earlier parts of the process. To reflect the risk associated with launching its various strategies, the enterprise needs to make judgments regarding the extent to which the various strategies entail technological and customer risk. With these five pieces of information in mind, the enterprise can determine which strategy in each market is best; then it can allocate its resources accordingly.

Exhibit 13.7 shows the combined risk-adjusted customer value (the customer value index) and shareholder value (shareholder value created) that each strategy creates. The higher the combination of shareholder and customer value, the better the strategy. In this case, strategies P (hold share), T (gain share), and C (gain share) offer the greatest investment attractiveness for the Progressive, Traditional, and Commercial Markets, respectively. First priority for investment is the Progressive Market, second priority is the Commercial Market, and the lowest priority is the Traditional Market.

Finally, Exhibit 14.3 shows the Implementation Map. This is in the format of the Integrated Strategy Map, showing the priorities for action. On this chart, however, the actions have been replaced with the identity of the functional group or process team responsible for their implementation. The enterprise is now ready to implement its best strategy in each market.

The Market Value Process Workshop

Cleland Associates conducts hands-on, active learning, private workshops for enterprises who wish to use the Market Value Process to build their own strate-

Exhibit 13.7. Customer and Shareholder Value Map: Sports Medicine Instruments Business Area.

	Customer Value Index (Marketing Strategy)		
Shareholder Value Created (Financial Strategy)	Low	Medium	High
High	Invest —Selectively P(G)	Invest	Invest —Priority P(H)
10			
Medium	Invest —Selectively T(H), T(L) C(L)	Invest T(G), C(H)	Invest C(G), P(L)
0			
Low	Withdraw	Improve Financial Performance or Withdraw	Improve Financial Performance or Withdraw

Strategies P(H), T(G), and C(G) offer the greatest investment attractiveness for the Progressive, Traditional, and Commercial Markets, respectively.

gies. These intensive, two- or three-day programs deliver first-cut strategies similar to the one depicted in this Appendix. Sportmed launched its planning in one of these workshops. If you would like more information on these workshops, we invite you to call us.

Cleland Associates, Inc.
1550 Portola Avenue
Palo Alto, CA 94306
Phone: (415) 323-0953
Fax: (415) 323-6651

Exhibit 14.3. Implementation Map: Progressive Market.

Advanced features, accuracy, ongoing education, consultative selling, purchases, and manufacturing overhead are top-priority items.

Market: Progressive   Competitors: B, C, D
Scenario: "Business as Usual"   Strategy Emphasis: Quality
Objective: Hold Market Share   Future Slope: High: Q/P = 65/35

	Quality Strategy	Priority	Ownership for Implementation
P1	Advanced Features	1	Research & Development
P2	Multifunctions	3	Research & Development
P3	Accuracy	1	Research & Development
P4	Ease of Use	3	Research & Development
	Summary		Emphasize advanced features and accuracy
N1	Ongoing Education	1	Marketing
N2	Service	2	Customer Service
N3	Reputation	2	Marketing
N4	Consultative Selling	1	Sales
	Summary		Emphasize ongoing education and consultative selling
	Price Strategy		Sales
	Cost Strategy		
P1	Purchases		Manufacturing
P2	Direct Labor		Manufacturing
P3	Manufacturing Overhead		Manufacturing
P4	Research & Development		Research & Development
	Summary		Emphasize purchases and manufacturing overhead
N1	Marketing		Marketing
N2	Customer Service		Customer Service
	Summary		Make sure high quality requires our 36 percent non-product cost disadvantage
	Operating Profit Margin (When Strategy Is in Place)		15%

GLOSSARY

Bermuda Triangle. A position in the upper left corner of the Customer Value Map where a competitor is offering below-average quality for above-average price and is therefore losing market share. Its counterpart on the Cost Map is the upper right corner: above average in both product cost and non-product cost.

business attractiveness. The reward—market share and sales in year five—that customers give an enterprise for its position on the Customer Value Map.

carried value. A key result that is the output of a step in the Market Value Process and is carried forward as an input to a future step.

combined value. The amount of customer and shareholder value that a strategy creates.

combined-value problem. The failure of a strategy to meet customer needs with the precision necessary to create enough combined customer and shareholder value to make the strategy work.

core competence. A bundle of skills and technologies that enables the enterprise to provide a particular benefit to customers.

creative market definition. Figuring out the way to divide customers into groups having bigger differences in needs among them than any other way of defining can produce.

customer value. Quality for the price, where quality consists of both the product and non-product benefits the customer is seeking.

customer value index. Profiles the risk and reward of a strategy because it combines the market share and sales reward, flowing from an enterprise's position on the Customer Value Map, with the risk an enterprise takes to arrive at this position.

double-win one. The Innovator in a market scores a double win by simultaneously creating a high-slope, quality-sensitive market and becoming the quality leader in that market.

double-win two. An enterprise that follows the rule of twenty and two-thirds in building its price strategy scores a double win by simultaneously pricing low enough to please customers and high enough to satisfy shareholders.

double-win three. An enterprise that builds its quality strategy on pull-ahead moves scores a double win by simultaneously increasing its quality and its differentiation.

goals. An enterprise's goals are to create customer and shareholder value. An enterprise sets the objective—gain, hold, or lose share—in each market that best delivers this combined goal.

integrated customer value strategy. The steps to improve quality, price, and internal cost that an enterprise must take in order to support an objective—gain, hold, or lose market share.

market definition. A two-step process—a creative act followed by an analytic act—that precedes the development of strategy. The creative act is to develop a variety of alternative approaches to definition, such as geography (United States versus the rest of the world) or income (upper versus lower), that represent different ways to divide the enterprise's business area into markets. The analytic act is to determine which of several promising approaches is the best.

"market gets" line. The best straight-line fit for the points depicting the positions of each of the four competitors on the Customer Value Map. In this sense, it depicts what the market is "getting" from competitors.

Market Value Process. The process that *diagnoses* how well an enterprise is currently meeting its customers' needs, *builds a bridge* to cross the gap between current and desired performance, and *shows the payoff* measured by the combined customer and shareholder value the strategies create. It measures and maps the value an enterprise creates in both the product markets and the securities markets.

markets. Groups of customers whose price, product, and non-product needs are similar to one another's and different from those of other customer groups.

"market wants" line. The line that depicts the tradeoff between quality and price that customers are prepared to accept.

neutral cost line. The line along which the interplay between an enterprise's advantage and disadvantage in product and non-product cost gives a unit total cost position that is equal to the competitive average unit total cost.

non-product costs. The costs an enterprise incurs to offer its non-product quality—distribution, marketing, and selling.

non-product needs. Nonprice needs, usually less tangible than product needs, that surround the product needs. These may include up-to-date information provided by consultative selling, ready availability provided by a strong distribution system, top-notch customer service, and reassurance provided by the image and reputation of the seller.

non-product quality. The precision with which an enterprise's benefits package meets the non-product needs.

objective. A statement about how aggressive an enterprise wants to be in a market, expressed in terms of whether to gain, to hold, or to lose market share.

offering. A package of price, product, and non-product benefits designed to meet or exceed the customer's price, product, and non-product needs.

poststrategy customer value. The enhanced value an enterprise offers customers once its precision strategy is in place.

precision strategies. The word *precision* relates not only to the accuracy with which strategies meet needs but also to the brevity with which they are stated. They can be summarized in a single page. The summary should be so easy to absorb that any employee can use it when deciding how to put the enterprise's resources to best use. All precision strategies are integrated customer value strategies.

prestrategy customer value. The value an enterprise is offering customers prior to putting its precision strategy in place.

price. The price per unit actually realized from the transaction—not the list price from which negotiation begins.

product costs. The costs an enterprise incurs to offer its product quality—purchases, direct labor, manufacturing overhead, and research and development.

product needs. The nonprice needs that are at the core of the buying decision. These may include superior performance, solid reliability, broad variety, and ease of use.

product quality. The precision with which an enterprise's benefits package meets the product needs.

psychographics. The mind-set of the customer. In this book it means the customer's readiness to adopt innovation. A Progressive customer is an early adopter of innovation and is quality sensitive. A Traditional customer is a late adopter of innovation and is price sensitive.

quality. Includes both product and non-product quality and is measured relative to the competition as perceived by customers.

rule of twenty and two-thirds. A positioning on the Customer Value Map that combines a 20 percent quality edge with a price two-thirds of the distance between the market average price and the "market wants" line and thereby delivers simultaneously a premium price and a superior customer value.

shareholder value. The net cash flow a strategy generates over the strategy period plus the increase in value of the business during this period.

slope. The steepness of the "market wants" line on the Customer Value Map. In high-slope markets, quality is more than 60 percent of the buying decision. In moderate-slope markets, quality is between 40 and 60 percent of the buying decision. In low-slope markets, quality is less than 40 percent of the buying decision and price is more than 60 percent.

strategic fit. Measures the risk posed by the new customers and the new technology an enterprise faces as it moves to its desired position on the Customer Value Map.

strategy period. The time period needed to develop and implement a strategy and see the customer and shareholder value the strategy creates. The time frame for an enterprise's scenarios usually coincides with its strategy period.

Take No Prisoners. A position in the lower right corner of the Customer Value Map where a competitor is offering above-average quality for below-average price and is therefore gaining market share. Its counterpart on the Cost Map is the lower left corner, below average in both product cost and non-product cost.

value. See "customer value" and "shareholder value."

value-based revenue outlook. Building a value-based revenue outlook entails a two-step thought process. The first step is to use scenarios to envision market growth. The second step is to envision the enterprise's market share growth by measuring and mapping the change between the prestrategy and poststrategy value the enterprise offers its customers.

value leverage factor. The customer need—quality or price—in which a given move in one direction delivers more value for customers than an equivalent move in the other. For example, in a quality-sensitive market, quality is the value leverage factor. A 10 percent increase in the relative product and non-product quality that an enterprise offers creates greater customer value than a 10 percent decrease in its relative price. In a price-sensitive market, price is the value leverage factor. A 10 percent decrease in relative price creates greater customer value than a 10 percent increase in relative product and non-product quality.

NOTES

Preface

1. The Market Value Process is a service mark of Cleland Associates, Inc.
2. Robert L. Simison and Oscar Suris, "Alex Trotman's Goal: To Make Ford Number 1 in World Auto Sales," *The Wall Street Journal*, July 18, 1995, p. 1.

Chapter One

1. Kathleen Deveny and Suein L. Hwang, "Elsie's Executives: Borden's Bottom Line Has Been Damaged by Conflicting Styles," *The Wall Street Journal*, Jan. 25, 1994, pp. 1.
2. Stephanie Losee, "How Compaq Keeps the Magic Going," *Fortune*, Feb. 21, 1994, pp. 90–92.

Chapter Two

1. Robert Bruce, "Alexander Graham Bell," *National Geographic*, 1988, *174*(3), 358–385.
2. Theodore Levitt expanded the concept of surrounding needs to four concentric circles—increasingly intangible needs were in the outer rings—in *The Marketing Imagination*, Chapter 4 (New York: Free Press, 1986).
3. The Profit Impact of Market Strategy (PIMS) Program, founded by Sidney Schoeffler, pioneered the development of the Customer Value Map. Robert Buzzell and Bradley Gale

discuss the PIMS approach in *The PIMS Principles: Linking Strategy to Performance* (New York: Free Press, 1987). Bradley Gale developed this tool further in *Managing Customer Value: Creating Quality of Service That Customers Can See* (New York: Free Press, 1994).

4. Steven C. Wheelwright and Kim B. Clark explore the design, build, and test cycle in *Revolutionizing Product Development: Quantum Leaps in Speed, Efficiency, and Quality* (New York: Free Press, 1992).

Chapter Three

1. Derek F. Abell explores this three-dimensional view in rich detail in *Defining the Business: The Starting Point of Strategic Planning* (Englewood Cliffs, N.J.: Prentice-Hall, 1980).

2. Johnnie L. Roberts, "Lockheed's Efforts to Sell Dialog Unit Hit Snag from New Technology," *The Wall Street Journal*, May 6, 1988.

3. Mike Langberg, "The Cost of Success," *San Jose Mercury News*, Aug. 16, 1993.

4. Gary Hamel and C. K. Prahalad make an excellent case for this in *Competing for the Future: Breakthrough Strategies for Seizing Control of Your Industry and Creating the Markets of Tomorrow* (Boston, Mass.: Harvard Business School Press, 1994).

5. Geoffrey A. Moore not only discussed the importance of informed intuition but also enlarged the psychographics approach from two to five markets and explored in each the importance of price, product, and non-product needs in *Crossing the Chasm: Marketing and Selling Technology Products to Mainstream Customers* (New York: Harper Business, 1991).

6. Edward de Bono's fine book *Lateral Thinking: Creativity Step by Step* (New York: HarperCollins, 1970) showed that to solve the problem of connecting nine dots in a box using only four straight lines without raising the pencil from the paper, one can succeed only by extending the lines "outside the box." This image has become a symbol for creative problem solving.

Chapter Four

1. Elizabeth Olmstead Teisberg, *Strategic Response to Uncertainty* (Cambridge, Mass.: Publishing Division, Harvard Business School, 1991).

2. Peter Schwartz does a fine job of describing scenarios as plays in *The Art of the Long View: Planning for the Future in an Uncertain World* (New York: Doubleday Currency, 1991).

3. Phillip Robinson, "Congratulations, Apple, for Making a Mac That's Much More Than a Mac," *San Jose Mercury News*, May 8, 1994.

4. Don Clark and Joan E. Rigden, "H-P, Intel Form Broad Alliance on Computers." *The Wall Street Journal*, June 9, 1994.

5. H. Mintzberg, *The Rise and Fall of Strategic Planning: Reconceiving Roles for Planning, Plans, Planners* (New York: Free Press, 1994).

Chapter Five

1. Gary Hamel and C. K. Prahalad offer this definition and enlarge on core competencies in *Competing for the Future: Breakthrough Strategies for Seizing Control of Your Industry and Creating the Markets of Tomorrow* (Boston, Mass.: Harvard Business School Press, 1994).

2. Michael Porter expands the ideas of building quality and cost strategies as generic competitive strategies in *Competitive Advantage: Creating and Sustaining Superior Performance* (New York: Free Press, 1985).
3. Wendy Bounds, "George Fisher Pushes Kodak into Digital Era," *The Wall Street Journal,* June 9, 1995.

Chapter Six

1. Adrian J. Slywotzky and Benson P. Shapiro discussed marketing as an investment rather than an expense in *Leveraging to Beat the Odds: The New Marketing Mind-Set* (Harvard Business Review, Sept.–Oct. 1993, pp. 97–107).
2. Robert Frank, "Adding Some Fizz: Coca-Cola Is Shedding Its Once-Stodgy Image with Swift Expansion," *The Wall Street Journal,* Aug. 22, 1995, p. 1.

Chapter Seven

1. Advertisement in *The Wall Street Journal,* July 28, 1992, p. A7.
2. Bill Saporito, "Behind the Tumult at P&G," *Fortune,* Mar. 7, 1994, pp. 74–82.

Chapter Eight

1. Kevin J. Clancy and Robert S. Schulman, *Marketing Myths That Are Killing Business: The Cure for Death Wish Marketing* (New York: McGraw-Hill, 1994).
2. H. Thomas Johnson and Robert S. Kaplan give an entertaining description of the importance of using activity-based costing in *Relevance Lost: The Rise and Fall of Management Accounting* (Boston, Mass.: Harvard Business School Press, 1987).
3. For an example, see Leonard M. Fuld, *Competitor Intelligence: How to Get It—How to Use It* (New York: Wiley, 1985).
4. For a full discussion of this topic, see M. Hammer and J. Champy, *Reengineering the Corporation: A Manifesto for Business Revolution* (New York: Harper Business, 1993).
5. Stephanie Losee, "Mr. Cozette Buys a Computer," *Fortune,* Apr. 18, 1994, pp. 113–116.
6. Stanley M. Davis coined the creative expression "mass customization" and enlarges on the topic in *Future Perfect* (New York: Addison-Wesley, 1987).
7. This discussion draws on a fine article by Robert H. Hayes and Gary P. Pisano, "Beyond World-Class: The New Manufacturing Strategy," *Harvard Business Review,* Jan.–Feb. 1994.

Chapter Nine

1. Peter M. Senge explores the importance of changing counterproductive mental models in *The Fifth Discipline: The Art and Practice of the Learning Organization* (New York: Doubleday Currency, 1990).

2. Robert Buzzell and Bradley Gale enlarge on the topic of differentiation in *The PIMS Principles: Linking Strategy to Performance* (New York: Free Press, 1987).

3. Peter Drucker, "The Five Deadly Business Sins," *The Wall Street Journal,* Oct. 21, 1993.

4. Bradley T. Gale has developed a highly original "life-cycle" categorization of purchase attributes; his system increases differentiation potential from the two categories used here (high and low) to seven. See his thorough book *Managing Customer Value: Creating Quality and Service That Customers Can See* (New York: Free Press, 1994).

5. Laura Landro, Elizabeth Jensen, and Thomas R. King, "All Ears—Disney's Deal for ABC Makes Show Business a Whole New World," *The Wall Street Journal,* Aug. 1, 1995, p. 1.

Chapter Ten

1. Kathy Rebello, "Newton's 'Ferrari' Effect," *Business Week,* June 6, 1994, p. 89.

Chapter Eleven

1. George Stalk Jr. and Thomas M. Hout pioneered this topic in *Competing Against Time: How Time-Based Competition Is Reshaping Global Markets* (New York: Free Press, 1990).

2. Jared Sandberg and Bart Zeigler, "Web Trap: Internet's Popularity Threatens to Swamp the On-Line Services," *The Wall Street Journal,* Jan. 18, 1996, p. 1.

Chapter Twelve

1. Pascal Zachary, "His Way: How 'Barbarian' Style of Philippe Kahn Led Borland International from Glory to Jeopardy," *The Wall Street Journal,* June 2, 1994, p. 1.

2. Alfred Rappaport enlarges on the concepts of prestrategy and poststrategy value as part of his thorough treatment of shareholder value in *Creating Shareholder Value: The New Standard for Business Performance* (New York: Free Press, 1986).

3. G. Bennett Stewart III develops this topic at great length in his landmark book *The Quest for Value: The EVA (TM) Management Guide* (New York: Harper Business, 1991).

4. See James M. McTaggert, Peter W. Contes, and Michael C. Mankins, *The Value Imperative: Managing for Superior Shareholder Returns* (New York: Free Press, 1994).

Chapter Thirteen

1. Many believe that H. Igor Ansoff is the father of strategic management; he advanced this concept in *The New Corporate Strategy* (New York: Wiley, 1988).

2. Myron Magnet, "The Marvels of High Margins: Goodyear Tire & Rubber," *Fortune,* May 2, 1994, pp. 73–74.

Chapter Fourteen

1. John P. Kotter and James L. Heskett document that one of the keys to performance is a top management group that shares values concerning the importance of satisfying the needs of customers, shareholders, and employees in *Corporate Culture and Performance* (New York: Free Press, 1992).
2. For an excellent explanation of the nominal group technique, see Andre L. Delbecq, H. Van de Ven, and David H. Gustafson, *Group Techniques for Program Planning* (Middleton, Wisc.: Green Briar Press, 1986).
3. Ronald Henkoff, "Keeping Motorola on a Roll," *Fortune*, Apr. 18, 1994, pp. 67–68.

INDEX